FISHING
Hawaii Style

Volume 1
First Edition

A Guide To Saltwater Angling

By Jim Rizzuto

Illustrated By Leslie Hata

FISHING HAWAII STYLE Ltd.
HONOLULU, HAWAII

FISHING HAWAII STYLE is a wholly owned
subsidiary of HAWAII FISHING NEWS.

Distributed by HAWAII FISHING NEWS, Honolulu, Hawaii

Library of Congress Catalog Card Number: 87-083673
ISBN Number: 0-944462-01-4

Send all inquiries to:

HAWAII FISHING NEWS
P.O. Box 25488
Honolulu, Hawaii 96825

First Edition Published in 1983

Second Impression	1984
Third Impression	1984
Fourth Impression	1986
Fifth Impression	1988
Sixth Impression	1989
Seventh Impression	1991
Eighth Impression	1994
Ninth Impression	1998
10th Impression	2002
11th Impression	2005
12th Impression	2011

Design and Production by HAWAII FISHING NEWS

Foreword

To my knowledge "FISHING Hawaii Style" is a book unlike any other ever compiled. The unique talents of author Jim Rizzuto and illustrator Leslie Hata merge in a style that all fishermen, young and old, will find both interesting and informative. This collection of techniques and tips will surely prove invaluable to all saltwater anglers around the world.

Jim Rizzuto (Head of Lower and Middle Schools, Hawaii Preparatory Academy) combines his lifelong fishing experience with his experience as an educator. As Jim puts it, "I am an educator and teacher; that is my role. And whether I teach math, human relations, fishing or any other subject, I think education is fundamentally important for both vocation and leisure activities."

Jim, who began fishing on the banks of Delaware when he was barely big enough to hold a rod, has captured virtually every game fish known to man. And he has experienced all types of angling: fly-fishing, bait casting, trolling, big game, light and ultra-light. In this book he shares with you the knowledge he has gained over the years.

Leslie Hata, a graduate of California College of Arts and Crafts, displays his special talents as an artist with a pen and ink technique that clearly illustrates the author's intentions. Leslie's own experience and knowledge as an angler are revealed in the over 400 illustrations that make up "FISHING Hawaii Style," Volume 1.

Being an avid angler myself, I feel extremely fortunate to have had the opportunity to work with these two very talented friends.

We dedicate this book to you, the angler. Good luck . . . and good fishing!

CHUCK JOHNSTON
Hawaii Fishing News, publisher

Preface

A young boy and an old man sat on black boulders at the edge of the sand. The man's face was a dark leather gift from the sun and from his father. The young boy's face glowed fresh with youth and health. The partners tended two fishing rods, wooden butts braced in cracks between hard, square rocks.

The rods were bent, but only from the strain of line pulling against lead sinkers anchoring baits beyond the surf: traps waiting to snare unwary fish.

A long time they sat like that, the boy's impatience rising as time passed steadily with no fish to interrupt it. The boy's mood formed words: "This isn't much fun."

The old man smiled. He'd heard the boy say that often during the past years, but he'd also seen the boy wild with excitement when fighting a hooked fish or while just packing his fishing gear in eager anticipation of another adventure.

And he knew that, despite the temporary impatience, the boy was just as hooked as any fish.

It was the boy who spotted the rod tip jerking. He withdrew the rod from the crack, waited for another firm tug, and then lifted the rod up quickly to spear the fish's jaw with the hook point.

The fish raced away, dragging line from the reel as the metallic voice of the spool shrieked in alarm.

Then quickly, the fish was gone. Whether the line broke or the hook pulled out does not matter now, thirty years later. The fish was gone, and the boy felt the pain of frustration and disappointment.

The man, putting his hands on the boy's shoulders, looked into the young eyes as they blinked to hide tears and said, "The great game fish are powerful enough to escape from everything but your memory."

The boy did not fully understand what had been said, but the words stayed with him year after year. And with time he came to realize that the words were true not only about fish caught but also fish lost.

The story reveals the two reasons why this book was written — because young anglers learn from their fishing companions and because an angler's memories are as powerful as the great game fish that inspire them.

Acknowledgments

This book represents the combined skills and diverse talents of a wide range of exceptional people. Among them are fishermen, artists and editors—and some who are all three.

Thanks goes to Leslie Hata for a truly remarkable assortment of accurate drawings that could only have been produced by an artist and fisherman who is master at both crafts. Thanks also go to Catherine Flynn for typography, Sylvia Rodgers for copy editing, and Bob Paxton for layout and design.

I'm also indebted to many fishermen who have shared their ideas, methods and techniques. These include many professionals—men and women who live by their knowledge of the sea. For their great help, thanks go to captains Zander Budge (*SPOOKY LUKI*), Rob Englehard (*IHU NUI*), Peter Hoogs (*PAMELA*), Jack Ross (*CAPTAIN JACK*), Kenny Hughs and Mike Fairfield (*MAVERICK*), Francis Ruddles (*VICI*), Myrna Holdredge (*ULTIMATE*), and Steve Kaiser and Juan Waroquiers (*MEDUSA*). Other fishermen and women who have shared their lore are Karin Nickola, Charlie Teves, Wally Lam, Ernest Theodore, Ken Ozaki, Sef Propios, Kimo Libero and Mike Sakamoto.

The late Deal Crooker deserves the thanks and respect of all of us, though his great voice no longer rattles our CB radios with advice and encouragement.

And a very special thanks goes to the man who made it all possible—Chuck Johnston. His faith, understanding and commitment are the heart and soul of this effort.

Table of Contents

Basic Information on Fishing Tackle and Techniques

Knots and Nots 1
Tying a Hook to the Line 1
Attaching a Sinker to the Line 1
Knots for Joining Two Lines 2
Special Joints and Solutions to Other Knotty Problems 2
Wire Leaders 6
Homemade Wire Eye Former 7
Snap Connectors 7
Double Eye Connector 8
Getting Hooked 9
Weights 10
Fishing Rods 13
Fishing Reels 18
The Way You Keep Your Tackle 19

Spinning Tackle Techniques

The One-Handed Rod 22
The Two-Handed Rod 24
How to Fight a Fish on Spinning Tackle 26
Casting with Lures 28
Spin Fishing with Jigs 32
Deep-Water Jigging 34
Spoon Feeding Fish 36
Twelve Lucky Tricks for Whippers 38

Table of Contents (continued)

Fishing With Bait
Live or Otherwise 40
Rigged Whole Baits 43
Thirteen Tips for Casting with Bait 46

Information on Bottom Fishing
The Key to Success 48
Downriggers! 50

Big Game Basics
Baiting the Big Ones 52
Twenty Tricks for Trolling Live Bait 55
Rigging a Swimmer Bait 58

Plastic Resin Trolling Lures
How to Mold and Pour Your Own Resin Trolling Lures 60
Getting the Lead In and Other Lure-Making Tricks 65
Big Game Trolling with Lures 68
Sharpening a Big Game Hook 74
Twenty-One Details in Rigging Big Game Trolling Lures 74
Braking and Breaking 76
Rigging Up and Out 77

Fishing the FADs
Tips on How to Fish the FAD Buoys 80

Safety: First and Always
Keep Safe While Fishing 83

Tackle Box
Take Along What's Right for the Job 85

Virtues of Sport Fish
Playing Favorites 86

Hawaii's Game Fish — Where and How to Catch Them

'O'io (Bonefish) 88
'Omilu and Papio (Bluefin Trevally) 88
Kaku (Barracuda) 92
La-i (Leather-Skin Jack) 95
Weke and 'Oama (Yellow or Samoan Goatfish) 96
Weke-'Ula (Red or Sacred Goatfish) 99
Awaawa (Ladyfish or Hawaiian Tarpon) 101
'Aha (Giant Needlefish) 102
Wahanui (Fork-Tailed Snapper) 103
Hahalalu (Young, Big-Eyed Scad) 103
Akule (Big-Eyed Scad) 106
'Opelu (Mackerel Scad) 108
Aku (Skipjack Tuna) 111
Ono (Pacific Ono or Wahoo) 114
Mahimahi (Dolphin Fish) 116
Uku (Grey Snapper) 119
Tuna and Billfish (Hydrodynamic Refinement) 121
Ahi (Yellowfin Tuna) 122
A'u (Pacific Blue Marlin) 126
Kahala (Amberjack) 128
Ulua (Giant Trevally — The Ultimate Shore-Casting Challenge) 129

Seasickness
The Offshore Blues 139

Cleaning Your Catch
Fish Preparation Begins with the Hookup 140

Fishing Hawaii Style
Oh, The Good Old Days 142

Let's Go Fishing
After All, Fishing Is Amusement 145

ATTACHING A SINKER TO THE LINE

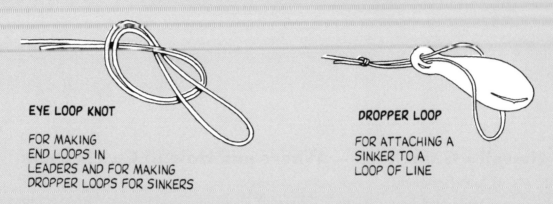

EYE LOOP KNOT

FOR MAKING
END LOOPS IN
LEADERS AND FOR MAKING
DROPPER LOOPS FOR SINKERS

DROPPER LOOP

FOR ATTACHING A
SINKER TO A
LOOP OF LINE

**FINISHED
DROPPER LOOP**

THIS SIMPLE RIG HAS MANY DIFFERENT USES. IF YOU
CAN MAKE THIS RIG, YOU HAVE ENOUGH KNOT-TYING
SKILL TO MAKE MANY OTHER TYPES AS WELL.

BASIC "DUNKING" RIG

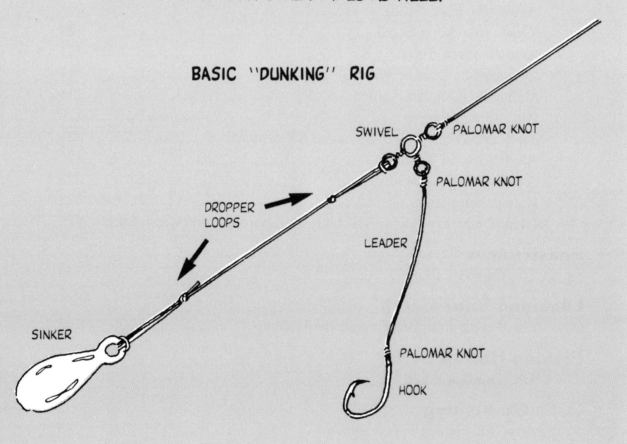

SWIVEL

PALOMAR KNOT

PALOMAR KNOT

DROPPER
LOOPS

LEADER

SINKER

PALOMAR KNOT

HOOK

Basic Information on Fishing Tackle and Techniques

Knots and Nots

Every new fisherman would like to have the chance to fish with someone who has fished for many years. But people who know how to fish like to fish with other people who know how to fish.

Many old-timers grumble when asked to take a beginner fishing. Youngsters are a lot of bother, they say.

What bother? Mostly just things like tying on hooks and swivels and sinkers.

And not just at the start of the fishing trip. Beginners get stuck a lot. They lose a lot of fishing tackle when their hooks get caught on rocks and coral along the bottom.

That means breaking the line and losing the hooks, swivels and sinkers. And that means starting all over again!

A novice who knows how to tie his own knots is a good fishing companion. He only needs advice, not help.

Tying a Hook to the Line

It is easy to learn how to tie knots. In fact, in shore fishing you really need to learn how to tie only one knot. The one knot you need is a knot that will keep a hook tied to your line. This same knot will tie on a swivel or a sinker or a snap.

This simple knot is called the "palomar knot."

First, double the end of the line about six to eight inches. Next, slide the hook onto the double line.

Now, tie an overhand knot in the doubled line, but do not tighten.

Finally, pass the loop of the doubled line over the hook (or swivel or lure), and then pull tight.

Perhaps some of you are in the habit of using the clinch knot or improved clinch knot. Take my advice and use instead the palomar knot. I've switched over and am catching fish I used to lose.

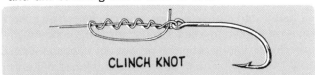

CLINCH KNOT

The palomar knot is better than the clinch knot for a couple of reasons. First, because the line is doubled, it is harder for the knot to break or for fish to bite through it. Second, in tying the palomar knot you avoid one of the major problems of the clinch knot: weakening the

leader by the resistance of the knot being formed. Clinch knots sometimes bind while being formed, injuring the leader in the process. This difficulty even occurs when the leader is lubricated.

The palomar is also slightly quicker and easier to tie than the clinch knots.

Also, the palomar knot is slightly smaller, making a less bulky presentation to the fish.

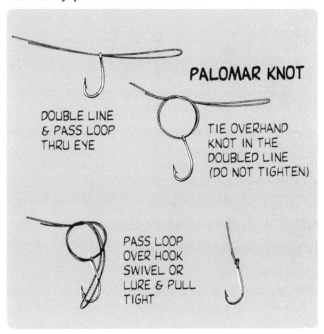

PALOMAR KNOT

DOUBLE LINE & PASS LOOP THRU EYE

TIE OVERHAND KNOT IN THE DOUBLED LINE (DO NOT TIGHTEN)

PASS LOOP OVER HOOK SWIVEL OR LURE & PULL TIGHT

To tie on a sinker, you should learn another knot. This knot, called the "eye loop" knot, is even easier. The diagram shows the steps better than words can.

When you want to tie a sinker on your line, make a dropper loop. Do this by starting with a 10-inch piece of line. Make a loop with the knot very close to the end.

Push the loop through the eye of the sinker, then push the sinker through the loop. This will keep the sinker from sliding off the loop.

Now tie a swivel to your line with a palomar knot (or any other knot you've learned). Tie the sinker loop to the swivel in the same way you put the loop on the sinker.

Now you have the sinker on the line. You can make a "dunking" rig in two more steps. Tie a hook to a length of leader using the palomar knot. Then tie the leader to a swivel with another palomar knot.

Knots for Joining Two Lines

To join two monofilament lines or leader sections, use the blood knot. This knot is made by overlapping both ends of two lines, wrapping each end five times around the standing line and tucking the ends into the line loop formed by the two wraps.

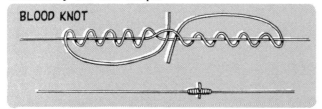

BLOOD KNOT

The "joiner knot" (see diagram) is an especially good knot for tying two leaders or lines of different diameters. The diagram shows how it is tied better than any verbal directions can.

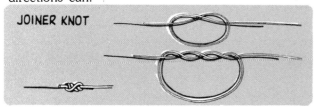

JOINER KNOT

So far, the emphasis has been on joining monofilament lines and leaders since nylon monofilament is the most common material now used. Braided dacron, however, also makes an excellent fishing line, is preferred by many trollers and is easy to join without knots.

Special Joints and Solutions to Other Knotty Problems

No knot in a fishing line can ever restore the line to 100 percent of its original strength. We'd all catch a lot more fish if we could find ways of repairing our lines with magic — or if we were rich enough to throw away all of our line when it broke and just start over.

For the big game fisherman who uses braided dacron line, there is a way to join different pieces with no loss of strength. The trick is to learn how to use a splicing needle with the steps shown for making a simple joint in an accompanying series of illustrations.

Monofilament nylon, however, has taken over the trolling grounds by approbation. Nearly every big game fisherman has made the switch to modern formulations of this clear, smooth, single-strand line.

Despite its many plusses, the single major disadvantage of nylon monofilament is the problem of joining a new section to a spoolful of line when a substantial amount of the spool has been lost to a strong fish.

The best knot you can use is a blood knot, served over with dental floss. The traditional blood knot is well known as a bond that approximates the original strength of the line by 80-to-90 percent. The dental floss whipping increases the strength of the knot in several

ways. Before serving the knot, leave very long tag ends, at least an inch or so, instead of clipping off the ends close to the knot, as most books advise. Clipped ends sometimes lead to knot failure by slipping back through the knot under strain, causing the joint to unravel quickly. Whipping floss tightly around the long ends prevents them from backing out through the knot under the strain of a long battle with a big fish. Furthermore, by binding down the tag ends against the mainline on either side of the knot, you add some of the strength of the tag end to the line. I've yet to have a whipped blood knot fail under stress. Each time I've tested this knot, the line has broken elsewhere first. The waxed dental floss serving makes the knot slip more easily through the guides, decreasing the amount of punishment the knot takes as it is dragged back and forth through the rollers during a see-saw battle with a tough fighter.

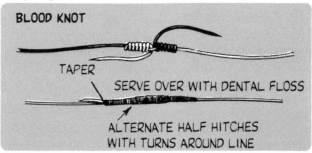

BLOOD KNOT

TAPER

SERVE OVER WITH DENTAL FLOSS

ALTERNATE HALF HITCHES
WITH TURNS AROUND LINE

When tying on a new section of nylon, always make sure the section is considerably longer than the length of line you'll actually have outboard when you are trolling. This saves the knot from being stressed until you actually need it to pull in a fish.

My own preference is to use both monofilament and braided line for trolling. I like to pack the reel with dacron but use nylon monofilament for the outboard section. This means splicing monofilament to braid, a job too tough for any knot I've ever tried.

With a few precautions, the splice can be done by inserting the monofilament up inside the dacron, then whipping the last several inches of overlap with tight wraps of waxed floss. Some special steps do have to be taken to insure maximum strength, because there is some inherent cause for failure, as Rip Cunningham pointed out to me one day. Rip is editor of *The Salt Water Sportsman* magazine. He had seen the dacron-nylon splice in my book *Modern Hawaiian Gamefishing* and had tested it on a line-breaking machine. The joint, as he had spliced it, failed at much too low a percentage of the line strength, primarily because of a phenomenon called "necking." The braided dacron thinned out and broke at the point where the nylon ended inside.

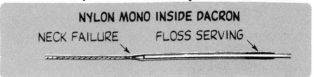

NYLON MONO INSIDE DACRON

NECK FAILURE   FLOSS SERVING

I showed Rip how to beat this. An example should nicely do the job of explaining. Suppose you want to join a section of 50-pound test dacron braid (hollow core, please) to a section of 50-pound nylon monofilament. First, cut several feet of 80-pound test, hollow core, braided dacron and splice one end to the 50-pound test braided dacron. This splice should give you 100 percent of the breaking strength of the 50-pound dacron. So far, you've given up nothing. Now, taper the end of the 50-pound monofilament by shaving it with a single cut from a sharp knife held at a low angle. Slip this tapered end up inside the 80-pound test for about a foot, and whip the 80-pound test dacron down tightly around the monofilament with tight wraps of floss for about two inches. The tapered end of the monofilament reduces the necking effect, to be sure, but since the nylon is inside the 80-pound test, you can afford to lose a substantial percent of the strength of the 80-pound test to necking and still have it stronger than the 50-pound line on either side.

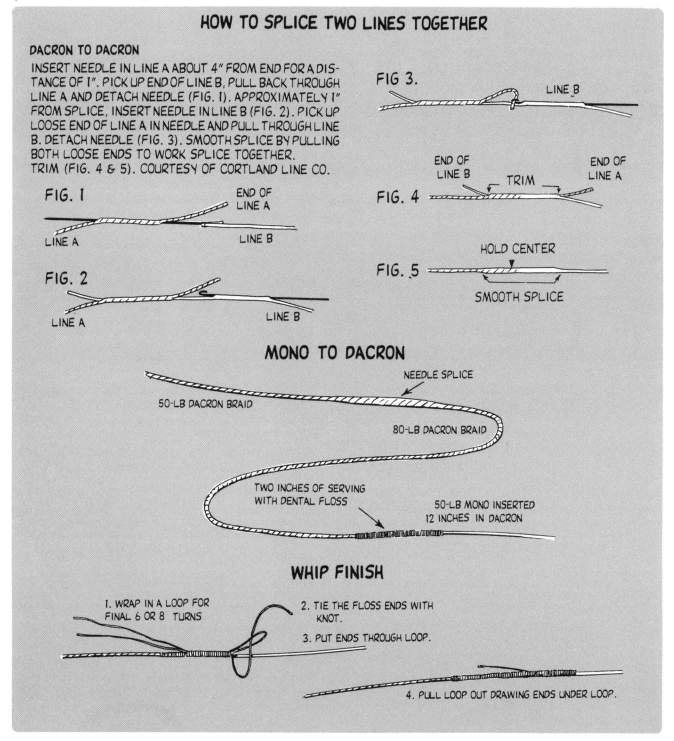

HOW TO SPLICE TWO LINES TOGETHER

DACRON TO DACRON

INSERT NEEDLE IN LINE A ABOUT 4" FROM END FOR A DISTANCE OF 1". PICK UP END OF LINE B, PULL BACK THROUGH LINE A AND DETACH NEEDLE (FIG. 1). APPROXIMATELY 1" FROM SPLICE, INSERT NEEDLE IN LINE B (FIG. 2). PICK UP LOOSE END OF LINE A IN NEEDLE AND PULL THROUGH LINE B. DETACH NEEDLE (FIG. 3). SMOOTH SPLICE BY PULLING BOTH LOOSE ENDS TO WORK SPLICE TOGETHER. TRIM (FIG. 4 & 5). COURTESY OF CORTLAND LINE CO.

FIG. 1

END OF LINE A
LINE A
LINE B

FIG. 2

LINE A
LINE B

FIG. 3.

LINE B

END OF LINE B   TRIM   END OF LINE A

FIG. 4

HOLD CENTER

FIG. 5

SMOOTH SPLICE

MONO TO DACRON

NEEDLE SPLICE
50-LB DACRON BRAID
80-LB DACRON BRAID
TWO INCHES OF SERVING WITH DENTAL FLOSS
50-LB MONO INSERTED 12 INCHES IN DACRON

WHIP FINISH

1. WRAP IN A LOOP FOR FINAL 6 OR 8 TURNS
2. TIE THE FLOSS ENDS WITH KNOT.
3. PUT ENDS THROUGH LOOP.
4. PULL LOOP OUT DRAWING ENDS UNDER LOOP.

So much for joining two sections of line; how about marrying your line to your swivel? Through laziness (at least, that's my excuse), many fishermen do not take advantage of all the potential strength allowed them by the IGFA rules which permit the use of a double line. Whether you splice an end loop in dacron or use a bimini twist to form a double line in monofilament, the joint that forms the double is a bond testing nearly 100 percent of the line's breaking strength. So far, there is very little loss. When tying a double line to a swivel, you can afford to give up a high percent of strength, merely because you are now at 200 percent of the original test of the line. Therefore, when you tie in a clinch knot, which cuts back the line strength to, say, 80 percent, you are still joining your line to your swivel at 160 percent of the strength of the mainline. If you use a double line and you are careful to make sure the knots are not damaged in use, you should never break a line at the swivel.

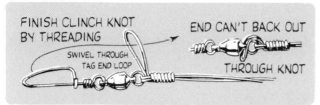

FINISH CLINCH KNOT BY THREADING
SWIVEL THROUGH TAG END LOOP
END CAN'T BACK OUT
THROUGH KNOT

If you do use a double, by the way, there is a neat little trick that Jack Ross showed me that will make the knot fail-safe. Clinch knots sometimes fail by having the tag end back out of the knot under continuous tension during a long battle. When you use a double line, this tag end is actually a loop. Finish the clinch knot by dropping your swivel through the loop. Even if it starts to back out, it will seize up against the swivel and be held firm.

In each of these cases, going an extra step is all you need to make sure you've got all the strength you can get from your line.

Stranded wire leaders, the kind used by big game fishermen for trolling with lures, are joined to hooks and swivels with end loops. The end loops require special sleeves made of soft metal. The sleeves are crimped to the leader using a special type of pliers. Most marlin fishermen prefer to weave the leader into a flemish eye and then use two sleeves for extra security.

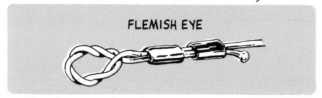

FLEMISH EYE

Use sleeves to form loops in heavy monofilament as well.

Beginners (and some experts) often have problems with their knots, even when they know what knots to tie and how to tie them.

Here are ten rules to keep in mind, regardless of what knots you tie.

(1) Before tying any knot, examine your line for fraying and scrapes. Cut off any suspect line and start with a fresh section a few feet (more if necessary) above your old knot.

(2) Examine the eye of the hook and swivel for rough spots before you tie your line or leader to it. Rough spots can scrape the line or leader as you tighten the knot. This scraped and weakened section lies hidden under the knot itself, where it remains undetected.

(3) Use plenty of "working line" when tying a knot. The working line is the section actually being held, bent, twisted and formed into the knot.

(4) Lubricate the working section with water or saliva as you draw it tight. Wetting allows the line to clinch up smoothly and evenly with a minimum of line kinking.

(5) Tighten the knot with a steady pull rather than a jerk. The amount of tension will, of course, depend on the strength of the line or leader. Pull with just enough tension to snug the knot until it is well formed.

(6) And do pull the knot tight. Don't leave it loose thinking (incorrectly) that a loose knot has less continuous strain and hoping that reduced strain means longer knot life. It doesn't.

(7) Don't trim the finished end too close to the knot. Leave at least a sixteenth of an inch (more with heavier tests) to avoid having the end slip out of the knot under heavy strain.

(8) Whenever possible, use the heat of a match to ball the end of the line. The resulting knob will add extra insurance against having the knot slip. When heating the end of the line, protect the line or leader, itself, from the heat to avoid weakening it.

(9) No knot ties perfectly with a full 100 percent of the line strength, though some are fairly close. Even the best knots will break before the line does, because the knot actually tends to cut itself.

(10) To get maximum strength, where practical, use a double line for the last section. Do this by doubling the main line back on itself and securing it with either a bimini twist, a braid, or a spider hitch. The hair braid is as close to a 100 percent knot as any can be. The bimini twist, if tied correctly, is also an outstanding join; unfortunately, many people tie it too loosely and it slips on itself.

This doubled section ties the swivel with a knot well over 100 percent of the mainline.

A cautionary note about the use of saliva as a lubricant: Some feel there is just enough acid in saliva to attack the leader and weaken it. I've never seen any test results that prove this. If you are at all concerned, dip the knot in water before snugging it tightly and don't use saliva. You just might not want to take the chance that in this case "spitting on it" may turn out to be bad luck, rather than good.

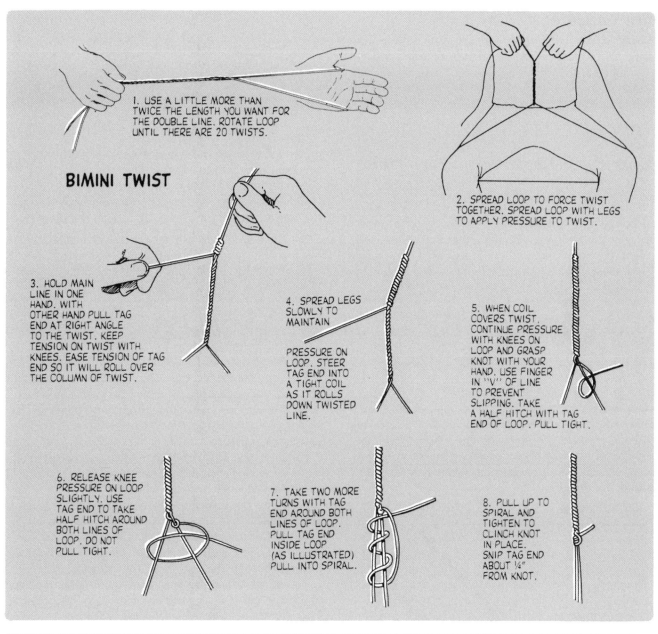

BIMINI TWIST

1. USE A LITTLE MORE THAN TWICE THE LENGTH YOU WANT FOR THE DOUBLE LINE. ROTATE LOOP UNTIL THERE ARE 20 TWISTS.

2. SPREAD LOOP TO FORCE TWIST TOGETHER. SPREAD LOOP WITH LEGS TO APPLY PRESSURE TO TWIST.

3. HOLD MAIN LINE IN ONE HAND. WITH OTHER HAND PULL TAG END AT RIGHT ANGLE TO THE TWIST. KEEP TENSION ON TWIST WITH KNEES. EASE TENSION OF TAG END SO IT WILL ROLL OVER THE COLUMN OF TWIST.

4. SPREAD LEGS SLOWLY TO MAINTAIN PRESSURE ON LOOP. STEER TAG END INTO A TIGHT COIL AS IT ROLLS DOWN TWISTED LINE.

5. WHEN COIL COVERS TWIST, CONTINUE PRESSURE WITH KNEES ON LOOP AND GRASP KNOT WITH YOUR HAND. USE FINGER IN "V" OF LINE TO PREVENT SLIPPING. TAKE A HALF HITCH WITH TAG END OF LOOP. PULL TIGHT.

6. RELEASE KNEE PRESSURE ON LOOP SLIGHTLY. USE TAG END TO TAKE HALF HITCH AROUND BOTH LINES OF LOOP. DO NOT PULL TIGHT.

7. TAKE TWO MORE TURNS WITH TAG END AROUND BOTH LINES OF LOOP. PULL TAG END INSIDE LOOP (AS ILLUSTRATED) PULL INTO SPIRAL.

8. PULL UP TO SPIRAL AND TIGHTEN TO CLINCH KNOT IN PLACE. SNIP TAG END ABOUT ¼" FROM KNOT.

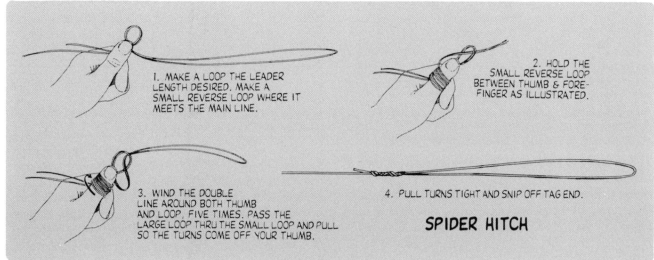

1. MAKE A LOOP THE LEADER LENGTH DESIRED. MAKE A SMALL REVERSE LOOP WHERE IT MEETS THE MAIN LINE.

2. HOLD THE SMALL REVERSE LOOP BETWEEN THUMB & FORE-FINGER AS ILLUSTRATED.

3. WIND THE DOUBLE LINE AROUND BOTH THUMB AND LOOP, FIVE TIMES. PASS THE LARGE LOOP THRU THE SMALL LOOP AND PULL SO THE TURNS COME OFF YOUR THUMB.

4. PULL TURNS TIGHT AND SNIP OFF TAG END.

SPIDER HITCH

Wire Leaders

Cable wire is very handy because it is strong and flexible. It is made of seven strands of wire twisted tightly together to form a single strand. It can be used as a leader when you are after any fish that has sharp teeth or rough scales that can wear through or cut nylon.

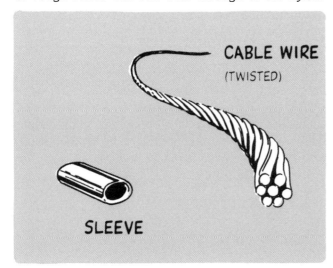

In order to form an end loop in cable wire, you need special sleeves and a special tool. the sleeves are short pieces of tubing made from metals that won't corrode or cause a reaction with the wire. The special tool looks like a pair of pliers with very long handles. You use the tool to squeeze the sleeves tightly around the wire; this is called "crimping."

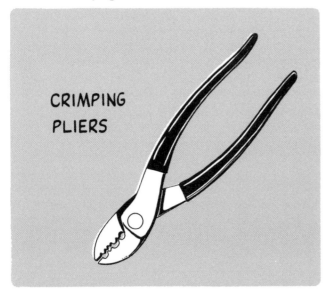

To form an end loop, slip a sleeve onto the wire, then double the wire back on itself and slip the end of the wire back through the sleeve. Don't let the end of the wire stick out of the sleeve because the thin strands at the end are very sharp and if they stick out they will either catch on your clothing or tear your skin when you grab the leader.

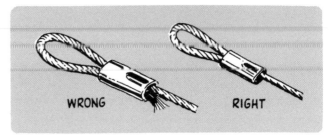

Some fishermen use two sleeves. One holds the wire to keep the loop from slipping. The other is there just to cover the end to keep it from hurting you.

Other fishermen like to turn the end back through the sleeve, sticking it in just far enough to be covered when the sleeve is squeezed. In order to do this, you must choose sleeves big enough inside to allow the cable to go through the sleeve three times.

The long handles on the crimping tool give you extra pressure for squeezing. But they do need some help. Always brace one end of the crimper up against a solid object, like a table top, when you squeeze. This gives you extra pressure.

Another type of wire which is often used in fishing is made of a single strand of stainless steel. You don't need sleeves when you are making a leader from this type of wire as the end loop is made by twisting the wire around itself.

With stainless steel leaders you should always start your end loop with a "haywire twist." The twist is needed to keep the end loop from slipping.

To make the haywire twist start by forming the loop of the eye using a large nail or other cylindrical object. Then twist the wire so each end is wrapped evenly around the other. After you've made three or four wraps this way, finish off with the barrel twist.

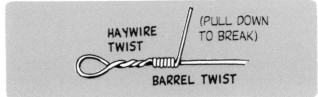

To finish the loop, don't cut the wire with a tool, but break the wire by pulling the end down toward the main section. The break will be clean and smooth, so you won't cut yourself on it.

Now that you've seen how easily a kinked wire breaks, always remember to keep wire from kinking when you are using it. Putting a sharp bend in a section of stainless steel wire weakens it to the strength of spaghetti.

Homemade Wire Eye Former

To make a round eye in wire easily, you'll want a special eye former, which you can make. Take two finishing nails, each the size of the eye you want to make. Drive them into a board so they are the same distance apart as the thickness of the wire you want to bend. Then, with a hacksaw, saw off the nailheads. (They'll only get in the way.) You need to leave behind only short stubs — ¼-inch to ½-inch pieces are fine.

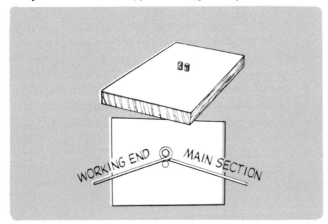

To make an eye, slip your wire between the two nails. Then taking the working end of the wire, turn it all the way around one nail and back through the slot between the nails. The two nails will hold the wire firmly and assist you in making the bend.

Now take the main section of wire and bend it back against the unwrapped nail.

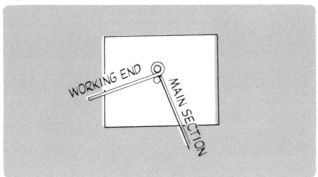

Then take the loop off the nails.

Next, grasp the loop with a pair of pliers. (Smooth-jawed pliers are best because they don't scratch the wire or leave behind a rough surface.) Then turn the working end of the wire around the main section about four times. It should wrap easily if you have left yourself four or five inches of wire to work with.

PULL DOWN TO BREAK

Once you have four or five wraps, pull the working end of the wire down toward the main section. The wire should break easily right next to the main section leaving behind no sharp edge.

Snap Connectors

One of many items you can make with the wire eye former is the snap connector. Snap connectors are, of course, quite useful for many purposes, such as attaching sinkers to leaders or leaders to mainlines.

To start a snap connector, make an eye in a section of wire, using the directions given earlier (step 1). Next insert in the slot between the nails that section of the wire whose distance from the eye is equal to the length that you want the snap connector to be. At that point, bend the wire back on itself as in a hairpin (step 2).

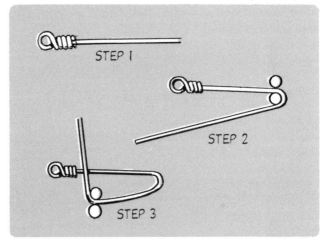

STEP 1

STEP 2

STEP 3

Now insert into the slot that point of the working end that is about two-thirds the distance from the bend to the eye. At that point bend the wire at a 90 degree angle so that the working end of the wire crosses nearly perpendicular to the shank (step 3).

Next grasp the nearly finished snap with pliers; then bend the working end of the wire one complete turn around the shank (step 4).

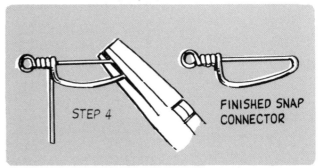

STEP 4

FINISHED SNAP CONNECTOR

Nip off the end of the wire close to the shank, and you've got a snap connector that will stand up to a lot of pressure yet still be easy for you to open.

But just as the snap is easy for you to open, it is also easy for a fish to open with its mouth. So never use a snap connector where a fish can open it.

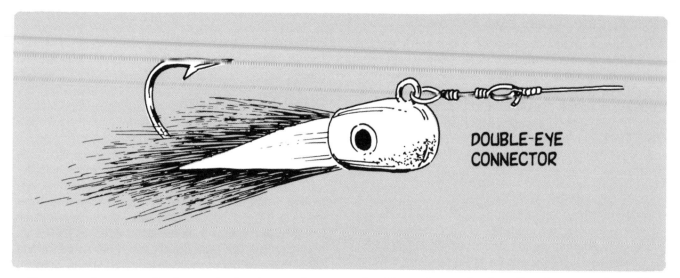

DOUBLE-EYE
CONNECTOR

For example, never attach your leader to your lure with a snap, despite the fact that this is the way most factory-packaged wire leaders are made.

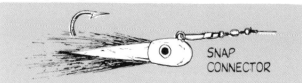

SNAP
CONNECTOR

An experience we had jigging for yellowfin tuna around the "F" buoy off Kona will explain why. Using spinning tackle, we were hooking quite a few fish, and they were running big — five to 70 pounds. After a half-hour fight, one of my crew lost a good fish within sight of the surface. When he reeled in the slack line he noticed that the snap was open. He thought he'd forgotten to close it. From then on he was very careful to make sure to close the snap, but he lost another fish when the snap opened again. By squeezing down on the lure with their throat muscles, the fish were opening the snap.

It's hard to believe until you've seen it happen, but I guarantee it will eventually happen to you. So you should attach your leaders directly to your lures. However, if you want some freedom of motion, attach your leader to the lure using a split ring or double-eye connector.

Double-Eye Connector

To make a double-eye connector make a round eye on a piece of wire. After you've made the one eye, make another eye at the other end of the wire, but this time slip the lure onto the eye before you make the wraps around the main section.

You can tie your leader (if nylon monofilament) directly to the connector. If you are using a cable-wire leader, crimp the leader onto the connector with a sleeve. It's a permanent attachment, of course, and you have to cut the leader to change lures. But at least, it won't be the fish that is changing the lures for you.

The double-eye connector gives you a free-swinging attachment point on lures that need a loose joint for action.

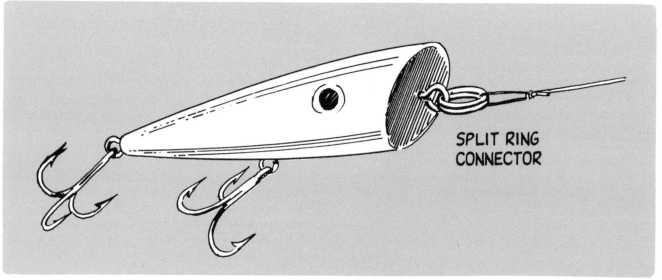

SPLIT RING
CONNECTOR

Getting Hooked

It's the hook that makes a fisherman an "angler." And, it is the best fishermen who know all the angles and how to use them.

You see, "angle" is an old English word for fishhook. Fishermen may use nets or spears, but it is the angler who fishes with a hook.

Those early hooks were simple pieces of bent wire or, in Hawai'i, artistic creations of shell and bone. Today, fishermen have many different kinds to choose from, each with a special purpose. Each kind is just right for one type of fishing; the best hook for one kind of fishing may be the worst for another.

Some hooks that easily catch one type of fish won't catch another type, except by accident.

We'll explain why this happens. But first, you have to learn the names of the parts of the hook. If you don't, you won't understand what we are talking about. **Figure 1** shows what each hook part is called.

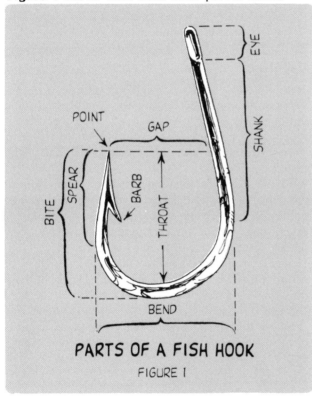

PARTS OF A FISH HOOK
FIGURE 1

The two most popular styles of hooks used in Hawai'i are the limerick and the Tankichi. Each has an entirely different use.

Let's look at the limerick first.

The limerick (**Figure 2**) is used to catch fish that are nibblers. Weke, moana and most other small reef fish pick up the bait gently. They hold it in their mouths carefully. They chew off bits and pieces so gently that you may not even know they are there.

When they reach the last little bite, they feel the hook. Then they spit it out and swim away.

If you want to catch a nibbler, you need a hook with several special features. It has to be made from light wire. The fish doesn't feel a heavy weight when he picks up the bait.

It has to have a straight point. When you feel the nibble, you jerk your line. This is called "setting the hook." A hook with a straight point drives straight into the fish's jaw when the hook is set.

The hook should be as small as possible. That needs some explaining. It is the gap size that tells you whether a hook is the right size for the size of the fish. Pick two different styles of hooks with the same gap size. You will see that the limerick hook is the smallest style of hook with that gap size. The limerick has several other very important features. It is made from a metal that doesn't rust easily. A limerick hook lasts a long time. It comes in many different sizes. The difference between two sizes is very small, which makes it easy to get just the right size for the fish you want to catch.

The metal of a limerick hook is soft. If you get stuck in coral, pull hard. The soft wire will straighten out just enough to let you pull the hook free. But the light wire can cause problems. The hook point may bend or break. Always check the hook point to see if it needs to be straightened or sharpened with a file.

The limerick has a medium length shank. You can buy styles of hooks with a shorter shank, but they are hard to get out of a fish's mouth after he's been caught. You can buy longer shank hooks, but they scare the fish away. The length of the limerick shank is just right.

And limerick hooks are cheap. You can buy cheaper hooks, but you can't buy good hooks that are cheaper. So, buy hooks that are shaped like the limerick style when you want to fish for nibblers.

Tankichi hooks are for a different type of fish and fishing. Look at the Tankichi hook, and you can see many differences from the limerick.

Like the limerick, the Tankichi (**Figure 3**) is used for bait fishing. But not for nibblers. The Tankichi is for fish that bite and run. Many Hawaiian fish, like papio, kaku and 'opakapaka, grab a bait and hurry on to find their next meal. They aren't thinking about spitting the bait back out. That's for the frightened little nibbler fish to do. The tough fish with big mouths aren't afraid that one of their brothers will try to eat it before they can.

The Tankichi hook is for grabbers.

Other types of fish, like the 'o'io, are part nibbler and part grabber. They pick up the bait. Then they taste it to make sure they like it. They roll it around in their mouths to get all the flavor. And then they go off to find another meal as they swallow the bait.

The Tankichi hook is for the tasters, too.

This hook works for grabbers and tasters because of its shape.

The Tankichi is a big hook with a rolled-in point. It has a small gap. It is made out of heavy wire. It is almost

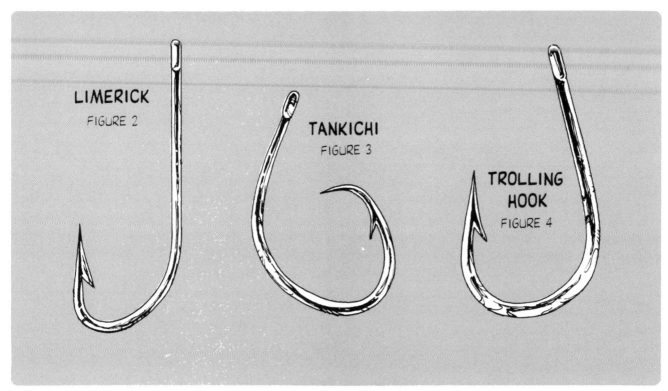

LIMERICK
FIGURE 2

TANKICHI
FIGURE 3

TROLLING
HOOK
FIGURE 4

in the shape of a circle. All of these features make it work.

What happens when a fish grabs the bait and starts to run with it? The hook is pulled to the corner of his mouth or to the edge of his jaw. The jaw slides into the gap. The jaw is locked into the gap of the hook even before the point stabs the fish. More pulling makes the hook turn. This pushes the point into the jaw. Now the hook is wrapped around a bone and the fish cannot escape.

The fisherman does not jerk the line to set the hook. The pull of the fish has set the hook all by itself.

The rolled-in point helps to keep the hook from getting caught in the coral. The heavy wire shank is too strong to bend. You need a strong shank to hold a strong fish.

Tankichi hooks are, unfortunately, very expensive.

Other types of hooks are used for other types of fishing. Trollers use sea demon hooks, sea mate hooks, tarpon hooks, tuna hooks, and southern and tuna hooks. These are all large hooks with extremely heavy wire.

Trolling hooks (**Figure 4**) are shaped a little bit like a limerick and a little bit like a Tankichi. In trolling, both the bait and the fish are moving when the fish strikes. That's different from nibbler fishing. In nibbler fishing, the fish isn't moving. The angler moves the hook to catch the fish. And that's different from grabber fishing. In grabber fishing, the fish is moving but the hook isn't.

So the hook you choose depends on how you will use it. And if you pick the one that is right for your fishing, you'll get to use it a lot.

Weights

Weight. Without it, you can't fish. You need it to cast your bait or lure out to where the fish are. You need it to pull your bait underwater and down to the level where the fish feed. You need it to hold your bait on the bottom.

And because a fishing weight must do three different jobs, there are many different kinds of fishing weights. Each is the best choice for certain types of fishing, for certain types of fish, for certain kinds of fishing tackle and for certain kinds of fishing conditions.

Fishing weights are usually called "sinkers." It's not hard to guess why they have this name. Without them your line would not sink down deep enough to be seen by a fish.

Sinkers are almost always made from lead. Lead is heavy; it is cheaper than most other metals; and it won't rust.

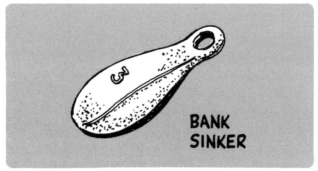

BANK
SINKER

The most common type of sinker is the bank sinker. It is shaped like a football with a large ring on one end.

The football shape is streamlined for long casts. The ring makes the job of tying the sinker to the line easy. Bank sinkers are made in sizes as small as 3/8ths of an ounce (you could fit three of these in a teaspoon) for whipping with light spinning tackle. Larger sizes of one, two, three and four ounces are for dunking with heavier spinning rods and reels. Big bank sinkers from five ounces up to 20 ounces are used for bottom fishing in deep water from boats.

Because of its football shape, it slides easily along the bottom when you reel it in, but it also rolls easily along the bottom when there is a strong current. You want your bait to stay in the place you picked when you made your cast. If it rolls, it may get stuck on the bottom. If it doesn't get stuck, it will roll back up in shallow water.

The pyramid sinker was made to hold bottom better in currents. It does not slide easily along the bottom. It digs into the sand.

The coin sinker is my favorite for most types of bait fishing. Unfortunately, coin sinkers are hard to find. Few fishing stores carry them. Coin sinkers look just like flat coins made out of lead. They have a wire ring molded into the edge for tying to the line.

Their flat shape makes them cut through the air easily for long casts and also stops the sinker from rolling in the current. The coin sinker holds bottom better than the bank sinker. The flat shape also makes the sinker "plane" up from the bottom when you reel it in fast. Because it planes, the coin sinker does not get stuck in the coral as easily as other types.

Slide-bait fishermen use very big sinkers with wire hooks. The heavy weight helps the fisherman make very long casts. The weight also makes the line sink very fast in the deep water where ulua swim. The hooks on the sinker catch in the coral and hold the bait in one spot. Because the wire is soft, the hooks straighten out and let go when the fisherman pulls hard.

Egg sinkers are used to make fish-finder rigs. The egg sinker has a hole through the middle. The line slides easily through the hole. When a fish picks up the bait, the line pulls through the middle of the sinker. The fish does not feel the weight of the lead. Many fish run away if they feel the weight when they nibble on the bait.

Some sinkers are made for trolling. Ringed sinkers are long and slender. They have rings at both ends, and their torpedo shape makes them pull easily through the water. One ring is for tying on the line. The other ring is for the leader.

Keeled sinkers are another type especially made for trolling. They have more weight on one side of the sinker than on the other. This lopsided shape keeps them from spinning when they are pulled through the water. They won't spin even when they are used to troll baits that spin.

Split shot sinkers are used for small fish on very light tackle. These are little round balls of lead cut almost in half. They are attached to the line by putting the line in the crack and squeezing the lead. The split shot closes and grabs the line tightly. They are usually used for float fishing. When fishing with a float, you want just enough weight to make the bait sink fast. But you don't want so much weight that it pulls the float under. Split shots are usually just right.

Clinch-type sinkers also have a split in them. They also are attached to the line by squeezing the lead together. Usually, they have ears on each end. The ears are bent over and squeezed tightly against the line. They are moved up or down the line easily without tying or untying knots.

A new kind of sinker is the rubber core sinker. It is like a clinch-type, but it has a piece of black rubber molded into the center. It attaches to the line by twisting the rubber. When the rubber is untwisted, the sinker drops off the line easily. The rubber core sinker can be used over and over again.

The first sinker I ever used was none of these. It was a sinker my father taught me how to make, and I used it for cane pole fishing. I made it from a toothpaste tube. Some types of toothpaste, hair creams and medicines are sold in tubes made from soft metal. When the toothpaste was all used up, we cut the containers into thin strips. Wrapping a strip or two around the line gave it enough weight to pull the bait down. A bobber held the bait off the bottom. The strip lead sinker works just as well now for cane pole fishing as it did then.

A fisherman's tackle box should contain several different kinds of sinkers. That way he always has the right type for any kind of fishing he wants to do.

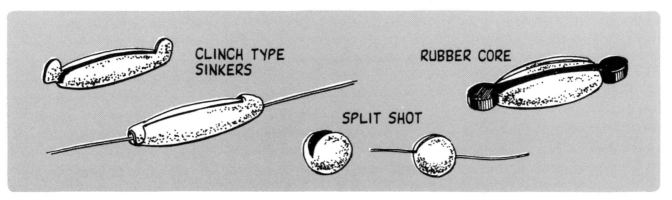

CLINCH TYPE SINKERS

RUBBER CORE

SPLIT SHOT

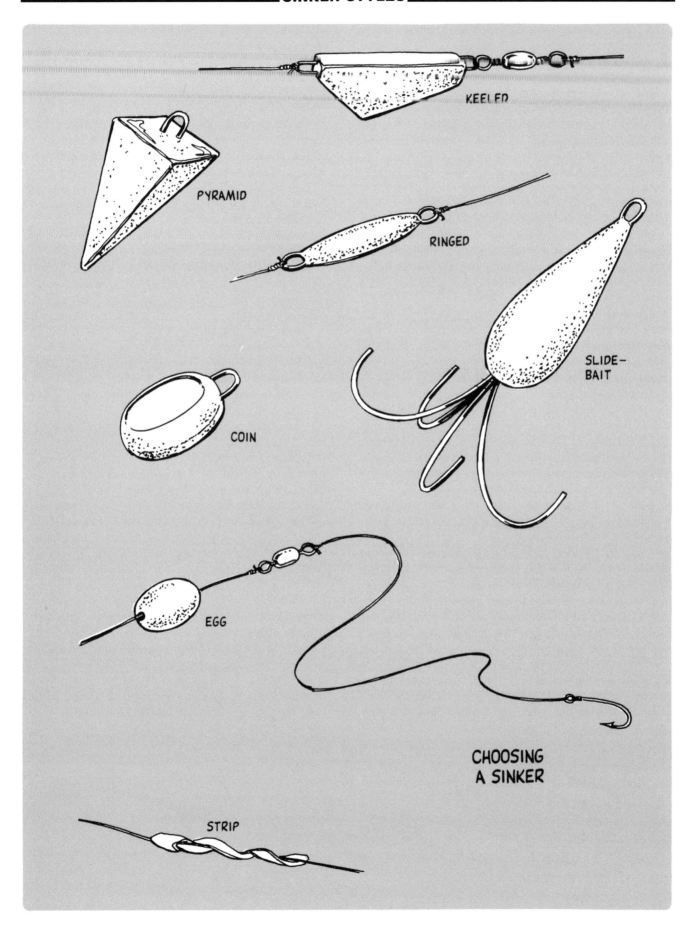

KEELER

PYRAMID

RINGED

COIN

SLIDE-BAIT

EGG

CHOOSING A SINKER

STRIP

Fishing Rods

A salesman at a fishing tackle store told me something when I was a youngster that I've remembered for thirty years. He said, "Fishermen don't choose fishing rods, but fishing rods choose fishermen."

He meant that many people don't know what they want when they go to a store to buy a fishing rod. They end up buying a rod because it's the right price. Or maybe because it's the right color. Or even because it's all the tackle store has. In any case, the fisherman didn't make a choice. The rod he bought was forced on him by reasons that didn't have anything to do with fishing.

In order to choose the correct outfit for spinning, you have to know what you are going to throw and what you are out to catch. You can buy spinning rods, reels and lines balanced to toss the lightest lures for the smallest fish or heave huge baits for surf-cruising giants.

Then again, the bait or lure you throw also depends on what you hope to catch. Though it is true that the smallest bait will occasionally be sucked in by the biggest fish, the small bait/small fish is really only rarely waived by the ocean's hungriest big game.

What kind of fishing are you going to use it for? Do you need it for trolling? Whipping with small lures? Casting heavy lures? Dunking? Slide bait fishing? What size and type of fish do you expect to catch on it? Will you use it on a boat or from shore? How will you carry it from home to the fishing grounds — car, bike, on foot?

Each answer will have some effect on the type of rod you choose.

You should also know what kinds of fishing rods there are to choose from. To do this, you may have to visit many different fishing tackle stores. Advertisements in fishing tackle magazines can give you more ideas. You may also want to write to fishing tackle companies for their catalogs. The new catalog from the Shakespeare Fishing Tackle Group has nearly 200 different types of fishing rods in it alone. And that's just one manufacturer!

Studying catalogs and advertisements can be a very good starting point because they explain what each rod is for and what its good points are. They also give you an idea of how much money you can expect to pay for rods of each kind with parts made from different kinds of materials.

Many different companies make rods that are like rods made by other companies. Once you've decided on what you want, you may find that a rod like it is made by Shakespeare, by Daiwa, by Garcia-Conolon, by Browning, and by many other companies.

Let's go through the steps of choosing a simple spinning rod like the one pictured.

Rods like this are made in lengths from five to seven feet, to cast lures from one-sixteenth of an ounce to two ounces, on lines from 2-pound test to 15-pound test. They are made from solid fiberglass, hollow fiberglass, fiberglass combined with graphite fiber, graphite fiber alone, or boron fibers alone. They come ferruled or unferruled. The butts and foregrips may be one-handed or two-handed and made from wood, cork, or several different types of artificial rubber materials.

The choice sounds complicated, but not if you know what you want to use your rod for. If you were a dedicated fisherman with a lot of money, you would buy a different rod for each different use. You'd buy an ultra-light spinning rod five feet long to use 2- to 4-pound test line for casting one-sixteenth to one-quarter ounce lures in hopes of catching fish weighing up to two pounds. Then you'd buy a light spinning rod six feet long to use 5- to 8-pound test line for half ounce or three-quarter ounce lures in hopes of catching fish from two to four pounds.

So chances are you'll want to buy one rod that will do the job of three. It won't do each job as well as the one rod best designed for that job, but it will do all of the jobs well enough to keep you fishing.

Your compromise is a one-handed spinning rod about six feet long. A one-handed butt is between six and eight inches long. Two-handed butts are around 15 inches long. They are for casting heavier lures and fighting bigger fish.

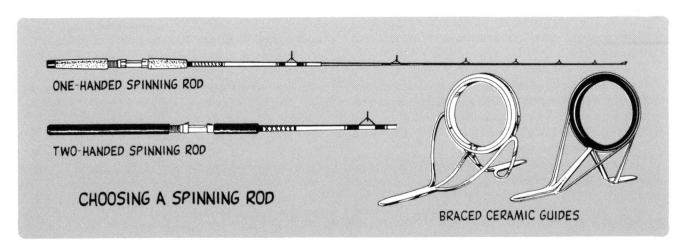

ONE-HANDED SPINNING ROD

TWO-HANDED SPINNING ROD

CHOOSING A SPINNING ROD

BRACED CERAMIC GUIDES

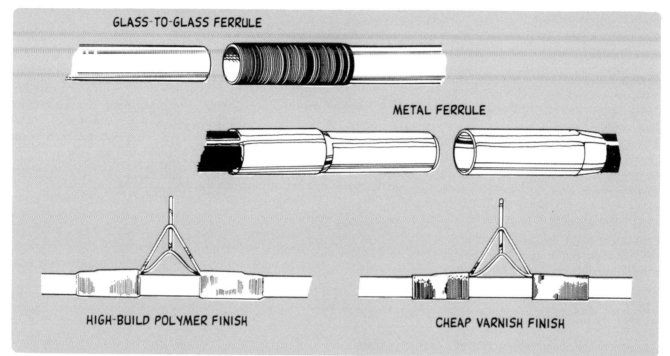

GLASS-TO-GLASS FERRULE

METAL FERRULE

HIGH-BUILD POLYMER FINISH

CHEAP VARNISH FINISH

Your rod should be designed for use with ½-ounce to 1-ounce lures and 6- to 12-pound test line. Manufacturers generally put a label on the rod right above the foregrip. This label tells you the best lure weight and the best line strength for the rod.

Hollow fiberglass rods do a satisfactory job. Glass and graphite are a bit better since they are stronger and have more action. Graphite is better yet. But you need not feel that you must buy a rod made from a material more expensive than fiberglass. Fiberglass rods are so good that you may never want more expensive rods even when you can afford them.

Wood butts are unsatisfactory on light spinning rods. Choose butts and foregrips of cork or artificial rubbery material. The latter look like sponge except that the bubbles are so small you can barely see them. Cork is satisfactory but will gradually break apart after many years of hard use. The best cork is the kind with very small holes. Cheap cork has large holes.

Rod guides can be made from many different materials. The best guides have rings of chrome-plated stainless steel, tungsten carbide or ceramic material like aluminium oxide.

Any of these rings are satisfactory. The cheapest are made of chrome-plated stainless steel, and many fishermen even prefer them to the more expensive rings. The stainless steel rings are light in weight and attractive. They remain bright with very little care, and they stand up to a great deal of hard use.

Tungsten carbide is tougher but looks dull and grey. Ceramic rings are heavier. If you compare a ceramic ring with a stainless steel ring of the same size, the ceramic ring has a smaller opening, which cuts down on casting distance.

I have rods with all three types of guides and like them all. Many manufacturers now make rods with stainless guides except at the tip. The tip guide is often tungsten carbide or ceramic just because of the extra friction caused by the strain of the line as it bends over the tip ring.

The best action rods are one-piece with no ferrule.

A one-piece rod is usually hard to carry in cars. The best two-piece rods have glass-to-glass ferrules. When they are put together the glass joins evenly and you can't even see the ferrule.

The ferrule should not be in the exact middle of the rod. In other words, it should not be three feet from the end of a 6-foot rod. You want the ferrule to be as far from the tip of the rod as it can be without making a piece too long to carry in a car. The ferrule should be four or four and a half feet from the tip.

Now look at the finish. Good rod manufacturers now use a type of plastic varnish that is very thick, strong and attractive. the rod looks like it has been coated with honey. Look at the edges of the wrappings. On a rod with a good finish the wrappings should look like they are part of the glass. The edge of the wrapping should not stand up like a small step. This type of finish lasts a long time. You should not buy a rod if the finish is just a light coating of varnish over the wraps.

Once you've done your homework and know just what you want, then go look for it. If you can't find it at one store, keep looking. If what you want costs a bit more than what you expected to pay, it's worth saving your pennies to get the extra. And if the color of the rod isn't exactly what you hoped for, just remember this: no fish ever looked at a fishing rod before deciding whether or not to bite.

At the lightest end of the practical scale for Hawai'i is the spinning rig chosen to cast light lures in the 1/16th- to 1/8th-ounce range. These will usually be small jigs targeted for papio between a half pound and three pounds.

Tackle chosen to whip with jigs for papio will also serve a broad range of other uses. The same combination can handle up to, perhaps, an ounce of lead as part of a bait fishing rig for weke, moana and other kinds of near-shore shallow-water fish.

To cast a light lure, you must use light line; that's the real starting point. A light lure just won't pull a heavy line off the spool no matter how much force you put into your cast. The line is too stiff and has too much air resistance. Light jigs work best with lines of 8-pound test or less, but it is seldom practical to go below 6-pound test for Hawai'i's fishing. True, a good caster might stretch the upper end of this range as high as, perhaps, 12-pound test, but it takes the best premium grade of monofilament line to help out. Expert ultra-light casters use lines of only 2- or 4-pound test, but these folks are fanatics!

With lure and line selected, rod and reel must balance to match. Reel size is indicated by its line capacity. A good rule of thumb is to choose a reel holding approximately 200 yards of whatever strength line you choose. More about features to look for later: size is the issue here.

The rod I'd choose to complete this light spinning rig would be a 6-footer, perhaps a few inches more. For best casting action, it would be one-piece or have its ferrule approximately one-third of the distance from the butt — still down in the thick part of the rod rather than in the more limber mid-section where the stiff ferrule can upset the natural curve.

Most rod manufacturers now mark each rod with the weight of lure it is designed to cast and the strength of line rated to be used.

That's the basic light "whipping" rod. For heavier whipping, or for "dunking" (still-fishing with a bait held in place on the bottom with a weight), you'll want an outfit capable of reaching maximum casting distance with weights between one and three ounces and lines from 12- to 20-pound test.

My choice for this rod is a medium action 9-footer. Fast taper is best — in other words, with a fairly stout butt section stepped down rapidly to a light tip. Such a rod would almost have to be a two-piece rod for ease of transporting, but a one-piece rod has nicer all around action. My 9-footer comes apart just above the foregrip (I made it that way) and leaves an unsegmented section about seven and a half feet long. When I travel between islands, I carefully pack all my rods in an 8-foot cardboard tube begged from a carpet salesman. Travel has never hurt any of my equipment.

The reel should carry around 250 yards of 15-pound

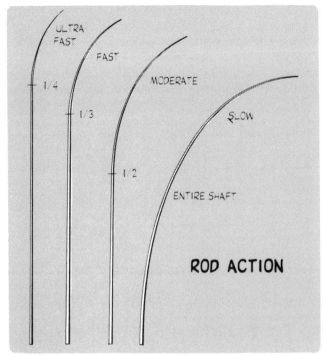

ROD ACTION

test line. This rod would be good for whipping with a 1-ounce plug or with a torpedo weight fished with a bait strip behind an 18-inch leader. It will also toss off a 50-yard cast with a 2-ounce sinker for dunking baits like shrimp, squid or cut strips from aku, akule or 'opelu.

Fishing from a boat, I've seen a rod like this take 40-pound ono and, on a near-shore whipping expedition (from a boat), a 50-pound ulua. When big fish like this are the quarry, a spare spool of 20-pound line, easily slipped on the reel, upgrades the power of the outfit. Spare spools with lines of graduated tests markedly increase versatility with a very minimum expenditure of money. The extra spool can be carried in your pocket.

The heaviest spinning tackle available is based on big reels now manufactured to handle, perhaps, as much as 400 yards of 25-pound test line. Paired with a stiff action 10- or 11-foot rod, such a combination can cast as much as five or six ounces of lead nearly 100 yards.

Such a heavy-duty outfit might be chosen for ulua, but most ulua fishermen prefer the conventional revolving spool reels instead of spinning reels when this much size and power are needed. True, spinning tackle is easier to use, but once mastered, conventional tackle works better with heavy lines.

A popular compromise outfit is an intermediate rig between the light-whipping and medium-dunking combinations already mentioned. It is composed of an 8-foot rod with the same size reel as the medium dunker, a reel holding about 250 yards of 15-pound line. With extra spools carrying 12- and 20-pound line, the fisherman has three different kinds of fishing methods available to him with only slight sacrifices in effectiveness.

Quality? First a philosophy. Choose the best equipment you can afford. Buying "cheap" tackle guarantees that a beginner will stay a beginner, or worse yet, be a quitter. Have a clear idea of the kind of fishing you intend to do before you shop for your equipment. Then, buy from a store that specializes in fishing tackle; the latter usually has a better selection of tackle and a salesman with more reliable advice and information. Once you know what to look for in a reel or rod, you can compare prices for the same quality equipment at discount stores.

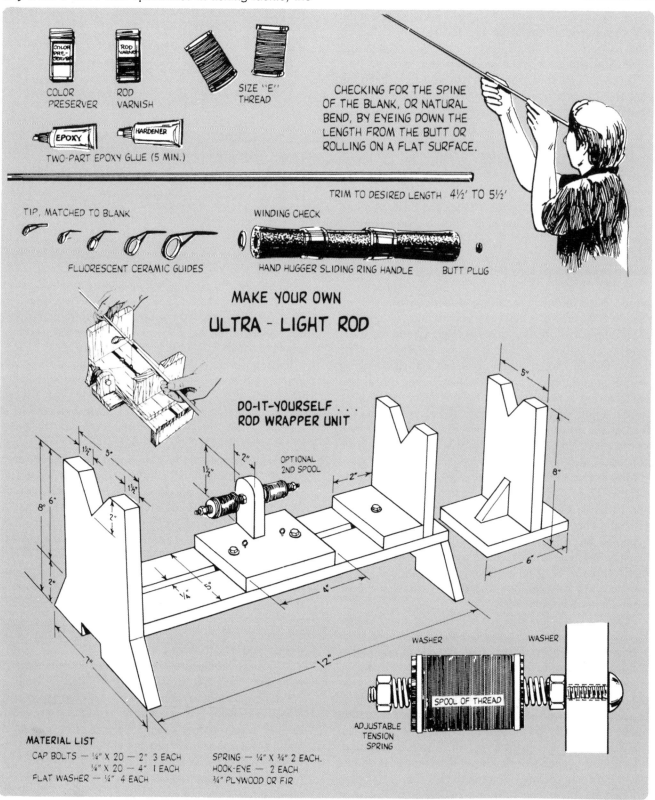

COLOR PRESERVER

ROD VARNISH

SIZE "E" THREAD

TWO-PART EPOXY GLUE (5 MIN.)

CHECKING FOR THE SPINE OF THE BLANK, OR NATURAL BEND, BY EYEING DOWN THE LENGTH FROM THE BUTT OR ROLLING ON A FLAT SURFACE.

TRIM TO DESIRED LENGTH 4½' TO 5½'

TIP, MATCHED TO BLANK

FLUORESCENT CERAMIC GUIDES

WINDING CHECK

HAND HUGGER SLIDING RING HANDLE

BUTT PLUG

MAKE YOUR OWN
ULTRA - LIGHT ROD

DO-IT-YOURSELF . . .
ROD WRAPPER UNIT

OPTIONAL 2ND SPOOL

WASHER

WASHER

SPOOL OF THREAD

ADJUSTABLE TENSION SPRING

MATERIAL LIST

CAP BOLTS — ¼" X 20 — 2" 3 EACH
¼" X 20 — 4" 1 EACH
FLAT WASHER — ¼" 4 EACH

SPRING — ¼" X ¾" 2 EACH.
HOOK-EYE — 2 EACH
¾" PLYWOOD OR FIR

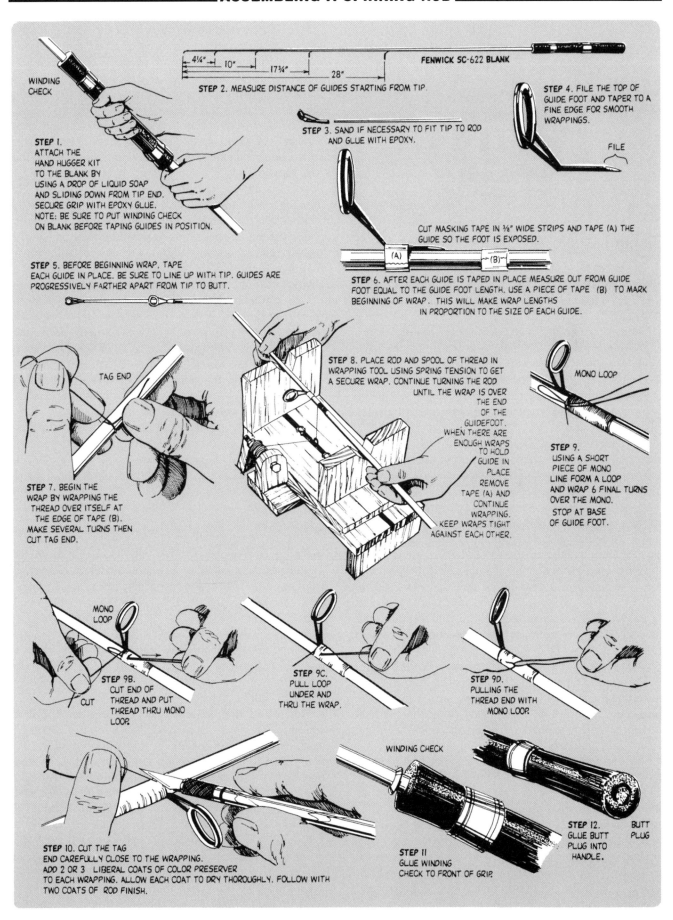

FENWICK SC-622 BLANK

STEP 2. MEASURE DISTANCE OF GUIDES STARTING FROM TIP.

4¼" 10" 17¾" 28"

WINDING CHECK

STEP 1.
ATTACH THE
HAND HUGGER KIT
TO THE BLANK BY
USING A DROP OF LIQUID SOAP
AND SLIDING DOWN FROM TIP END.
SECURE GRIP WITH EPOXY GLUE.
NOTE: BE SURE TO PUT WINDING CHECK
ON BLANK BEFORE TAPING GUIDES IN POSITION.

STEP 3. SAND IF NECESSARY TO FIT TIP TO ROD AND GLUE WITH EPOXY.

STEP 4. FILE THE TOP OF GUIDE FOOT AND TAPER TO A FINE EDGE FOR SMOOTH WRAPPINGS.

FILE

STEP 5. BEFORE BEGINNING WRAP, TAPE EACH GUIDE IN PLACE. BE SURE TO LINE UP WITH TIP. GUIDES ARE PROGRESSIVELY FARTHER APART FROM TIP TO BUTT.

CUT MASKING TAPE IN ½" WIDE STRIPS AND TAPE (A) THE GUIDE SO THE FOOT IS EXPOSED.

(A)   (B)

STEP 6. AFTER EACH GUIDE IS TAPED IN PLACE MEASURE OUT FROM GUIDE FOOT EQUAL TO THE GUIDE FOOT LENGTH. USE A PIECE OF TAPE (B) TO MARK BEGINNING OF WRAP. THIS WILL MAKE WRAP LENGTHS IN PROPORTION TO THE SIZE OF EACH GUIDE.

TAG END

STEP 8. PLACE ROD AND SPOOL OF THREAD IN WRAPPING TOOL USING SPRING TENSION TO GET A SECURE WRAP. CONTINUE TURNING THE ROD UNTIL THE WRAP IS OVER THE END OF THE GUIDEFOOT. WHEN THERE ARE ENOUGH WRAPS TO HOLD GUIDE IN PLACE REMOVE TAPE (A) AND CONTINUE WRAPPING. KEEP WRAPS TIGHT AGAINST EACH OTHER.

MONO LOOP

STEP 9.
USING A SHORT PIECE OF MONO LINE FORM A LOOP AND WRAP 6 FINAL TURNS OVER THE MONO. STOP AT BASE OF GUIDE FOOT.

STEP 7. BEGIN THE WRAP BY WRAPPING THE THREAD OVER ITSELF AT THE EDGE OF TAPE (B). MAKE SEVERAL TURNS THEN CUT TAG END.

MONO LOOP

STEP 9B. CUT END OF THREAD AND PUT THREAD THRU MONO LOOP.

CUT

STEP 9C. PULL LOOP UNDER AND THRU THE WRAP.

STEP 9D. PULLING THE THREAD END WITH MONO LOOP.

STEP 10. CUT THE TAG END CAREFULLY CLOSE TO THE WRAPPING. ADD 2 OR 3 LIBERAL COATS OF COLOR PRESERVER TO EACH WRAPPING. ALLOW EACH COAT TO DRY THOROUGHLY. FOLLOW WITH TWO COATS OF ROD FINISH.

WINDING CHECK

STEP 11 GLUE WINDING CHECK TO FRONT OF GRIP.

STEP 12. GLUE BUTT PLUG INTO HANDLE.

BUTT PLUG

Fishing Reels

The modern spinning reel is a bargain, especially when compared with its ancestors, all of those imports that first intruded on the American scene in the late 1940s.

Today's spinning reels are only slightly more expensive in price, yet only a fraction of the true monetary cost when you correct that price for inflation. And what you get is a reel with improvements in every major feature. We'll talk about some of these improvements as a guide to the features to look for when purchasing a reel.

The skirted spool. By changing the spool design to surround the rotating head, rather than fitting inside it, reel designers have accomplished several improvements. They made a spool that was slightly stronger and better able to resist the crushing impact of stretched nylon line choking down on the reel. But far more important than strength, they made a unit that gives greater protection to the delicate main gears.

The skirted spool keeps out sand and water. When a reel is resting in a rod holder or sand spike in anticipation of a strike, the open face of the reel is directed upwards. The same is true during the cast. In the original design, the rotating head was a bucket ready to collect water — salt water, that is, the kind that corrodes gears and renders drag washers useless.

The skirted spool encloses the main housing and turns back the water. Just as important, it keeps the sand out. No more of that ringing noise that heralds sand grains flying around and scraping the insides of the bell-shaped housing.

High-speed retrieve. The rotating head on modern reels turns four or five times for every crank of the reel handle. Originally, spinning reels were built with two- or three-to-one ratios.

The difference is a great advantage in lure presentation. I have whipped for papio shoulder to shoulder with anglers using older model reels and out-fished them for no other reason than that my reel zipped the lure back faster, leaving the papio less time to make up its mind and giving the lure a much more exciting action.

Actually, depending on the type of fishing you do, the fast retrieve could be a handicap or an advantage. Low-speed retrieves do have more power. This helps if you want to crank under heavy tension. But light-tackle fishing is generally done with finesse rather than force, and the extra crank power is of nebulous value, especially since you want to use your reel merely to pick up line, not as a winch. The lifting force is really done with a pumping action of the rod and not by turning the reel handle.

What is most important about the high-speed reel in fighting a fish is its ability to retrieve line more quickly when a fish turns and heads toward you during the fight.

Even when there is no special need for the speed of a high-speed reel, the fact that it takes fewer handle turns to bring in the bait or lure for another cast means a savings in arm and wrist power over a long fishing day.

Corrosion resistant finishes. One reason modern reels last longer is the durability of their exterior surfaces, especially here in Hawai'i where warm salt water has more salt in solution and carries it at a temperature more likely to activate its corrosive power.

Baked enamel housings can last forever if washed thoroughly with a wet rag, then coated with the residue left by wiping with a lightly oiled cloth.

It is especially important to do this to the entire surface, including that part most frequently overlooked, the reel foot. After using a spinning reel, it should be wiped free of all salt water and the reel seat on the rod rinsed out thoroughly. Otherwise, the corrosion starts quickly under the reel seat hoods and the finish of the reel deteriorates from there.

Most corrosion problems involve the spool, especially the edge over which the line passes on the cast. No amount of care will keep a baked enamel spool surface from attack by salt water, especially since the salt seeps down the face of the spool between the stored line and is held there.

Modern reels have spools with polished metal surfaces, uncoated with any finish. Since the surface is uncoated, there is no way for salt water to intrude between the "protective" finish and the metal of this spool to start corrosion.

Hardened line rollers. The bail arm on the first spinning reel I ever owned was just a loop of chromed wire. The manufacturer never understood how rapidly nylon line could cut through common metals. Within one or two fishing trips, my prized purchase was permanently disabled: one could almost say it was disabled right from its improper conception in the mind of a designer who just didn't understand his art.

On modern reels, the line passes over a special roller guide of hardened stainless steel, tungsten carbide, or, in some new models, ceramic. Because the guide rolls, it spreads what little wear there is evenly. The metal is hard enough to last a long time, yet the roller can be replaced at the first sign of grooving.

Gasketed gear housings. A standard attempt to prolong the life of early spinning reels was to pack the gear housing with heavy grease, thereby supposedly making it nearly impenetrable to salt water. It was a great idea in theory, but it never really worked. Many of the better modern reels, like the Mitchell 900 series have special gaskets in place between the two pieces of the gear housing to seal out water and dirt. The result is a reel design rarely needing internal lubrication and only needing to be opened occasionally for inspection.

Many other improvements fall in categories so simple one wonders why they were never thought of before. For example, manufacturers now label each spool with the line capacity worked right into the surface design so you will always know how much of what strength line to buy when filling the spool, even after you've misplaced your manual. One reel, the Zebco Omega, even has an indicator dial you can set to remind you of the pound test of the line on the spool, an especially helpful feature when you have more than one spool for your reel.

This same Zebco Omega has a radically different drag system that promises to increase reliability. Instead of working through drag washers built into the spool itself, and thereby exposed to water seeping in, the drag works by pressure on the main shaft, completely sealed off in the main housing. Drag changes are effected by turning a knob at the rear of the reel.

Still another feature of this Zebco Omega is the self-centering bail, a new development on many other brands of reels as well. The anti-reverse mechanism is built to stop the rotation of the rotating head right at your finger tip, thereby positioning it perfectly for casting.

The finished product of this evolution is an entirely different generation of equipment. So different, in fact, that reel makers will gladly warranty their reels for five or more years. This is a striking contrast to the many original spinning reel designs that carried not a warranty, but a warning that they were **not** to be used in salt water.

The Way You Keep Your Tackle

Some feel that a fisherman is known by the tackle he keeps when, in fact, he is known by the way he keeps his tackle. Mishandled and improperly cared for fishing equipment is the mark of a careless and imprudent fisherman regardless of how much he was willing to pay for his rods, reels and lures in the first place.

Even moderately priced equipment, when well managed, performs better than the highest-priced paraphernalia if the latter is a conglomeration of corroded guides, frayed lines, seized reels, battered lures and rusted hooks.

In fishing, looking good is an important guide to working well. Rusted hook points don't hook fish.

Battered lures won't attract them, if the damages alter the seductive action or appearance. Seized reels freeze and snap lines instead of letting them flow with the pull of a running fish. Frayed and fuzzy lines break at the slightest pull. Guides that are corroded into open mouths full of jagged teeth will chew and shred lines.

All can be eliminated with care. Here's how.

Rods should be rinsed with a hose after each use. It's really the metal parts that need attention. Once rinsed, roller guides should get a quick spray with lubricant, followed by a spin with the finger to make sure they turn easily.

Check ring guides, when dry, with a piece of fine mesh nylon such as stockings are made of. Corrosion will snag the mesh. If no stocking is handy, run the edge of a thin-bladed knife around the ring. Grooving or corrosion will catch the blade. Good guides let the blade glide smoothly.

The rod should be disassembled at the ferrules to make sure they work easily. Ferrules and reel seats should be wiped with an oily rag to lubricate and leave a protective film.

Guides should be perfectly smooth or be replaced. Changing guides is a simple matter, and the skill is fun to learn, yielding a custom-finished product.

Whether on board boat, in the car or at home, rods should be stored in special rod racks or rod holders. Proper storage decreases the likelihood of damage and prolongs the appearance and life of the equipment.

Reels should never be washed with a hose. The blast of fresh water forces the salt water deeper inside. It also soaks the drag washers, rendering them unreliable. Drag washers are designed to be free of all lubricants, even water.

Never immerse a spinning reel in salt water. Total submersion drives salt water down into the housing (you'll see the air bubbles streaming from the seams in the reel where sections of the casing join). Removing this unwanted salt water to halt its corrosive effects means taking the reel apart, rinsing the salt water off each part and relubricating the reel.

Swivels and snaps should be soaked in fresh water to remove all traces of salt.

Lures and leaders should be kept separate from their used counterparts until they can likewise be rinsed free of salt. The best arrangement is a bath in a bucket of fresh water as soon after use as possible. Some fishermen keep a bucket of fresh water aboard ship just to rinse lures, hooks and leaders as soon as they are pulled in at the end of fishing. Lures, hooks and leaders that receive this treatment last forever.

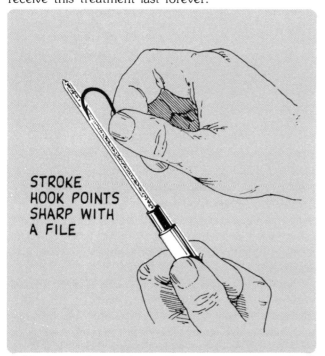

STROKE HOOK POINTS SHARP WITH A FILE

Hooks need special care. Frequent attention to hook points with a file keeps points penetratingly keen.

Flip your anti-reverse lock to "on" and leave it there — always — whether your reel is in use or stored. You never want the reel handle to spin backwards; this will cause tangles. Besides, you don't need to turn the crank backwards to release line; flip open the bail or loosen the drag.

When you break off a sinker or lure, you have lost the tension it applies to the line as you reel in. The result is loose and tangled line piled unevenly on the reel spool, which will jumble up in the next cast. In this instance, provide tension by grasping the rod ahead of the rod grip with your right hand and holding the incoming line between two fingers, applying as much pressure to the line as needed to lay it on the spool smoothly as you reel in the line with your left hand.

Fishing tackle gets tougher with every new development, but no matter how rugged it gets, you still must take proper care of it if you want to get all the useful life built into it.

These are the major suggestions you'll need to get the maximum life out of your gear. There are many others you'll discover as you move from beginner to expert.

DON'T USE GUIDES AS HOOK-KEEPERS. MANY ANGLERS MAKE THE MISTAKE OF HOOKING THEIR LURES IN THE ROD GUIDES FOR SAFEKEEPING. THE FRAMES ON THE GUIDES WEREN'T MADE TO STAND UP TO THIS KIND OF STRAIN, AND THE PLATING OF THE FRAMES CAN BE EASILY MARRED IN THIS WAY. THE RESULTING DAMAGE IS A SPECIAL NUISANCE BECAUSE GUIDES ARE NOT REPLACED EASILY OR CHEAPLY.

WRONG!

IF YOUR ROD DOES NOT HAVE A HOOK-KEEPER, SLIP THE HOOK INTO THE FORWARD HOOD ON THE REEL SEAT. BE SURE NOT TO HOOK THE LURE OVER THE SPREADER BARS ON THE REEL. NOT ONLY WILL THIS SCRATCH THE FINISH ON THE BARS, BUT THE HOOK CAN TANGLE IN THE LINE ON THE REEL SPOOL. IF THE LATTER HAPPENS, IT WILL DAMAGE THE LINE.

RIGHT!

PROTECT YOUR GUIDES BY SPRAYING WITH A RUST-INHIBITING LUBRICANT

If you are careful to keep salt water out of your reel, lubrication of the main housing should only be needed once or twice a year. You do this with a special reel grease formulated to stick to the gears and axles.

As a matter of fact, don't even immerse your reel in fresh water. Manufacturers discourage washing reels by submersion because wet drag washers malfunction, and the fresh water will actually drive some of the salt water deeper into the reel rather than rinsing it away.

Drag washers must be kept dry, but more importantly, free of all dirt and grease. Drag washers depend on a pre-determined and controlled degree of friction to perform correctly in allowing line to slip off the reel when a fish pulls.

The best procedure for washing a spinning reel is to wipe off all exposed parts and surfaces with a wet rag. Remove the spool and be sure to wipe the hidden surfaces thereby exposed.

With a wet rag you'll remove all of the salt without wetting any part that should be kept dry. To clean the reel surface thoroughly, be sure to remove the reel from the rod and clean the reel foot as well.

You may use a hose to rinse the rod, but the rod blank itself is made of non-corrosive materials and needs no special washing.

Don't ever lay your reel in the sand. Just one sand grain will do serious damage. If sand works its way into the internal mechanism, it will chew up gears or, at least, scratch the finish of the reel and provide a place for corrosion to begin.

You'll know when you have sand where it doesn't belong. The reel will signal the invasion by ringing like a bell when you crank the handle. Unfortunately, there is no good way to remove this sand at the fishing site. It sticks to your reel grease and can't be washed away with fresh water because the grease doesn't wash away (you purposely selected a type of grease that repels water). When you return home, you'll have to clean the affected parts with a petroleum solvent (kerosene, for example) and relubricate.

Glass ferrules need not be washed or lubricated and such rods should be stored connected, to protect the ferrule ends.

Inspect your line as part of your rod care, because it may tell you something about the condition of your guides. The first sign of problems is a roughened surface; the line appears cloudy. If you hold it up to the light, you will see scratches on the surface.

If your rod guides are in perfect condition the cause of the roughened line will certainly be contact with rocks, coral heads and other underwater snags the line encounters in use.

There are several other possible causes, however. The first is the condition of the rod guide rings. Inspect these rings regularly by this simple method. Insert the blade of a knife into the ring and touch its inner surface,

the same surface the line contacts. Now slide the blade back and forth across the ring. If it catches, your line has started to groove the ring and the ring will return the favor; the guide must be replaced.

Replacing guides presents problems since matching the manufacturer's thread color may be difficult. Get a top quality rod with ceramic, stainless steel or tungsten carbide guides in the first place and you won't have to worry about the problem.

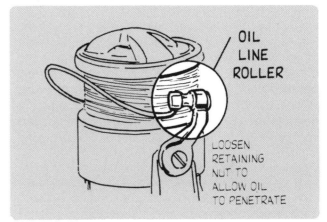

OIL LINE ROLLER

LOOSEN RETAINING NUT TO ALLOW OIL TO PENETRATE

Two reel problems also cause abraded lines. The line roller on the bail may be corroded or may not be revolving. The finish on the reel spool may show roughened spots of corrosion started by scratches or chips. In either case, you must replace the offending part.

Know your reel inside and out. Get a parts manual and learn to strip your reel before you even use it the first time. This is a good check to make sure every part was properly lubricated by the manufacturer at the outset. It will also teach you the features of a quality reel so you will know what to look for when you make the next purchase.

Don't buy a reel without a parts manual. It not only tells you how to field strip it, but gives advice on maintenance and lists parts numbers in case replacement is necessary because of wear or damage.

Discard abraded line; it is weak. But don't replace the whole spool full. Strip off the length of line you release on a cast, then another 10 yards. Replace this length by knotting on a new piece with a blood knot.

Why replace this total amount? You don't want your knot to be in the casting section of your line, where it causes friction and reduces casting distance. The extra 10 yards buries the knot deeply enough to keep it from catching on loops pulled off in casting.

Learn how to splice, braid or knot on new sections. If your line is a braided nylon or dacron, hold it up to the light when dry and look for the fuzz. Your line should be as smooth as a pencil and not fuzzy like a pipe cleaner. If the line is mono, it should be clear and shiny. When the surface takes on a frosty look, it has been scraped and chafed and should be replaced.

Spinning Tackle Techniques

The One-Handed Rod

Casting is easier to learn than it is to teach. Like riding a bike or batting a baseball, casting is done by the muscles without your mind really thinking about what you are doing. With practice, your hands, fingers and arms will learn to take over the job and do it right just from the feel of your equipment and the way it moves.

When you begin to learn how to cast, knowing the proper steps will help you avoid some mistakes. But don't be afraid to make mistakes. You'll make many until you get the rhythm and timing of the motion. Just practice in a good spot where you have lots of room around you in all directions. My favorite place to teach casting is a football field. There are no windows to break if a cast heads off in the wrong direction. Also, the yard markers help students see how far they are casting and how much they improve with each cast.

Be sure you start with balanced tackle. Your rod, reel and line must be the right ones for the size of the lure you want to cast. For example, you may never learn to cast a ⅛-ounce sinker on 30-pound test line with an 11-foot rod. But that same sinker would sail a hundred feet on 2-pound test line with a 5-foot ultra-light rod.

My favorite combination for teaching young fishermen to cast is a 6-foot spinning rod with a small openfaced spinning reel that holds about 150 yards of 8-pound test line. The casting weight is a ¾-ounce lead sinker. The rod and the reel are a good match. The line is light enough to cast easily but strong enough to keep from breaking if the line catches during the cast. The weight is a little heavier than you might normally use when fishing with this rig, but the extra weight makes casting a little easier for beginners. It gives good distance in slow motion with very little power.

SPOOL
BACKING
MAINLINE

FILL THE SPOOL TO THE CURVE OF THE LIP.

One important thing before you begin casting is to be sure your reel is filled to the curve at the lip of the spool. If the reel is filled too much, loose loops will flip off during the cast and tangle. If it is not filled enough, the line will bind against the lip and prevent it from slipping off easily.

Begin your cast by holding the rod correctly. If you are right-handed, you'll cast with your right hand and reel with your left. We'll describe right-handed casting, so if you are left-handed, just reverse all the information you read, replacing left for right and right for left. Grasp the rod in your right hand with the leg of the reel between your second and third fingers. The reel should hang down below the rod. Your thumb should be on top with your index finger (your pointer) kept straight. your grip on the rod should be firm but not so strong that you feel your muscles tighten or strain.

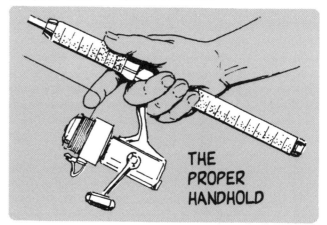

THE PROPER HANDHOLD

Hold the line with the tip of your index finger. You'll need to experiment a little to know exactly how to do this. Depending on how long your fingers are, you may hold the line slightly differently from the way other fishermen might. Hooking your finger slightly will help hold the line if it seems to want to jump off your fingertip.

With the line on your fingertip, open the bail of your reel. Your fingertip is now the only thing keeping the line from flipping off the reel.

Point the tip of your rod straight in front of you at your casting target. The rod should be parallel to the ground. The casting weight should hang down about six inches from the rod tip.

The first part of your motion is called the "backcast." During the backcast, you'll swing the rod up into casting position and the lure will bend the rod to put some extra spring tension into it.

While you are learning, do the steps in slow motion until you have confidence in your rhythm. Begin the backcast by lifting the rod straight up over your head. Start slowly and speed up a little as the rod swings back behind your head. Keep your elbow near your side, but not touching.

When the rod is straight up over your head, the lure will swing back behind the tip and begin to bend it backwards. The backcast should continue a bit more until the rod is at about a 45-degree angle (halfway between vertical and horizontal).

Without stopping the motion, push your casting arm forward and the rod will begin swinging forward. As you push your arm. you will straighten your elbow and push down with your wrist.

So far it's been easy. The hand, arm and wrist movements are a cinch to learn. The hard part is timing the exact moment to let go of the line. You will almost certainly get it wrong the first dozen times you try. That's very natural. Release the line just as the rod straightens and points to your target. Just straighten the curl in your index finger and the line will let go.

As you release the line, stop the swing of the rod. Otherwise, you'll strike your rod tip on the ground. Also, the line slips through the guides more easily if the rod tip is pointing toward your target.

As the line runs off the lip of the spool, keep your index finger close enough to the line so that you can feel it tapping your finger each time the spool rotates. Keeping in touch with the line is called "feathering." Feathering the line helps you control the distance you cast.

Repeat these steps in slow motion until you feel you have the rhythm. Then gradually speed up, putting in more power and distance. Once you have the feel of the heavy weight, change weights, trying a ½-ounce sinker and then a ¼-ouncer. The ability to cast light weights is the mark of the expert.

And so is accuracy. To catch fish you need to be able to put your lure right in the spot where you think they are feeding. To help you develop accuracy, try target casting. A hula hoop or a loop made out of rope can be used as a circular target. Lay the target on the ground close to the outer end of your casting range. That means if your best distance is 100 feet, set your target at about 75 to 80 feet. Then practice until you can drop your casting weight into the circle. If long-distance accuracy is very hard for you, move your target closer and develop your skill over shorter distances.

With dry-land casting, there's one nagging problem — loose line loops. When you are casting in water, the water holds back the lure and keeps tension on the line while you are reeling in. You won't have that tension as your weight hops and skips its way back to you over the grass. To make sure your line lays on the reel correctly while you're reeling in, hold the rod with your right hand above the foregrip and pinch the line between your fingers as you reel.

You can add a lot of fun to your casting practice by competing against your friends to see who can hit the target most often. But the best test is how close you can get to a fish.

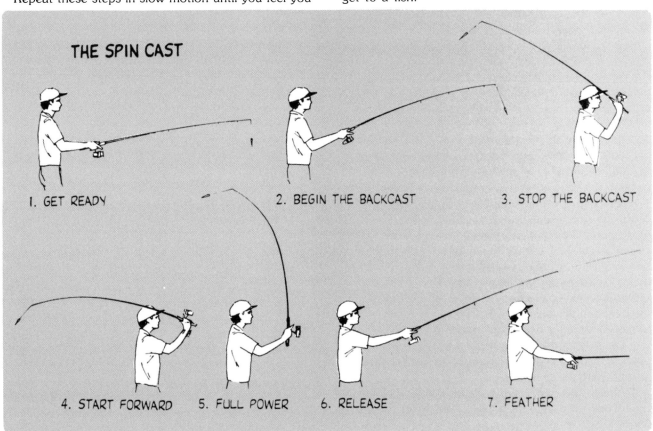

THE SPIN CAST

1. GET READY
2. BEGIN THE BACKCAST
3. STOP THE BACKCAST
4. START FORWARD
5. FULL POWER
6. RELEASE
7. FEATHER

The Two-Handed Rod

The surfline is a favored place for fish to feed. Small fish try to escape from larger game fish by hiding in the white foam and shallow water. The tumbling waves churn up the sand, pulling crabs, shrimp and other crustaceans free from their loose footing. These, too, become easy prey for game fish.

Surf fishing requires a long two-handed rod and the ability to cast a bait or lure a respectable distance. Casting is not difficult once you've learned the rhythm of body and arms working together.

First, grasp the rod properly with both hands. Your right hand should hold the rod at the reel seat with the foot of the reel held comfortably between the second and third fingers. The right-handed position is much like that used on a one-handed spinning rod. As with one-handed casting, the "pointer," or index finger, is used to control the line. The index finger holds the line until it is released during the cast, and it continues to "feather" the line during the cast to control distance.

1. The left hand should grasp the butt near the end of the rod. The rod butt should be the right length for the fisherman. The distance between the middle of the reel seat and the end of the butt should be just about the width of your shoulders. Some fishermen prefer a longer butt to give them a little more leverage and to lift the rod tip higher over the waves when the rod is held in a sand spike.

Surf-spinning rods come in sizes ranging from seven to 13 feet. A good rod for beginners is eight or nine feet long and capable of casting weights from one to three ounces. It should be matched with a reel holding about 250 yards of 15- or 20-lb test line. Such an outfit will land most fish caught in the surf, though it won't stand much of a chance with a large ulua.

While you are learning how to cast with such an outfit, choose a sinker with a weight on the heavy end of the recommended range. The heavier weight allows you to "lob" a cast in slow motion until you get the feel of casting.

2. Start the cast by standing with your feet spread about the same distance apart as your shoulders. Your toes should be pointed at about right angles to the direction you are casting. Your knees should not be locked rigidly tight but should be loose enough to allow them to flex during the cast.

During a full cast, your rod will begin by pointing in the direction you want to cast. Then you'll swing it back to help flex the tip. Then you'll power it forward to send the sinker flying toward your target. That's a two-part process, with the first part called the "backcast" and the second part the "forward cast."

To begin the cast, point the rod at your target with the tip held parallel to the ground. The sinker should be about two to three feet from the rod tip, which allows a pendulum action.

3. Lift with your right hand, pulling the rod up and backwards. As the rod tip swings back over your head, your left hand begins to swing forward until both hands are about the height of your ear. The rod should swing back until it is about parallel to the ground behind you. The butt should now be pointing toward the target.

4. Your cast should never stop. As soon as you reach the end of the backcast, push forward with your right hand and pull down with your left. This action will flex the rod into a full-powered bend.

5. As the rod is coming up (until it is vertical to the ground), the right arm straightens until it is only slightly bent.

6. Just after the rod passes through the vertical position, release the line by straightening your index finger. The lure will head up and out in a good-distanced arc. If you release the line too soon, the weight will go up rather than out. The cast will land too short. If you release the line too late, the lure will go out on a flat path and hit the water too soon.

At this point, your arms should be nearly straight out in front of you. Throughout the cast, your body should twist slightly as you push with your shoulders.

7. After the line is released, be sure to follow through with your body swing and to continue the swing of the rod in an arc until it is nearly parallel to the ground. Actually, when your rod stops, it should be pointing to a spot just above your target.

You can control the distance of the cast by feathering the line with your finger. In other words, you can keep the finger near the side of the spool where it can touch the line as it comes off the reel.

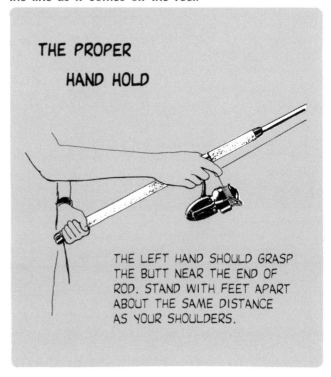

THE PROPER HAND HOLD

THE LEFT HAND SHOULD GRASP THE BUTT NEAR THE END OF ROD. STAND WITH FEET APART ABOUT THE SAME DISTANCE AS YOUR SHOULDERS.

When your sinker hits the water, pull the rod butt back against your body and brace the butt against your forearm. Then crank the handle forward to snap the bail shut. If you are fishing with a lure, you are now ready to retrieve it to make it look alive. If you are fishing with a bait, you may want to pause before you snap the bail; this lets the sinker pull the bait down to the bottom. After the sinker is resting on the sea floor, you can reel in the slack line until you feel the sinker holding back against the bottom. You need to have a tight line or you won't be able to feel the fish nibble.

If you are using a soft bait, you may want to change the way you cast. Soft baits can be jerked off the hook on a snappy cast, especially at that point where the backcast stops and the forward cast begins. In bait fishing, many fishermen don't use a backcast at all. They begin their cast with the rod pointing back behind them parallel to the ground. They are careful to use a gentle swing, putting more power into the cast as the rod comes up.

The cast we've described is a traditional one used by most surf-casters, and it will get you the distance you'll need for most types of fishing. Remember, the fish you are after are kinds that like to hunt within casting distance of the surfline.

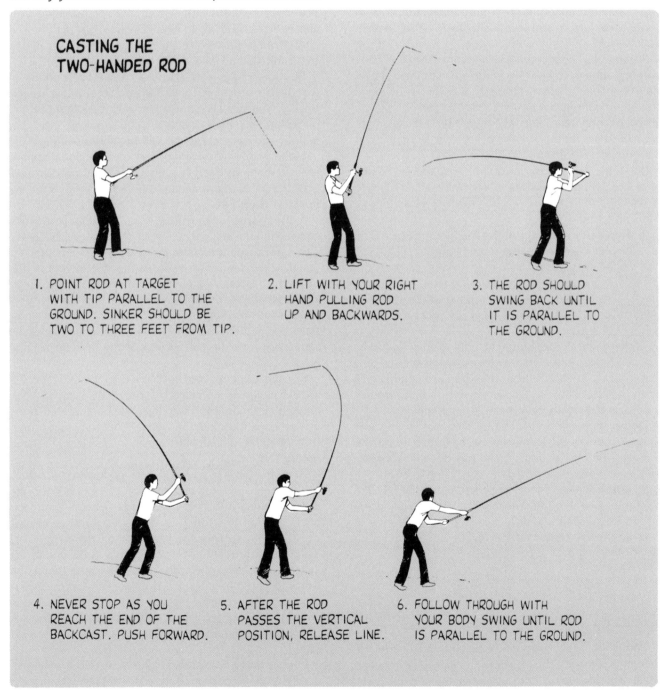

CASTING THE TWO-HANDED ROD

1. POINT ROD AT TARGET WITH TIP PARALLEL TO THE GROUND. SINKER SHOULD BE TWO TO THREE FEET FROM TIP.

2. LIFT WITH YOUR RIGHT HAND PULLING ROD UP AND BACKWARDS.

3. THE ROD SHOULD SWING BACK UNTIL IT IS PARALLEL TO THE GROUND.

4. NEVER STOP AS YOU REACH THE END OF THE BACKCAST. PUSH FORWARD.

5. AFTER THE ROD PASSES THE VERTICAL POSITION, RELEASE LINE.

6. FOLLOW THROUGH WITH YOUR BODY SWING UNTIL ROD IS PARALLEL TO THE GROUND.

How to Fight a Fish on Spinning Tackle

Spinning tackle was invented to make casting easy. As a result it isn't really very well designed for fighting a fish. But, if you follow some simple rules and avoid making some common mistakes, you'll be able to land some very big fish with your spinning rod and have a lot of fun in the process.

Let's look at some do's and don'ts.

1. **Be ready.** In any type of fishing, the strike of a fish is almost always a surprise when it happens. Even though you don't know the exact moment a fish will hit, you must be prepared for it. Your equipment has to be ready to do its job, and your mind has to be set to react as it should.

Having your equipment ready means that your hook is sharp enough to bury itself into a fish at the slightest jab; your knots are well tied; your line is in good condition; your leader is well chosen to prevent chafing on rocks, fins, teeth and scales; and your drag is tight enough to set the hook while being loose enough to let the line go without breaking it.

Being mentally ready means that you are set to pull your rod tip up the instant a fish strikes. You need to strike back to drive the hook into the fish before the fish can spit it out.

2. **Keep your rod tip high.** The higher your rod tip is, the more control you have over your fish. The high line angle keeps the fish closer to the surface and keeps the line above the bottom and away from sharp snags. The high tip also puts a bend in the rod. The bend helps in that it keeps constant pressure on the fish.

To keep the tip up, brace the butt against your wrist or (with longer butts) your forearm. You can raise your arms over your head if the water you are fighting in is really shallow. In most cases, however, raising your reel until it is level with your head is high enough.

However, you'll want to break this rule to do three things: to pump the fish when pulling in line, to bow to the fish when he is running, and to work the fish when he's near you.

3. **Don't winch.** Many beginners make the mistake of cranking away on the reel handle without paying any attention to what the fish is doing — whether it is causing the line to pull off the reel or letting the line go slack. The result is a badly twisted line.

To use your rod and reel correctly, don't crank when the fish is pulling line off the reel. As a matter of fact, you should never crank when the line is under a lot of strain. That's because you never use the reel to pull the fish toward you.

To pull the fish toward you, lower the rod tip until it is pointing to a spot above where the fish is. Reel in line while you are doing this. Lowering the rod tip takes

some of the pressure off the line so you should be able to reel some line in.

Now lift the rod tip back up until it is over your head. This action, called "pumping," should pull the fish toward you a few feet. Lower the rod tip again, repeating the process.

Sometimes the fish is so stubborn you can't pull him toward you. Keep trying, and you'll eventually wear him out.

Remember: use the rod as a lever to pry the fish toward you, and only use the reel to gather up line when it has very little strain on it. Never reel while the drag is slipping.

4. **Keep a tight line.** When you are pumping your fish, reel fast enough to keep the line tight and the rod bent slightly. If you give the fish loose line, he can spit the hook out or dive down toward the bottom.

By attaching a weight to your line (say, a chunk of wood) and using your rod and reel to pull that weight toward you across your lawn, you can practice the pumping and reeling action. You'll quickly see that neither rod nor reel alone will get the job done.

Make your rhythm smooth so that the line does not jerk the hook in the fish's mouth. Ragged pumping will tear the fish's jaw, opening a hole that can cause the hook to drop out.

5. **Respond.** Sometimes you'll get your fish halfway in and he'll get a new burst of energy. He'll race away from you with strength just when you thought you'd licked him. You need to be able to reduce the pressure on your line quickly before the fish breaks it. When he starts running, lower the rod tip quickly. This takes some of the pressure off faster than any other thing you can do. It also reduces the drag on the line by removing some of the friction of the line against the guides.

For the same reason, bow to a jumping fish. The line should never go completely loose. You want to keep enough strain on the line to keep the hook seated in the fish's mouth. But you don't want to have so much strain that the hook will break free when the fish jerks his head during the jump.

Keep the bend of your rod directed toward the fish. A running fish will sometimes race to one side or the other, making a loop of line. A fast fish can then loop back and spit the hook out. You want to keep turning with the fish so that the loop doesn't form.

6. **Be patient.** More fish are lost near the end of the fight than at any other time. The fisherman thinks the fish is too tired to get away. Both the fish and the fisherman are excited from seeing each other. The line is shorter and tighter, giving less margin for error. A quick, strong movement by the fish will often let him get away.

During these final stages, take it easy. For example, don't tighten your drag. If the fish wants to take line, let him. Every run he takes will make it easier for you to land him.

You will still need to keep your rod tip high, but in a different way. At the start of the fight, you held your rod nearly straight up. The fish was far away so the angle between your rod and line was nearly a right angle. When the fish is close, you still want to keep the right angle, but you can do this with a rod that is more nearly parallel to the ocean.

7. **Use the sea.** Waves are a great help in landing a fish but only if you use them right. Let the incoming wave push the fish toward you while you reel to keep a tight line. Some fishermen like to back up to keep their line tight while the fish is riding a wave. When an outgoing wave pulls against your fish, just try to hold it in place. You may need to release some tension, which you can do in several ways. You can reduce the pressure by lowering the rod, or by walking toward the fish, or even by reaching your arms forward to give an extra foot of line.

8. **Use a net or gaff.** Once you've got the fish whipped and at your feet, you can still lose him if you don't have some way to take him out of the water. Your line may not be strong enough to lift him out of the water or drag him up the beach. The hook may not be anchored well enough in the fish's mouth to take the strain. Most fish caught on spinning tackle are small enough to be netted with a hand net. Hold the net stationary and slide the fish over the net, head first.

If a fish is too big to fit into a hand net, use a gaff. For example, you'll want to gaff barracuda and ulua. Both can be gaffed in the lower jaw (or behind the head) and dragged up onto the beach or up the side of a lava ledge.

With practice, spinning gear becomes a satisfactory weapon for fighting fish. And there are very few sports besides fishing where practice is so much fun.

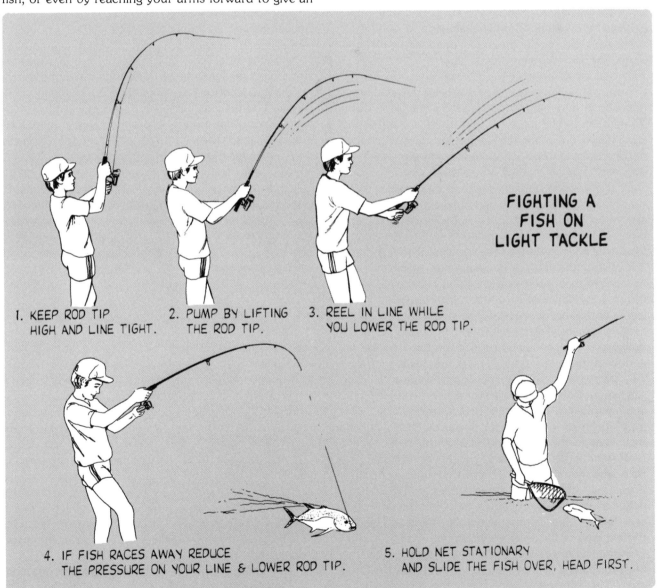

FIGHTING A FISH ON LIGHT TACKLE

1. KEEP ROD TIP HIGH AND LINE TIGHT.

2. PUMP BY LIFTING THE ROD TIP.

3. REEL IN LINE WHILE YOU LOWER THE ROD TIP.

4. IF FISH RACES AWAY REDUCE THE PRESSURE ON YOUR LINE & LOWER ROD TIP.

5. HOLD NET STATIONARY AND SLIDE THE FISH OVER, HEAD FIRST.

Casting with Lures

Fishing lures are magic. Like puppets, they create the illusion of something alive. Their tricky underwater action makes some fish hungry; the lures look like something to eat. Their unusual movements make some fish curious; they tease the fish until the fish grabs them to find out what they are. Their erratic dance makes some fish angry; they provoke the fish into killing.

Fishing with lures is very exciting because lures get fish excited. Fish that only nibble at baits will often charge a lure at high speed. Usually, the fisherman can see the strike because most lures are fished near the surface.

Using lures is an active kind of fishing for the fisherman. Lure fishermen move from place to place, trying new spots. Each new spot is a challenge. As they cast their lures over and over again, they get lots of exercise! It's not a sport for the lazy, even though the exercise is a relaxing form of recreation.

Hawai'i's fishermen use three main types of lures: plugs, jigs and spoons.

The plugs come in three different styles: splashers, darters and swimmers. The splashers make a lot of noise to attract fish from far away. Their front end is slanted to push water away from them when they are jerked hard. On some, the slanted front end is scooped out like a shallow cup. These lures make a popping and gurgling noise when they are pulled.

To fish a splashing plug, cast it as far as you can and reel it in at medium speed. Jerk the rod tip from side to side as you reel. Each jerk makes the lure jump forward then stop for just a split second. The lure will wander from side to side as it is reeled. This teases the fish.

To learn the best action for your splashing plug, watch a school of mullet playing on the surface. Watch the way they leap forward and jump from side to side. Listen closely and you'll hear them make gurgling noises as they splash water. If you are lucky, you may see a mullet school when it is frightened. Watch the way they act when they are chased. This is the action you want your lure to have. Splashing plugs are made to look and act like mullet because big fish like to eat mullet. The best splashing plugs are the Rebel poppers. They cast well, are made out of plastic for strength and have a head shaped for action and noise.

Darters act like splashers, but they don't make any noise and they have round heads that don't push water. If you just reel them in straight, they don't have any action at all. However, if you twitch your rod tip, as you reel them in, they'll dance all over the surface. The best darting plug is the Pfleuger ballerina.

Swimmers are usually made of very light wood with a metal or plastic lip that sticks out from under the lure's chin. The lightweight wood and the metal lip work against each other. The lip tries to pull the lure underwater. The light wood tries to keep it on the surface. The result is that the lure wiggles back and forth under water very rapidly. It looks just like a swimming fish.

Many companies make very good swimmers. The best of these are the Rapala, Rebel, Cordell, Redfin and Bagley Bang-O lures. These are sold in many sizes from the tiniest (about an inch long) up to lures that are 8 and 9 inches long. I have used swimmers to catch every kind of fish I have ever caught in fresh and salt water. Tiny swimmers are especially good for trolling in shallow water with light spinning tackle.

Never tie your line directly to the front loop of a swimming plug. This robs the lure of its action. Always use a small ring. It gives the lure freedom to wiggle the way it wants to.

Another type of swimmer is the MirrOlure. It is a heavy plastic plug that is shaped like a fish. Because it is heavy, it sinks. The line is tied to a ring on top of the "head" of the fish. If the lure is pulled very fast, it wiggles just a little.

A jig is a lure with a head made out of lead molded around a special hook. The shank of the hook is bent so the ring of the hook sticks out on the top of the jig. The traditional leadhead is painted and has a tail tied to its hook. The tail is usually made from the tail hairs of a buck deer. That's why many fishermen call these lures "bucktail jigs." The tail can also be made from feathers.

A new type of tail that is now very popular is molded from plastic. Some plastic tails are shaped just like fish. Others are shaped in a half circle like a curl. The curly tails ripple in the water when the jig is reeled in. Many fish must think the plastic tails taste delicious, for one result of using them is that small fish chew them right up.

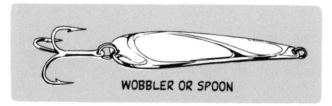

WOBBLER OR SPOON

Spoons are metal lures that have a hook attached to the rear with a ring. Spoons wiggle when they are pulled through the water. Most spoons are shaped just like the bowl of a teaspoon. The rounded shape gives them a lot of wobbling, side-to-side action. This is one reason spoons are often called "wobblers." When they are pulled fast, they start to spin. Fish don't seem to like spoons as much when they spin as when they wobble.

Very small spoons are excellent for all types of fish. The bright sides shine and attract fish from far away. The wobbling action makes a vibration in the water, which the fish seem to be able to feel.

The way a lure acts is the most important thing about it. Its action is its magic.

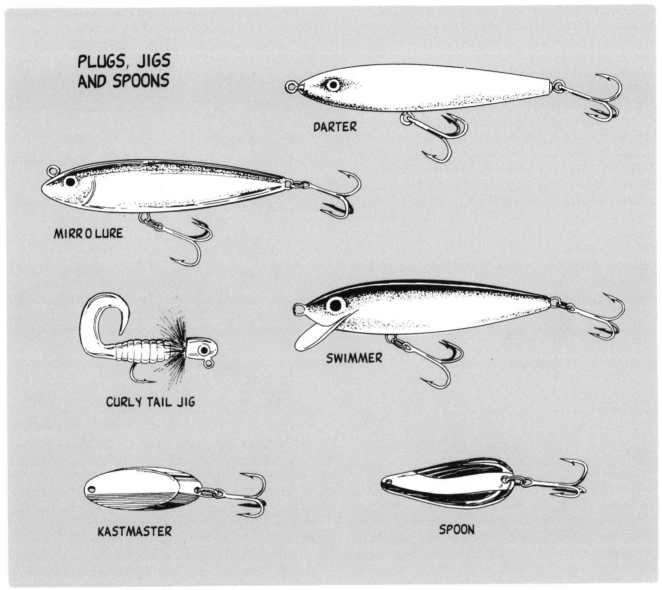

PLUGS, JIGS AND SPOONS

DARTER

MIRRO LURE

CURLY TAIL JIG

SWIMMER

KASTMASTER

SPOON

Over the past 30 years, I've read every fishing story ever written by Phillip Wylie. Wylie wrote fishing yarns good enough to be regular features in popular magazines of the classic era (like *The Saturday Evening Post*) as well as fishing adventures for the fin-fur-and-feathers journals. His tales about Florida fishing charter-men Crunch and Des were even the basis for an early television show broadcasted in the flickering black-and-white 1950s.

I remember one of Wylie's stories very vividly, even after 30 years. Its central theme was an intriguing question: If you had to choose just one fishing lure to use, and no other, what lure would it be? As I recall, Wylie fleshed out the tale by making the lure the essential ingredient in a survival kit for boaters lost at sea. That gives the question a believable context. After all, a survival kit isn't big enough to provide you with many choices, so your lure better work or it's you the fish will be eating next.

Wylie's hero chose the fixed hook leadhead jig, also called a bucktail jig.

BUCKTAIL JIG

Despite three subsequent decades of lure development, I think Wylie's hero would still make the same choice. But he would certainly be bewildered by the array of leadheaded jigs he would now have to choose from.

An explosion in the development of the jig has resulted in a tackle store variety numbering in the hundreds. Yet, the basic principle is the same and the basic lure is still among the most effective in the sea.

Wylie would, for example, be walloped by Seven-strand's new Clout lure as well as the many other modern kinds of brilliantly colored soft-bodied jigs.

To understand why, let's look at the traditional bucktail jig and its drawbacks. (After all, they were good, but no one ever said they were perfect.)

The making of the jig begins with the selection of a special jig hook. This hook type has its shank bent at right angles just behind the hook eye. A lump of lead is molded onto the hook at the bend. This lead knob becomes the head of the finished bait, and the hook eye sticks out at the top of the head. It is this configuration of lead and hook eye that makes this lure so special.

So far, we are describing the new lures just as much as the old lures, but now comes the difference.

The next step in making the original bucktail jig is to tie on a bunch of deer tail hair to the stub of lead projecting a fraction of an inch back from the head along the hook shank.

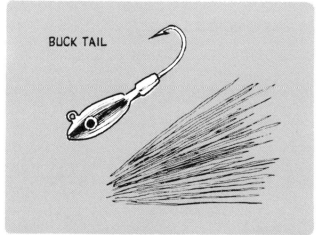

BUCK TAIL

Here's where the drawbacks begin. Drawback number one: though deer hair has a bit of breathing action as it is pulled through the water, it is basically stiff and lifeless stuff. Drawback number two: bucktail can be dyed in a variety of colors but the range is limited and most fishermen opt for the natural colors of white or brown. Drawback number three: the wrapping thread used to secure the bucktail to the hook is not proof against sharp teeth, so under the onslaught of fanged predators, jigs quickly lose their deer tails. Replacement is a nuisance.

Drawback number four: finishing the lure means painting the head. No matter how the original metal is fluxed to help the paint adhere and despite the number of coats and the final heat treatment, with normal use and natural abuse painted leadheads tend to lose their finish. Drawback number five: the cinched waist look of the finished product, having head and tail of different materials bound together with a bunch of string, is unappealing.

That catalog of drawbacks is enough to make you wonder why Wylie, and so many other fishermen, like jigs so much. But, remember, the major reason the lure works so effectively is its look and action as it is jigged through the water.

Modern jigs have enhanced the look and improved the action. Take the Clout for example.

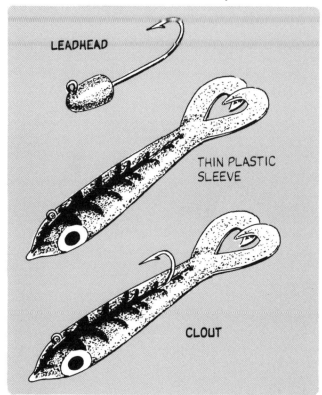

LEADHEAD

THIN PLASTIC SLEEVE

CLOUT

The Clout has a hollow plastic body and tail that slips over the unpainted leadhead. This thin plastic sleeve makes a fish-shaped bait which can come in any color and pattern necessary to copy any natural bait you (and your quarry) choose. Streaming behind the body is a pair of curly tails which ripple behind the lure as it moves.

The plastic shell provides the finish to the leadhead. It is a much more durable coating than brittle paint which has the tendency to split and pop off like a peanut shell.

The tough plastic of the Clout wards off sharp teeth well. Yet, after it has succumbed to many fierce strikes you can replace the whole unit — head, body and tail — by slipping a new shell over your leadhead lump.

The Clouts are exceptionally lifelike lures in the water, so it is no surprise that many different types of fish strike them readily.

Lest you think this has become an advertisement for Clouts, let's switch over to some other effective variations of the modern jig.

Many lures now marry the traditional painted leadhead to a new kind of body and tail made of molded plastic. The plastic shapes generally start as a body that is roughly fish- or shrimp-shaped and end either in a fantail or curlytail. The translucent bodies have a lifelike look.

Perhaps the most important feature is the soft and natural feel of the plastic. To understand why softness is so important, remember that the action of the jig is a series of forward darts alternating with free-falling plunges. Many, if not most, strikes come on the plunge. That means that a fish grabs the lure when there is no line tension to set the hook. Soft-bodied lures encourage the fish to hang on until the lure is brought forward for the next dart, thereby setting the hook.

GLEN EVANS
TALL TALE
BUCKTAIL

Fantail bodies give the jig an enticing wigwagging action when the lure is jerked forward. The fantail retards the movement, providing a tail and pivot point that exaggerates the leaping and dipping action. The best example of a fantail leadhead is the Glen Evans "Tall Tale Bucktail."

Curlytail jigs carry the rippling and swimming actions to their fullest extreme. The soft plastic curls straighten out from water resistance, but the elastic tension along the inner edge of the curve helps make the tail thrash back and forth in an undulating and wriggling action. These replicas actually seem to come alive the instant they hit the water.

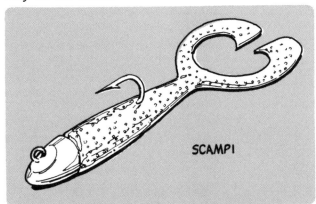

SCAMPI

The company making the widest range of sizes of curlytail jigs is Scampi. Scampi lures start at two inches and 1/16th of an ounce, but top off at a mammoth 12 inches and 1½ pounds (no misprint — that's 24 ounces).

The Super Scampi (4 ounces) and Jumbo Scampi (7½ ounces) are quick sinkers that plunge down to depths of 100 to 400 feet. The big Giant Scampi shows the versatility of jigs as a fishing weapon. This 24-ounce lure can probe depths of 500 to 600 feet.

The basic jig head is shaped like a bullet for quick sinking and straight running, but some jig makers have found a way to add a wobble to the rear end wiggle of the wriggling tail designs. One such is the Scrounger jig.

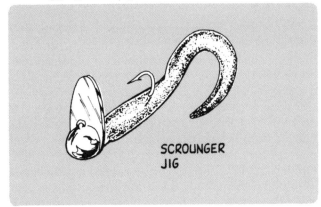

SCROUNGER
JIG

The Scrounger has a plastic lip fitted tightly to a groove that circumscribes the leadhead. This plastic lip deforms as the lure is pulled through the water, continuously tossing the lure from side to side. The resulting vibrations add sonic attraction to the jig's visual appeal.

TONY ACETTA
"JIGAROO"

Vibration is also the key to the special fascination fish have for the Tony Acetta "Jigaroo." This bucktailed jig, traditional in almost every other way, has a bright concave metal blade attached to the bottom by a loose link. The metal blade adds flash and movement to the jig's proven allure.

Other lures, like the Glen Evans "Shadrac," add flash by tying in strips and panels of metallic Mylar.

We could continue to pick our way through the contents of the serious jig fisherman's tackle box and continue to find variations in size, shape, color, materials and design. Yet, as we do so, the answer to the intriguing question we started with becomes a paradox. The best lure we could choose if we could choose only one? A leadheaded jig, of course. But which leadheaded jig? Our happy hero wants at least three more decades to research the question.

Spin Fishing with Jigs

The jig is the whipper's basic weapon, especially when the papio are running in the energetic 1- to 2-lb size.

The simplest jig is no more than a chunk of lead finished off with a wisp of hair and a touch of paint. But in the hands of an expert fisherman, it is transformed into a living creature, the way a puppeteer creates life in a stringed doll.

Fishing a jig is one of the most satisfying ways of angling any sportsman ever devised. But you get only as much out of the sport of whipping with a jig as you put into it. And what you need to put into it is the rhythm and timing of casting with well-balanced equipment as well as the mental tension of trying to outthink your quarry and convincing him that your jig is more than it seems. Your reward is the thrill of seeing a papio or kaku race out of hiding to gulp the illusion of life you've created.

Since the whole art of jig fishing is magic, legerdemain and sleight of hand, it follows that there are tricks to the trade.

Let's begin with a review of the basics. The jig is balanced to ride through the water with the hook point running up, positioned on the dorsal side of the lure. That's so the point is always safe from contact with obstacles, whether they be horizontal snags on the bottom or vertical protrusions like coral heads, rocks and sea weed.

As already described, the only real variables of construction in a jig are its size (and therefore its weight), its color and the type of material in its tail.

The lure's appeal to a fish is primarily determined by your particular method of working the lure. You can bounce or hop it, swim it straight, reel it fast or slow, run it near the surface, along the bottom, or vary it back and forth at all the depths in between.

The wise jigger fishes the same spot with several different retrieves before he gives up to move on. When whipping for papio, I use a series of entirely different actions on alternate casts. The first cast, I just crank the reel handle as fast as I can as soon as the lure hits the water. The jig runs on a straight course just under the surface. The next cast is a hopper — the retrieve is at about half speed. Though the speed of the reeling is kept constant, the rod tip is swept back and forth to make the lure dart forward and fall back.

On the third cast I hold the rod tip as high as I can and dance the lure right across the surface. It splashes, kicking up an audible commotion. Since it is repeatedly breaking free of the surface, it darts from side to side, never seeming to point in the same direction as before, acting like a frightened and confused bait fish. The penultimate retrieve is the deep hopper. I cast the lure, let it settle to within a few feet of the bottom without

reeling line, all the while barely twitching the rod tip so that the lure jerks slightly as it sinks. Then I sweep it forward with the rod tip, letting it settle back again as I quickly pick up slack line.

The last retrieve before I move on is the same fast surface runner as the first one. Often, the varied series has interested a fish that is now ready for action.

When the bottom is sandy, I throw in a retrieve that allows the lure to settle right to the bottom, pushing up a gentle puff of sand each time it hits. Papio and 'o'io will follow it, staring intently at it each time it rests idly in the sand, then smashing it on the third or fourth spurt as it jets forward across the sand.

Jigging requires monofilament line and leader. When kaku (barracuda) are the quarry, a light trace of wire is inescapable, but the chances of the lure attracting a papio or 'o'io are reduced nearly to zero.

The smallest jigs are the best. Jigs in the ⅛ to 1/16 ounce range have a tremendous amount of action and, therefore, an irresistible level of appeal.

Don't use snaps or swivels. Tie your line directly to the lure. Use a free-swinging loop type of knot that does not seize up against the eye of the hook and cut off the action. You want your lure to point up on the jerk forward, then dive straight down on the release. The bobbing action is much more tantalizing to fish.

Bait your jig. A thin strip of squid wriggles nicely. A tiny bit of shrimp adds some zest without interfering with the action. A small whole minnow hooked through the head can be unbeatable. The latter bait is especially valuable in jigging for kaku.

Watch the way the fish takes the jig. On the fast retrieve, sock the hook to him instantly since the fish has almost certainly swallowed the lure on the strike. With the slow retrieve, hit the fish immediately only if your jig is not baited. If it is baited, pause just a second, dropping the rod tip forward to give slack line so that the fish won't be alerted; then hit him.

Most strikes on hopper retrieves come as the lure is being jerked forward. At such times you have no choice but to set the hook instantly — in fact you are already unknowingly doing it as the fish hits. Occasionally, the fish will grab the jig on the drop. You may not even know it until the fish has realized his error and spits out the hook. Be sensitive to any change in the movement of the line as the lure drops, and hit it instantly if you get suspicious.

Choose the right colors. In Hawai'i, white or blue and white are often best, but yellow, black or translucent jigs are also great.

Follow these guidelines and, for the fish, the jig is up.

On the opposite page is an illustrated step-by-step procedure for molding your own favorite or custom leadhead jigs. We would like to acknowledge and extend our thanks to Charlie Teves for sharing this jig-molding tip with us.

MOLDING YOUR OWN LEADHEAD JIGS

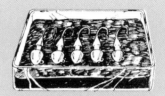

MATERIALS REQUIRED:
1. DOW CORNING 3120 RTV (RED) SILICONE RUBBER KIT
2. OLD PLASTIC LURE BOX
3. YOUR FAVORITE JIGS (FOR PATTERNS)
4. JIG HOOKS

1. POUR THE BOTTOM HALF OF THE MOLD BY MIXING JUST ENOUGH RUBBER AND DRYER TO FILL HALF THE LID.

2. WITH MOLD ON A LEVEL SURFACE WAIT UNTIL RUBBER STARTS TO THICKEN. CAREFULLY PRESS EACH JIG HEAD HALFWAY INTO RUBBER. ALLOW TO SET FOR 24 HOURS.

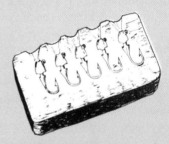

3. COAT THE FACE OF FIRST HALF WITH A THIN LAYER OF VASELINE. THEN MIX AND POUR SECOND HALF. AGAIN LET SET FOR 24 HOURS.

4. NEXT CRACK THE PLASTIC TRAY. THE TWO HALVES WILL SEPARATE EASILY BECAUSE OF THE VASELINE.

5. USE A SHARP KNIFE OR RAZOR TO CUT CHANNELS TO POUR LEAD INTO. MAKE IDENTICAL CONE-SHAPED CUTS IN EACH HALF.

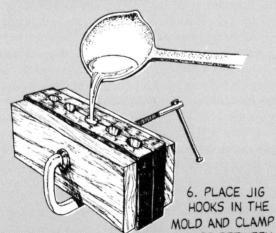

6. PLACE JIG HOOKS IN THE MOLD AND CLAMP IN A VISE BETWEEN TWO PIECES OF FLAT WOOD. DO NOT OVER TIGHTEN. POUR LEAD. LET COOL AND REPEAT PROCESS.

7. FINISH YOUR JIGHEADS WITH AN UNDERCOAT OF PRIMER AND ONE OR TWO COATS OF PAINT. ADD RUBBER TAILS, FEATHERS, FISH SKIN OR BUCK TAIL TO FINISH THE JIG.

Deep-Water Jigging

Deep-jigging is something I've read a lot about over the years. It has always seemed to me to be a natural method of fishing for Hawai'i. Unfortunately, the first few times I tried it I didn't have much success. Recently, however, my luck has changed.

To understand why deep-jigging has worked for me recently, you have to examine why my past efforts were failures.

Deep-jigging means plunking a heavy lure down to the bottom and bringing it back to the surface, yo-yo style. On the way back up, the angler reels and jerks his rod tip. The lure, if it is the right kind, darts upward then turns and dashes toward the bottom, only to jerk back upward again.

The right kind of lure must be used. A trolling jig that slides freely on its leader, for example, usually won't work. There isn't enough freedom in the leader rigging to allow it the necessary erratic up-and-down hop.

What's needed is a fixed-hook jig, the kind with a lead-head molded directly to a special hook. The eye of the hook acts as a kind of hinge that allows the lure to swivel instantly from a head-up dart to a head-down drop. In theory, deep-jigging with a fixed leadhead sounded like a great way to catch bottom fish.

So that's just where I started. But what kind of bottom fish should I catch? Knowing the kind you want to catch affects where you fish and how big a lure you choose.

Small jigs, the kind you choose for papio, just won't sink down very far. Anything under an ounce might as well have no weight at all if you are trying to reach a bottom that is down 30 feet or more.

And what kind of fish are going to hit big jigs? I found out the first couple of times I tried big jigs (2- and 3-ounce) in 100 to 200 feet of water. I had visions of uku (grey snapper), kahala (amberjack) and ulua (trevally), or at least papio.

Using jigs with plastic tails, in the approved (by nationally famous outdoor writers) way, I found that the bottom was paved with triggerfish and all manner of other tiny, toothy creatures which just loved to chew up plastic tails. You couldn't even get the lure back from a bottom drop in one piece. Little mouths had gouged great chunks out of the plastic bodies and needle teeth had shredded the carefully molded curly tails before they could even wiggle in front of a trophy fish.

On spinning tackle with 10- to 20-pound test line, I could get my 2- to 3-ounce bullet head lures down all right. I just couldn't get them back while they still looked alluring.

And then two things happened. First, I got a depth recorder. Second, I realized that the lure only had to go down to where the fish were and not to the bottom, and there is usually a difference.

The depth recorder read the bottom for me and told me not only just how far away the earth was, but also the kind of bottom it was (quite important) and whether there were any fish hovering above it. After all, if there are no fish big enough to be picked up on the recorder you are going to waste your time fishing that area. Wasting your time dragging a bait along the bottom is one thing. Wasting your time reeling and jerking is entirely another matter — quite an exhausting one.

The first fish I caught deep-jigging was a surprise and a pleasure. It was nothing I had expected. I recorded a school of fish hovering over a sandy bottom in about 170 feet of water. They were close enough to the bottom to make me worry about throwing away another plastic tail. So I rigged my bullet head (a yellow Glen Evans "Tall Tale Bucktail") with a section of octopus leg to replace the molded plastic tail that had already been lost to toothy critters.

WEKE ULA

The jig never reached the bottom. Before it could, I found myself fighting a 5-pound weke ula. You don't think of these big, bright-red goatfish as being the type of glamorous game fish that strikes artificial lures with abandon. Do think of them as good fighters (especially on spinning gear) and darn fine eating fish.

You can imagine that I was very happy to drop anchor up-current of the school (so as not to scare them with the anchor), chum the bottom with chopped 'opelu (we brought some along for bottom fishing bait to bring the fish under the boat), and plunk away with spinning gear until I had worked up a dozen or so fish.

Using strips from a freshly caught (on the way out to the bottom fishing hole) kawakawa was even better. A strip on the hook behind the bucktail was irresistible. And so was the jigging action. I really believe that I caught more fish by jigging than I would have with sinkers and plain hooks. You might argue with that, but you can't argue with all the fun I had with my spinning gear.

But that's not when deep-jigging really paid off for me. That first episode just encouraged me to keep trying.

Imagine trolling along and spotting (on your depth recorder) a giant school of fish milling around 100 feet down. The orange flasher on my recorder lit up in a rage of bright sparks blasting away next to the 100-foot mark. The fish were too deep to spot a trolling lure. And too uninterested to take the trouble to investigate the commotion of a boat passing overhead.

My partner and I quickly hauled in our trolling lures, broke out the spinning gear and armed the rods with jigs. We drifted back over the school and our jigs plummeted into the depths. Each of us prayed to the fish gods that the bright blips weren't just a school of 'opelu.

When we were sure the lures had dropped through the layer of fish, we started working them back up. After three upward sweeps, my lure just stopped. Nothing happened for a full 10 seconds. I felt like I was pulling on an anchor. Then the fish took off like a rocket.

I realized that the scream in my ears was partly from the reel and partly from my throat. The rest of it was from my partner's vocal chords. He was hooked up too.

Fifteen minutes later, we each did the honors in gaffing the other's bigeye tuna. We had drifted over an ahi ko'a loaded with bigeye of 20- to 25-pounds each.

DEEP-WATER "JIGGING"

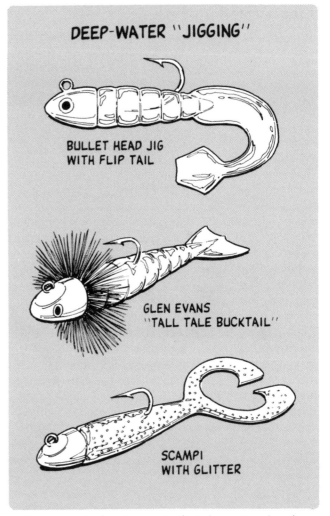

BULLET HEAD JIG
WITH FLIP TAIL

GLEN EVANS
"TALL TALE BUCKTAIL"

SCAMPI
WITH GLITTER

BIGEYE TUNA

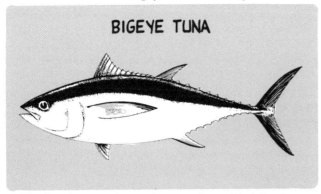

By the time we boated our pair, we'd drifted away from the school. Our first job was to find it again. Our second was to repair the damages.

I'd been using a 3-ounce bullet head Scampi lure with a double-twister tail. The tuna had ripped off the soft plastic tail. Fortunately, I had a big bag of 5-inch curly tails to replace them.

The bigeye tuna didn't seem to care about the change at all. They gulped the curly tailed Scampi just as fast as before. My partner had a white 2½-ounce Glen Evans "Tall Tale Bucktail." This one had a light grey molded tail shaped like the body of a shrimp. The plastic was a tougher formula than the others, and the lure was skirted with a fringe of bucktail.

We found that the soft-bodied lures had an extra advantage — fish gulped them down. Even when the first contact between fish and lure was just a bump, that bump was a good convincer that the lure was edible.

Whenever we felt a bump that wasn't a full take, we'd just drop the rod tip for a second to let the jig dive for the bottom. Then we'd sweep the rod tip up hard. The fish was always there. And when we finally landed it and looked for the hook, it was out of sight.

One recent development that has stimulated an interest in deep-jigging is the success of the Fish Aggregating Devices. The FADs not only gather fish at the surface, but they also attract fish all along a vertical column. Schools of bigeye tuna in the size range of 10 to 60 pounds can often be found at the buoys, stacked up at depths of 50 to 150 feet, depending on the time of day. These fish refuse to let a deep jig pass through their school unchallenged.

For me, perhaps the best part of deep-jigging is working a lure to make a fish hit and then feeling the strike when he does take it. I do a lot of trolling, and there is a lot of the feeling of a remote control operation about trolling. The action of the lure is really just a by-product of your transportation, not something you are really personally involved with.

You're not holding the rod when a fish hits. Yours is kind of a delayed reaction. Often, by the time you get your other lines in and finally get around to fighting a fish that hits a trolled lure, the most exciting part of the fight is over.

Don't get me wrong. I like trolling. But now that I know how and when to do it, I like deep-jigging just as much.

Spoon Feeding Fish

Few lures can really be called "secret weapons." That's because the good ones are too well known and well used to be thought of as "secret."

In Hawai'i, however, there really is a good lure that catches lots of fish when used right — yet it isn't used often or by lots of people. That type of lure is the "spoon."

A spoon lure is shiny piece of metal with a hook at one end and a ring for attaching the lure to your line at the other. Some spoons are flat as a knife blade. Most are curved like the bowl of a spoon, a shape that gives them their name. The shape and the weight of the spoon influence the action of the spoon being pulled through the water. Different shapes have different actions and must be worked differently.

Some fishermen like to use spoons better than any other type of lure; and they automatically reach for a bright silver wobbler when they open their tackle boxes. These spoon-chuckers have developed special tricks over the years. We'll share some of the tricks with you.

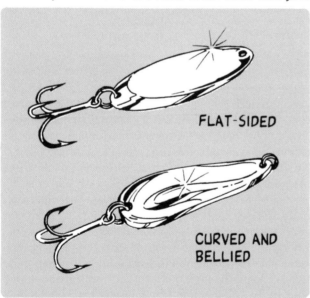

FLAT-SIDED

CURVED AND BELLIED

1. Small spoons sometimes work better than big spoons. This is especially true for casting with light spinning tackle over shallow reefs. The little ¾-inch spoons seem to be just the best bite for many types of reef fish, and the bigger game fish like them, too.

2. When using a small spoon, remember that the hook is extremely small and must be used carefully. If you use too much pressure, the hook might bend open and you'll lose your fish. Most spoons come with small treble-hooks. You might try changing to a double-hook

or a large single-hook for more strength. Sometimes changing hooks alters the action of the lure. The result may be for the better or for the worse. With experience, you'll find out what works best for your type of fishing.

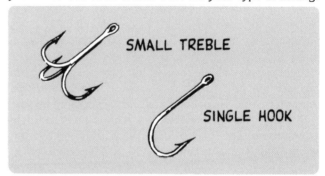

SMALL TREBLE

SINGLE HOOK

3. Big spoons sometimes work better than small ones. This is especially true when you are deep-jigging or when you have to cast very long distances with heavy line. When deep-jigging from a boat, big spoons sink faster and deeper, reaching down to where the bigger fish hang out. When casting in the surf, big spoons give you the reach necessary to get the lure into the clear water behind the waves. Many fish can't resist a fast-moving, flashing lure dodging back and forth into white water.

Some spoons are as much as 7 or 8 inches long, but these are generally not very good casters. Good spoons for deep-jigging and surf-casting are the 1- to 2-ounce lures.

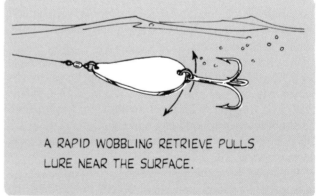

A RAPID WOBBLING RETRIEVE PULLS LURE NEAR THE SURFACE.

4. Try fast-swimming. Some spoons work best when pulled through the water rapidly. This is usually true for the flat-sided types of lures like the "Kastmaster" and "Mr. Champ" lures. A good speed is just fast enough to keep the spoons racing along without spinning. Sometimes, however, a spinning spoon can be a very good fish-catcher.

SOMETIMES IT TAKES A BIG SPOON TO GET OUT WHERE THE FISH ARE.

5. Try a jerky, start-stop retrieve. I like this one when I'm deep-jigging. The yellow-finned types of tuna which hang around fish aggregating buoys seem unable to resist a lure that darts upward and falls back. Don't let it drop back too much. If it does, the hook may tangle on the line. And when you are letting the lure drop, be ready for a jolt. At least half of the strikes you get will occur when the lure is falling back.

6. Try working the bottom. You can really only do this in sandy areas. Cast the lure, and let it fall until it stops. Then jerk the tip back six inches or a foot to make the lure jump forward and up from the bottom. Let it drop again until it stops. The shiny flashing and rolling action along the bottom imitates many kinds of feeding bait fish. It's an action big fish are on the lookout for. They'll spot the lure as it flashes, investigate when it drops back to the bottom, and snatch it when it darts forward. This action works because it takes advantage of a fish's curiosity and instinct.

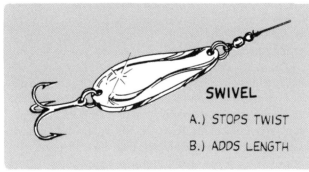

SWIVEL

A.) STOPS TWIST

B.) ADDS LENGTH

7. Attach a swivel to the front end of the lure. Most spoons have a split ring threaded through the attachment hole at the front of the lure. Add a swivel to this ring. The swivel does two jobs: it keeps the wobbling and whirling lure from twisting the line, and it helps protect the leader from sharp teeth.

With a swivel on the front of the lure, you may not need a wire leader. Even sharp-toothed fish may not be able to reach a nylon leader to cut it if the lure and swivel combination are long enough. Few fish will swallow the lure completely. Most will be hooked in the side or the front of the mouth.

8. Pick the right thickness of lure for your fishing. Spoons are stamped out of flat sheets of metal. The thicker the sheet, the heavier the lure. Thin metal lures have a lot of fluttering and spinning action at slow speeds, but they are very hard to cast. Lightweight lures are made for trolling for trout or salmon.

Thick metal lures are great casters, take a lot of beating from tough fish and wriggle enticingly at higher speeds.

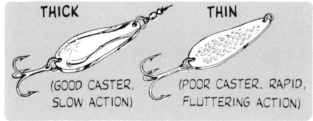

THICK

THIN

(GOOD CASTER, SLOW ACTION)

(POOR CASTER. RAPID, FLUTTERING ACTION)

9. When fighting a jumping fish with a spoon, keep the line tight when the fish clears the water. One great disadvantage of a spoon is the ease with which a fish can throw it. A jumping fish can often free himself by jerking his head and whipping the heavy lure around in an arc. Keep your line tight enough to prevent the fish from swinging the lure freely. You'll lose some fish if your line is too tight. You'll lose others if it is too loose.

10. Keep your spoons shiny. The best feature of a spoon is its flashing reflection, just like the bright flicker of a wriggling bait fish. Under most ocean conditions, bright spoons attract better than dark ones. However, in some types of freshwater fishing, dark spoons can be best — even black spoons are good for catching bass, while red and white "daredevils" are the standard lure for pike and pickerel. Not so in the sea.

After using spoons in salt water, wash them off with fresh water, dry them and store them in a dry place. Corrosion will make the lure less attractive, but, most of all, it will attack the split rings and hooks, making them too weak to hold the fish of your dreams.

11. Give the spoons a fair test. Fishermen often lose faith quickly. They'll toss a new lure out a few times and give up on it if it doesn't catch a fish on the first few casts. Then they'll flail the sea with their favorite lures for hours without getting even a touch — happy to do so because they believe in the magic of their tried and true lures.

Remember that all magic is trickery. Lures tease and tantalize, but most of all, they fool. Bright, wobbling spoons are among the best deceivers made.

Twelve Lucky Tricks for Whippers

1. When choosing a fishing rod, don't overlook that very important factor — sensitivity. The more sensitive a rod is, the quicker you'll feel the tap or tug that says you've got a bite and the quicker you'll be able to react to set the hook. Sensitivity is a judgment call; you won't find it measured and marked on the rod blank. To judge a rod's sensitivity, hold it in your hand at the reel seat just the way you would if you were fishing with it.

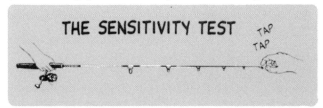

THE SENSITIVITY TEST TAP TAP

Then have someone else tap the tip. The lighter the tap you can feel, the more sensitive the rod. You'll never find a rod sensitive enough to transmit the stroke of a feather, but the closer you can get to it, the better.

2. Fish with confidence once you've learned the proper techniques. Very few fish are caught on the first cast or the first trolling pass. With confidence in what you are doing, you will fish harder, more seriously and with more concentration. The fisherman who fishes without commitment will occasionally be surprised by a strike, but most often he'll be sitting on the sidelines while his friends have the fun.

AS A PREDATOR APPROACHES, SPEED UP YOUR RETRIEVE.

3. When you see a fish trailing behind your lure, don't slow down or stop your reeling. Some fishermen feel that dropping the lure back will give the fish a chance to catch it. That's the wrong psychology. At the approach of a predator, a chased bait fish speeds up, even skittering out of the water, to try to escape. That action helps trigger the predator's striking response. Do the same with your lure. When a papio or kaku charges onto the scene, reel faster. The fish may not grab your lure, but, rest assured, he wouldn't have taken it had the lure died under his nose.

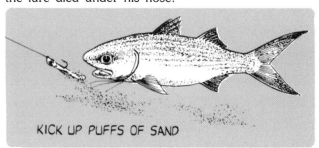

KICK UP PUFFS OF SAND

4. When fishing with jigs over sandy bottom, don't neglect the appeal of the "puff." Natural baits, like crabs, shrimp and small fish, kick up puffs of sand as they feed along the bottom and dart away to escape. Drop your jig on the sand. With the rod tip low, give the jig a hard jerk to kick up a puff. It's only natural.

GRUB BUG

5. Make a "grub bug" and test it out on your fishing grounds. You'll need a hook, a few brightly colored feathers and a piece of plastic worm about as long as the hook shank. Tie the feathers onto the hook about half way down along the shank. Then push the piece of worm down along the shank to cover the wraps. Fish the grub bug on a long leader behind a sinker. Or, pinch a split shot onto the eye of the hook and fish it like a jig.

6. Study your fishing grounds at the lowest tide on the chart. Extreme negative tides empty the reef of water and fish life, that's true, which makes the dry time the worst time for fishing. But it's the best time to spot those hollows, depressions, channels, coral heads and openings that will tell you where the fish will be hunting when the tide comes back in.

7. Study your fishing grounds with a snorkel, face mask and flippers. Get in among the fish to see what kinds are around, where they hide and what the sea conditions are doing to the bottom. Invading their territory will spook the fish for a while, knocking them off their feed and chasing some clear out to blue water. But you'll learn things about your fishing territory that will make it as much your home grounds as it is the fish's.

8. Fish the reef on an incoming tide. That's when the big fish, the ones that spend most of their lives in deeper water, are most likely to roam the reef. The reason? Water temperature and depth. Fish have definite preferences for certain water temperatures. Reef waters are normally too warm for deepwater fish, since the waters of the reef heat up from a day's soak in the sun. On a falling tide, these warm waters are pulled out to sea, pushing the cool water fishes away from them. Wave action at the reef edge mixes the warmer waters with the cooler sea. On the rising tide, this cooler mass pushes up over the reef again, bringing the big fish with it.

9. Fish the reef channels during the bottom half of the rising tide. Low reef waters concentrate fish in the deepest waters available to them. Quite often these fish are cruising back and forth as they wait impatiently for the waters to rise higher. They are eager. Keep whipping likely spots because new chances come as new fish take up positions in the channels.

10. Spread out across the reef during the top half of the rising tide. When the water is high, the fish might be anywhere since they are taking advantage of the temporary depths to search out food that usually isn't available to them.

11. Fish any tide at daybreak. Darkness covers and cools, keeping fish on the reef even in thin water. With the first stray rays of cold grey light, prowling fish steal around the reef to ambush unwary creatures.

12. Fish churning waters. White water, charged with bubbles, is enriched with oxygen. Fast-moving heavy-hitters, like papio and ulua, need lots of oxygen to support their energetic life-style. Tumbling water pulls prey fish and crustaceans away from the security of the rocks. Occasionally, the big fish feed right in the white water, but the bubbles reduce visibility to inches, leaving predators to chase shadows. A more productive zone is the clear water right at the edge of the white stuff. That's a great spot to cast into from a boat. Toss your lure right up into the suds then pull it clear so a rampaging papio can spot it.

When whipping with a jig, spoon or plug, make your rig a double-threat by using a dropper fly. One of the most remarkable shore-casting catches made in the world in the last two decades — a 73-lb striped bass, the new world record for surf-casters — was taken on a dropper fly. We don't have striped bass in Hawai'i, but we've got a lot of fish that will grab a dropper.

Here's how to use it. Let's say you're fishing with a jig on a monofilament-nylon leader. Tie the leader to your line with a blood knot. Make sure the tag end of your line that emerges from the blood knot is six to eight inches long. That's the end you'll tie your dropper fly to; even if the blood knot fails when you are hooked up to a big fish, the dropper fly is still firmly attached to your mainline.

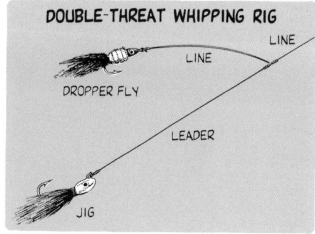

DOUBLE-THREAT WHIPPING RIG

To make a dropper fly, tie a bunch of hackle feathers to a hook, winding the shank with chenille of the same color. Finish the fly with colored thread to make a tapered head. Coat the head with shellac until hard, and dot some eyes on with the end of a matchstick (for the outer eye) and the head of a pin (for the inner eye). When twitching the jig through the water, the dropper fly will dance ahead with an action of its own.

The world-record striper was caught on a dropper fly fished ahead of a whole eel. The striper preferred the artificial to the natural. Why? Some piscatorial psychologists say the lure and dropper fly appear to a fish like one small creature attacking another. The big fish can't seem to resist the temptation to get into the act.

FISH CHURNING WHITE WATER
FOR FAST-MOVING HEAVY-HITTERS

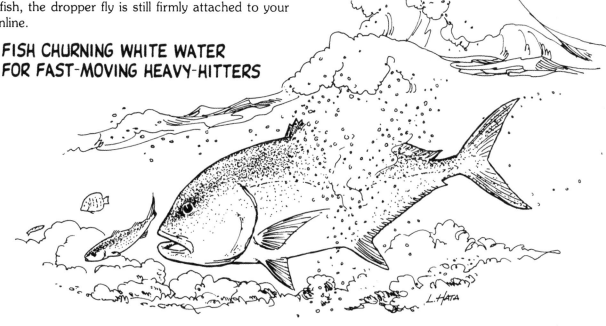

L. HATA

Fishing with Bait

Live or Otherwise

Why would a fish want to eat something made out of metal, wood, plastic, hair or feathers? That's the question the bait fisherman asks when he sees the rows and rows of lures in tackle stores. In his mind, something that tastes good, smells good and feels right is the best thing for getting a fish hungry enough to bite.

And for many kinds of fish, a fresh natural bait is not just the best way to catch them, it is the only way.

Hawai'i's fishermen have many different natural baits to choose from. Some kinds the fisherman can gather for himself; other types he must buy.

Take shrimp, for example. All fish like to eat shrimp. you can use shrimp to catch every kind of fish that swims near shore including papio, 'o'io, weke, moi — you name it.

The small Hawaiian shrimp is called 'opae and can be caught in brackish water streams and canals or along the pilings of docks and piers. 'Opae cling to pilings and rocks. You can dip them up with a hand net. More come out at night, so they are easier to catch in the dark. A bright light makes them easy to spot because their eyes shine in the beam of light.

Hook them under the collar behind the head. Use a small hook with very light wire. Don't poke the hook in far or you will kill the shrimp.

Dead 'opae will also catch fish. Use just enough bait to cover the hook. For small fish, use a small piece. On a larger hook, use a whole 'opae. For still larger hooks, use two or three 'opae on the same hook.

If you can't catch your own shrimp, you can buy large frozen shrimp at nearly every food store with a seafood counter. Local fishermen call these California shrimp, no matter where they come from. Break the shrimp into pieces just large enough to match the size of the hook.

Shrimp is soft and easily stolen by nibblers. It is also very expensive. Squid is a tougher, cheaper bait that is just as good for many kinds of fish.

In Hawai'i, many people make the mistake of saying "squid" when they mean "octopus." Don't be confused by the name. The real "squid" is sold under the Japanese name ika or the Italian name calamari.

To use a squid, you must cut it into strips. First, pull off the head. Most of the insides will come away with the head. Save the head because it is a good bait. Second, pull off the fins. They should come off easily. Once the fins are pulled off, the skin comes off very easily.

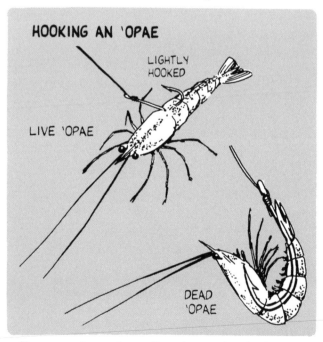

HOOKING AN 'OPAE

LIGHTLY HOOKED

LIVE 'OPAE

DEAD 'OPAE

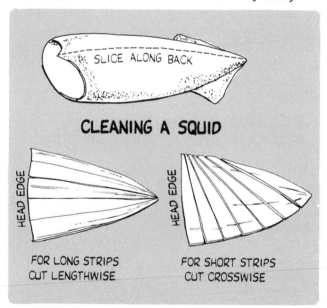

SLICE ALONG BACK

CLEANING A SQUID

HEAD EDGE

FOR LONG STRIPS CUT LENGTHWISE

HEAD EDGE

FOR SHORT STRIPS CUT CROSSWISE

If you can keep them alive, they make the best bait. To keep them alive, put them in a floating bait container. This type is a wooden box with openings covered with screening. The openings let new water in so the shrimp get plenty of oxygen. 'Opae will also stay alive for awhile stored in wet seaweed in a closed container.

Now you've got a clean white cone of meat called the mantle. Look for a V-shaped piece of mantle sticking out along the edge where the head was. Slice the mantle lengthwise starting at the V and going all the way to the tip of the squid. The mantle will fall open into a large flat triangle. For large strips, cut slices down the length. For shorter strips, cut diagonally across.

The head also makes good bait. Use it whole, or cut it into halves, or use just one tentacle on the hook.

Squid will last longer than shrimp if small fish try to nibble your bait. But octopus is best if you want your bait left alone until a big fish finds it.

Octopus (also called by their Japanese name tako) live in holes and caves in the reef. You can find them by looking for caves that have small bits of coral and shells lying outside their openings. Stick a spear into the hole and the octopus will grab it. He'll usually hold on long enough to let you pull him out of the cave.

You can kill the octopus quickly by cutting the nerve between its eyes.

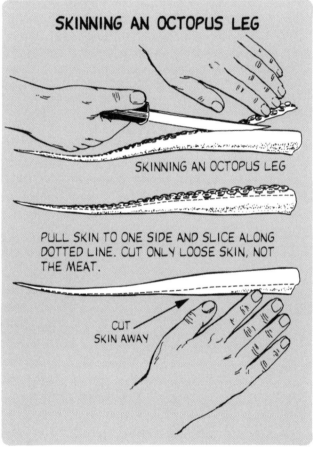

SKINNING AN OCTOPUS LEG

SKINNING AN OCTOPUS LEG

PULL SKIN TO ONE SIDE AND SLICE ALONG DOTTED LINE. CUT ONLY LOOSE SKIN, NOT THE MEAT.

CUT SKIN AWAY

Fresh octopus is an excellent bait for large papio and 'o'io. To prepare it, you must first skin it. The skin does not peel off easily but must be cut off. The tough meat of the arm slides easily inside the skin. Pull the skin to one side and slice it off. Then pull the rest of the skin to the other side and slice it off.

A piece of octopus bait will hold off the teeth of small nibbler fish all day. It is a favorite food of eels, unfortunately, and you can expect to catch a few when you use octopus for bait.

Slices of fish also make excellent baits. Slices cut from the tough and shiny bellies of aku and kawakawa are good for whipping and for still fishing. Many moi fishermen prefer aku or kawakawa belly for whipping in the rough surf where moi like to feed.

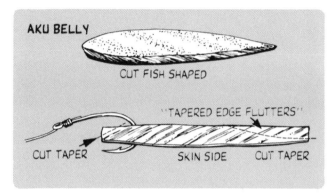

AKU BELLY

CUT FISH SHAPED

"TAPERED EDGE FLUTTERS"

CUT TAPER   SKIN SIDE   CUT TAPER

Slices of akule and 'opelu are excellent baits for still fishing. The meat is softer even than shrimp. When you cut a slice to use for bait, be sure to keep the skin on. The skin is a little tougher and holds the bait on the hook longer. Cut the baits by first fileting the fish. Then cut the filets lengthwise. Then cut down diagonally with the skin side down. In other words, cut the meat before you cut the skin.

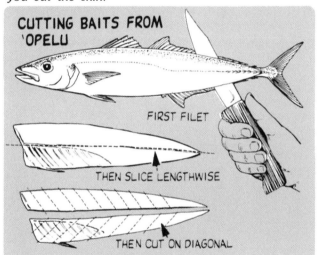

CUTTING BAITS FROM 'OPELU

FIRST FILET

THEN SLICE LENGTHWISE

THEN CUT ON DIAGONAL

Thin slices of weke are good bait for papio and kaku. Small whole weke, called 'oama, are the favorite food of both these fish.

Natural baits spoil fast in the Hawaiian climate of warmth and sunshine. To keep them from spoiling, keep them cold. Some fishermen use small insulated bags to carry their bait. The bags are easy to carry even for the fisherman who wades the reef. Put a small zip-lock plastic bag with a dozen ice cubes in the insulated bait bag, and it will keep the bait cooler a lot longer.

Some fishermen freeze their bait to make it last until they need it. While the bait is frozen it stays in good condition. But freezing does cause problems. Freezing softens the bait. Frozen akule and 'opelu, for example, do not stay on the hook as well. Octopus that has been frozen will absorb water. The loose white meat seems to draw in water and begins to look like jelly.

Fresh bait is the best bait. Old bait can be so bad that it might as well be made out of wood, plastic, metal or feathers.

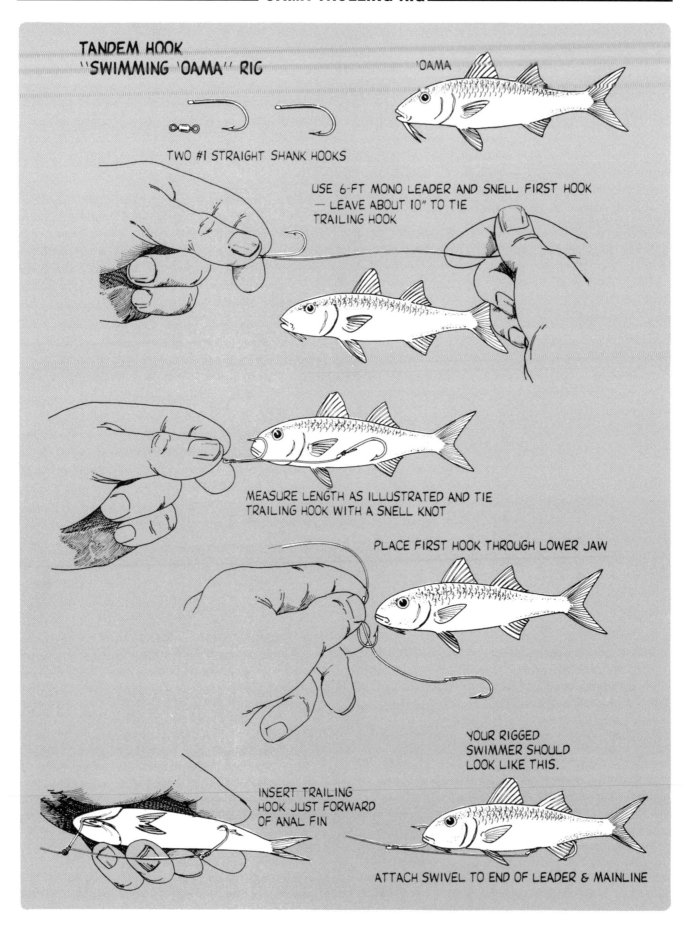

TANDEM HOOK
"SWIMMING 'OAMA" RIG

'OAMA

TWO #1 STRAIGHT SHANK HOOKS

USE 6-FT MONO LEADER AND SNELL FIRST HOOK
— LEAVE ABOUT 10" TO TIE
TRAILING HOOK

MEASURE LENGTH AS ILLUSTRATED AND TIE
TRAILING HOOK WITH A SNELL KNOT

PLACE FIRST HOOK THROUGH LOWER JAW

YOUR RIGGED
SWIMMER SHOULD
LOOK LIKE THIS.

INSERT TRAILING
HOOK JUST FORWARD
OF ANAL FIN

ATTACH SWIVEL TO END OF LEADER & MAINLINE

If a still-fished bait is good, a moving bait can be better — even for reef fish. A tandem hook "swimming 'oama" rig is very successful in trolling for papio, kaku, awa-awa, moana and big lai. The rig we've illustrated was suggested to us by Charlie Teves and Warren Kam. Charlie and Warren fish it on light spinning gear with 3- or 4-pound test line. They choose fresh or frozen 'oama in good condition and troll as slowly as necessary to keep the 'oama swimming upright without spinning.

Moving beyond the reef, trollers and drift-fishermen find that fresh whole baits such as rigged squid and 'opelu sometimes out-produce lures in fishing for mahi-mahi and ono. Chuck Johnston has found that rigged squid, especially, are good baits for trolling the fish aggregating buoys. According to Chuck, almost all artificial lures used today are sporting plastic skirts resembling the natural shape of the squid. This is proven testimony to the effectiveness of squid as a likely bait.

Because the fresh squid is a natural bait, it works best when trolled at speeds slower than the speed required for the artificial look alikes. This speed factor offers more good reasons to give fresh squid serious consideration: 1) Slower speeds mean less fuel consumption; at today's prices, this is a prime consideration. 2) The ideal trolling speed is between 2 to 8 knots; therefore, squid becomes an excellent bait for trolling or drifting near the buoys (FADs). 3) With the rough water conditions we frequently experience, slower boat speeds are more comfortable than faster speeds and create a lot less pounding.

Because the squid is a limp bait, it has to be rigged in such a way as to hold its natural swimming form while being trolled. Yet this natural softness makes it very easy for a predator to swallow the bait and simplifies the task of setting the hook.

One word of caution: fresh water, such as melting ice in a cooler, will soften the bait and cause it to discolor. Therefore, be sure to wrap it well and keep it out of direct contact with ice or water in the cooler. Squid should not be refrozen once it has thawed.

There are many ways to rig a squid. The one we will show you here is simple and durable and presents the bait in a lifelike manner.

Wire leader can be substituted for monofilament if preferred and, if it's ono you're after, it's mandatory.

All you need to rig a squid is a 15-foot leader, hook, 1/2-inch diameter ball cork, sleeve and crimping pliers. The size of hook and weight of leader should be in proportion to the size of the species you intend to catch. We've used a 12-inch long squid, 7/0 stainless steel hook and 150-pound test monofilament.

The complete squid can be rigged very quickly, and, when using baits of the same length, the rigged hooks and leaders can be rebaited in just a couple of minutes. Simply snip off the swivel, rebait, then reconnect the swivel to the end of the leader.

The rigged squid is a "skip" bait, though its action is really more like an effortless slide across the surface than a splashing and leaping skip.

Another effective skip bait for slow speed trolling can be rigged from a fresh 'opelu. (Avoid using frozen 'opelu — they are too soft and fall apart easily when towed.)

Select a needle-eye sea demon style hook about as big across as the depth of the bait's head at its eye. Bend the hook on to a wire leader with a haywire twist. Finish the leader with a simple barrel swivel, making a total length that will put the swivel in the 'opelu's mouth. Using a long bait rigging needle, draw the swivel up through the body and out the mouth. (See the illustration for the point of entry in the tail — a spot in the caudal peduncle where the skin is toughened by a row of scutes.) Sew the mouth shut with stitches that pass through the rear eye of the barrel swivel. The stitches should bind the bait firmly to the swivel to keep it from sliding back along the leader, and they should keep the mouth firmly shut to prevent water from entering and ripping the bait. The rigged 'opelu should be trolled just fast enough to keep it sliding across the surface without slapping. A bait that slaps its tail is, frankly, more attractive, but it will break up quickly from the repeated impact.

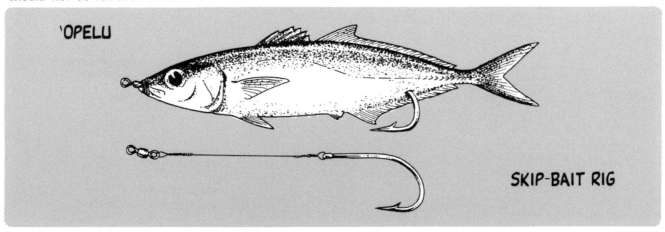

'OPELU

SKIP-BAIT RIG

CALAMARI SQUID RIG

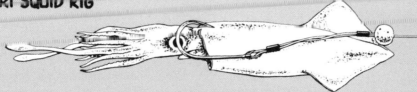

STEP 1   ATTACH THE LEADER TO THE HOOK AS ILLUSTRATED WITH SLEEVE. BE SURE TO LEAVE TAG END ABOUT 8" LONG. THEN, WITH BEND OF HOOK IN LINE WITH THE EYE OF THE SQUID, SLIDE SECOND SLEEVE AND CORK DOWN TO A POSITION JUST SHORT OF THE END OF THE TAIL. WHEN YOU HAVE DETERMINED THE RIGHT LENGTH, INSERT TAG END IN SLEEVE AND CRIMP. SNIP OFF EXCESS. THE CORK WILL NOW BE PREVENTED FROM SLIDING DOWN TOWARD THE HOOK.

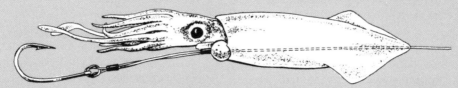

STEP 2   PUNCTURE A SMALL HOLE IN TAIL END JUST LARGE ENOUGH FOR LEADER TO PASS THROUGH. THREAD OTHER END OF LEADER UP THROUGH THE BODY CAVITY OF SQUID AND OUT THROUGH HOLE IN CENTER OF TAIL. CAREFULLY PULL THE LEADER THROUGH THE SQUID UNTIL THE CORK IS SEATED INSIDE TAIL END.

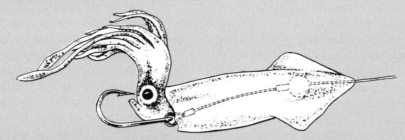

STEP 3   INSERT THE POINT OF THE HOOK THROUGH THE HEAD OF THE SQUID.

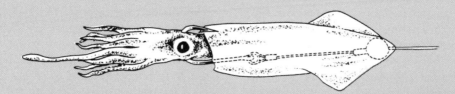

STEP 4   ONCE THE HOOK IS INSERTED, THE SQUID WILL STRAIGHTEN OUT. IF YOU MEASURE CORRECTLY BETWEEN THE CORK AND THE HOOK, THE HOOK WILL HOLD THE HEAD IN PLACE AND PREVENT IT FROM COMING LOOSE. THE CORK WILL NOW KEEP THE BODY FROM BEING PULLED BACK TOWARD THE HOOK. (SEE STEP 5 FOR TROLLING)

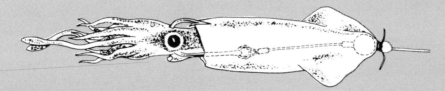

STEP 5   (OPTIONAL) TAKE SOME LIGHT BRAIDED LINE AND TIE THE TAIL END JUST ABOVE THE CORK. THIS WILL ENABLE YOU TO TROLL FOR LONG PERIODS BY PREVENTING THE HOLE IN THE TAIL FROM ENLARGING OR TEARING FROM THE DRAG THROUGH THE WATER. TRIM EXCESS BRAIDED LINE. (TYING IS RECOMMENDED FOR TROLLING AT HIGHER SPEEDS OR FOR LONGER PERIODS)

Sometimes a deep-swimming squid is much more effective than a skip bait. Here is a simple and fast way to rig the swimming squid.

You'll need a 1- to 2-ounce trolling jig wired with light cable as a leader. You'll also need a bait needle. That's it for the equipment, and the process takes just about five seconds.

Here are the steps:

1. Pick a jig with a plastic skirt and a cable wire leader testing roughly 100 to 125 pounds. The leader should be armed with a sharp stainless steel hook. The total length of the lure from the point of its head to the bend of the hook should match the length of the squid from the point of its body to its eye. The leader sleeve forming the end loop should be crimped tightly to make it as small as possible.

2. Slip the end loop of the leader into the eye of the bait needle.

3. Insert the bait needle under the squid's mantle at the head end and slide it up through the body cavity. Push the point of the needle out of the body at the exact tip of the squid's body.

4. Insert the lure into the mantle. Now draw the lure up inside the body by pulling on the leader of the lure with the bait needle. The lure should be pulled into the squid's body until the metal lure head rests snugly against the tough skin at the tip of the squid's body.

5. Finish up by passing the point of the hook through the squid's eyes and you are ready to troll.

This rig works well at all trolling speeds for several reasons.

The head of the lure distributes the towing strain over the full surface of the squid. The skin is not broken by stitches or towing threads.

The weight of the lure head pulls the lure underwater, even at relatively high speeds of 6 to 8 knots. Because the bait is underwater and not slapping along the surface, it does not break up as easily.

The lure head and the plastic tail fill up the squid's body, rounding it out to its natural streamlined shape. This shape is not only enticing to fish because of its natural appearance, but it makes the water flow naturally around the bait, eliminating much of the strain of skin friction.

During trolling, the salt water tends to toughen the squid. You'll find the bait is actually much softer at the start of your trip than two or three hours of trolling later.

When I know I am in an area where fish are known to be, I troll the squids at 2 to 4 knots. Such slow speeds let the squids run four to 10 feet under the surface (depending on the weight of the lure and the length of the trolling line). The depth and slow speed tend to make a very enticing presentation — not to mention the tremendous economy in fuel consumption. When I'm trolling squids, my outboard burns only about a gallon

of gasoline an hour! The savings on two or three trips will keep me in fresh bait for a year!

So far, rigged squid have filled my fish box with mahimahi, ono, rainbow runner, ulua, kahala, ahi and even a stray uku which hit a drifting bait while the boat was stopped to pull in another fish.

Another plus to this rig is its convenience. If a fish strikes the squid and tears it free from the lure, we are still rigged and ready for fishing since the lure is unveiled in all its glory. Several times we've had strikes that stripped the squid, but the fish returned a few seconds later to gulp the lure.

Don't overlook the potential of a rigged squid for high-speed trolling. We've hooked ono and mahimahi while trolling a rigged squid at our normal speed as part of a pattern of artificial lures. A curious fish that comes up behind a rigged squid to sniff it over will light up with anticipation from the trail of real food aroma.

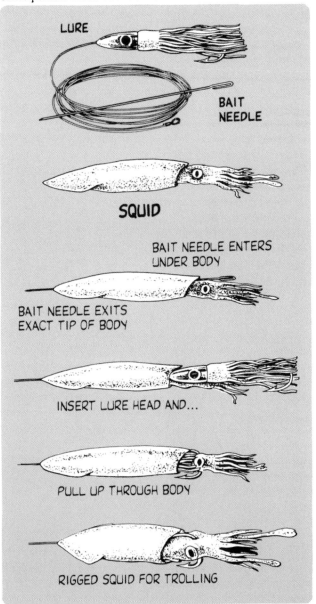

LURE

BAIT NEEDLE

SQUID

BAIT NEEDLE ENTERS UNDER BODY

BAIT NEEDLE EXITS EXACT TIP OF BODY

INSERT LURE HEAD AND...

PULL UP THROUGH BODY

RIGGED SQUID FOR TROLLING

Thirteen Tips for Casting with Bait

1. Anyone with a nose knows that live fish smell different from dead fish. Furthermore, the longer a fish has been dead, the more different it smells. That's true even if your smeller is only as good as a human nose. The difference is even more noticeable if your smeller is as good as the kind that a fish has. The fisherman who puts this information to work for himself will catch more fish.

The fish you are trying to catch can smell the difference between a live bait, a dead bait and an old dead bait. A fish can get extremely excited about the way a live bait smells, or it can be happy about the aroma of a fresh dead bait. Yet, it can work up an appetite for an old dead bait only if its belly has been empty a long time and there is nothing better around.

That's important information for you to know and use if you want to catch all the fish you should be catching.

2. Keep your bait alive if you can. Do this even if you are going to fish your bait dead, whether whole, in chunks or in strips.

Live baits are the best baits you can use for most kinds of fish. Live shrimp ('opae) and 'oama, for example, will catch more papio and other kinds of game fish than any dead bait.

Game fish are tuned to the smell of an excited live bait. At the Kewalo Basin holding tanks of the National Marine Fisheries Service, scientists performed a startling experiment. They put a live bait fish in a bucket to swim around for a while. Then they dribbled the water from the bucket into a large tank holding several ahi. After a short while, the ahi picked up the scent of the bait fish just from the bait smell in a few drops of water the bait fish had been swimming in. The ahi swam around their tank in great excitement as they searched for the source of the smell.

FLOATING BAIT BUCKET

3. To keep your bait alive, you have to keep the water in your bait bucket clean and full of oxygen. Clean any dead, crippled or bleeding bait fish out of your bait bucket. Change the water often. Better yet,

use the kind of floating bait bucket that lets you keep your bait immersed in the ocean's clean and well oxygenated water. If you use such a bait bucket, you'll need a second bucket as well. The floating bait bucket has holes that let sea water in and out. Your second bucket should be water tight so you can pull the perforated bucket out of the sea, leaking its water, of course, and then stick it into the watertight bucket.

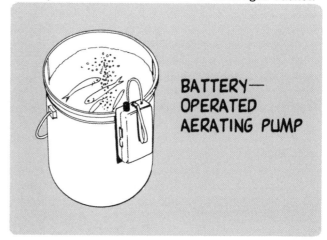

BATTERY— OPERATED AERATING PUMP

4. A simple, inexpensive battery-operated aerating pump also will help keep your bait alive and you won't need to change the water as often as you would without it. The pump attaches to the side of the bucket. From the pump, a small plastic tube runs down into the water. The pump shoots bubbles into the water, keeping it full of oxygen.

5. Keep the water as close to sea temperature as possible. Keep your bucket out of the sun, of course, and add new water periodically even if you are using a pump to supply oxygen.

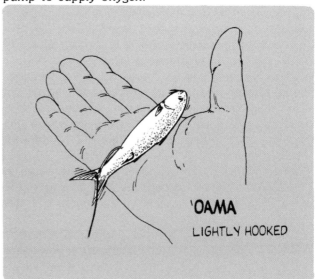

'OAMA
LIGHTLY HOOKED

6. To fish live baits, hook them loosely in a spot that won't kill them. Hooking shrimp or live bait fish just under the shell or the skin in the tail region, away from their vital organs, will help them stay alive longer.

7. Once a bait is dead, the substances in its body begin to change into other substances and the fluids that leak out of the body also change into other substances. It's these fluids that spread out through the water to signal game fish that food is around. Fresh dead baits give better signals than old dead baits.

That's not just a guess. We prove it all of the time when we fish for weke ula and other bottom fish in deep water offshore. If we bait one line with strips from a freshly caught kawakawa and another line with the same kind of strips from a bait that is only a few hours old, we'll catch two or three times as many fish with the fresh bait.

8. Keep dead baits as cold as you can. Don't leave your dead bait in the sun. Keep it on ice to slow down the chemical changes that happen after death. You can do this with a small cooler full of ice or an insulated fish bag.

9. Don't freeze your bait unless you have to. Freezing changes the texture of your bait — it makes it softer so it falls apart easier. Freezing also seems to change the bait's color, taste and smell. If you don't believe that, cut two pieces of fresh ahi. Put one in the refrigerator for two days, the other in the freezer. Thaw out the frozen ahi, and compare the way it looks, feels, tastes and smells with the refrigerated piece.

10. Some baits, like squid, must be used thawed because you can only get them frozen. And, frankly, there doesn't seem to be too much difference as long as you use the squid right away after it is thawed out. However, I have rarely used fresh-caught squid since it is so hard to get. The only fresh squid I've ever used has been some that I've jigged from a swimming school attracted to the lights of a drifting boat at night. Used live, these were tremendously successful for catching ahi, albacore and other types of fish that came up with the squid.

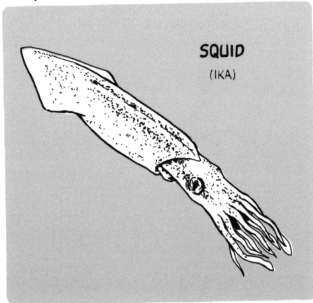

SQUID

(IKA)

11. Other baits, like octopus, are more readily available live and whole. If, for example, you catch an octopus, keep it alive and cut off legs as you need them. You'll have much better luck with them than with baits cut from frozen octopus.

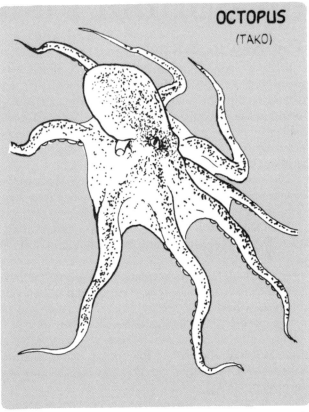

OCTOPUS

(TAKO)

Cutting the legs from a live octopus may seem cruel, but did you know that an octopus can grow back legs that it has lost?

A friend of mine used to capture an octopus at the start of each fishing trip to use for bait. Then he'd cut pieces off the legs as needed. At the end of the day, he'd toss the octopus back into the sea to grow more legs. His fishing area always seemed to have plenty of octopus even after they had disappeared from other spots.

12. Keep your baits away from water. If you store your baits where they will come in contact with fresh water (for example, on melting ice), they will change rapidly since the flesh soaks up the fresh water. Squid, for example, turns pink or purple in fresh water. If you keep your bait in salt water, the good smelling juices leak away. You want to keep those juices in the bait until it is on your hook and in position to trap a game fish.

13. Make sure you remove your bait from hooks, bait bags, tackle boxes, etc. at the end of your trip. Forget this rule, as I've done on occasion, and you'll be the most unpopular guy in the house, as family members will wrinkle their noses and prowl around asking "What's that smell?"

Information on Bottom Fishing

The Key to Success

What do you do when the fish aren't biting? You make them bite. What do you do when you can't find where the fish are? You make them come to you.

Sound like some fisherman's fantasy? For one type of fishing, it is the best kind of reality — a truth that's proved by big catches of fish as good on the dinner table as they are fun to catch.

The magic that turns the fantasy into truth is the Hawaiian "palu" bag. It works its sorcery by capitalizing on a fish's most instinctive vice: greed.

The palu bag is the key to success in bottom fishing. Its attractive power stimulates fish to look for your bait and gobble it greedily once found. Depending on the strength of underwater currents, the effect of the palu bag can reach for hundreds of yards and perhaps as much as a mile.

But there really is no mystery in what the palu bag is and how it is used. The palu bag is simply a sack that is filled with bait, lowered to the bottom and opened to disperse the bait over whatever area the currents will carry it.

Fishing with palu is similar to other practices around the world referred to as "chumming," but the difference is the use of a bag that carries the chum to a pre-selected place and trips open when the fisherman chooses. In most other types of chumming, ground up bits of bait are ladled over the side to attract fish feeding on the surface. The deep reef waters of the Pacific islands make surface chumming impractical, especially when the fish sought are at the bottom of 20 to 100 fathoms of water (and sometimes more).

The bag is made from a square of denim, eight inches on each side. Other materials can be used but denim is strong and has the right combination of stiffness and suppleness. Two adjacent sides of the square are sewn together to form a cone, with the fourth corner of the square acting as a flap. This flap is tucked in after the cone is filled with bait. It prevents the bait from spilling out.

The palu bag is attached to the line by a piece of string tied to the point of the cone. For fishing in very deep water (50 fathoms or more), the palu is tied to the line that will actually be used for fishing. This requires less work than sending the palu down on a separate line and hauling it back up.

When I fish in shallow water (30 fathoms or less), I prefer to use very light tackle (spinning tackle in some

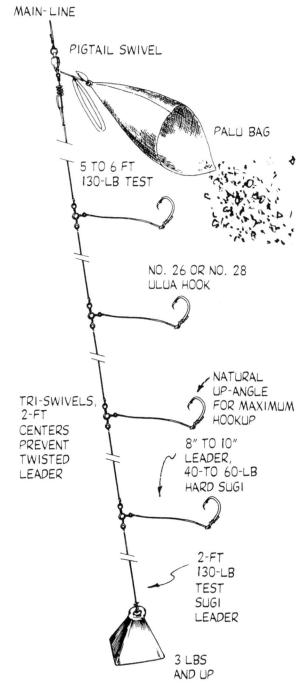

BOTTOM FISHING RIG

MAIN-LINE

PIGTAIL SWIVEL

PALU BAG

5 TO 6 FT 130-LB TEST

NO. 26 OR NO. 28 ULUA HOOK

TRI-SWIVELS, 2-FT CENTERS PREVENT TWISTED LEADER

NATURAL UP-ANGLE FOR MAXIMUM HOOKUP

8" TO 10" LEADER, 40-TO 60-LB HARD SUGI

2-FT 130-LB TEST SUGI LEADER

3 LBS AND UP

cases) and the palu bag is too cumbersome, so I do send it down on a separate line. Since the water is shallow, the line hits bottom quickly and is easy to retrieve.

The flap is usually enough to keep the bag closed until it is opened by a strong jerk on the line. For extra insurance, I knot a rubber band onto the attaching string of the bag. After the bag is filled and the flap tucked in, I loop the rubber band over the stuffed bag. The rubber band keeps the bag from opening accidentally.

What should you use for palu? The basic ingredient is any kind of flesh from fish, squid, shrimp, eels, crabs or clams. This can include head, guts, skin, bones, blood

— anything that provides the smell and taste of food. The palu meat should be chopped as fine as possible to spread through the water quickly and far. A meat grinder is very useful in getting the bait to the right consistency.

Other materials should be added to the palu to extend it and help it disperse. Some fishermen mix in sand to keep the palu near the bottom. Others use avocado because its oil is heavy and attracts some kinds of herbivorous fish whose excited activity interests bigger fish. Cooked sweet potato has the same effect and is traditionally used by some South Pacific cultures. In more cosmopolitan areas, fishermen use crumbs from stale crackers, oats or other dry cereals.

Some clue to what early Hawaiians used for palu is in the double meaning of the word. Palu not only means bait, but refers to a relish made by chopping up fish parts, including the head and viscera and combining with roasted kukui nuts and limu (seaweed). The mixture is then set aside for a few days to "ripen." The mixture, strongly flavored by the spoiled flesh, is used to season other foods.

When making palu for fishing, mix the ingredients in a bucket and add enough water to make the mixture

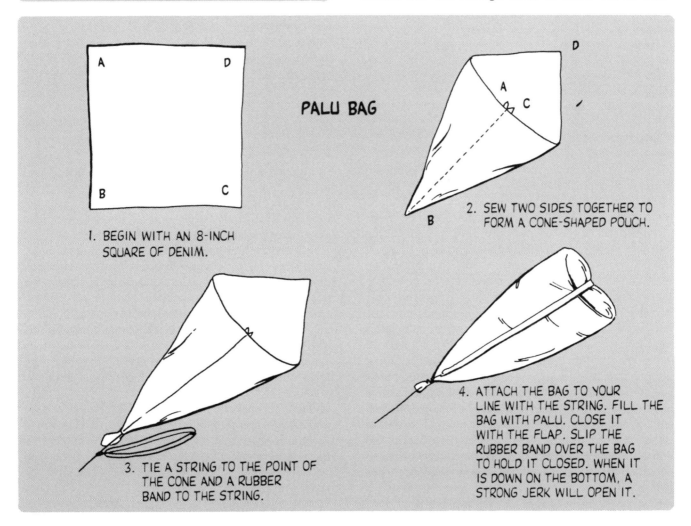

PALU BAG

1. BEGIN WITH AN 8-INCH SQUARE OF DENIM.

2. SEW TWO SIDES TOGETHER TO FORM A CONE-SHAPED POUCH.

3. TIE A STRING TO THE POINT OF THE CONE AND A RUBBER BAND TO THE STRING.

4. ATTACH THE BAG TO YOUR LINE WITH THE STRING. FILL THE BAG WITH PALU. CLOSE IT WITH THE FLAP. SLIP THE RUBBER BAND OVER THE BAG TO HOLD IT CLOSED. WHEN IT IS DOWN ON THE BOTTOM, A STRONG JERK WILL OPEN IT.

runny. The loose consistency makes the aroma spread more rapidly through the water.

I've used palu successfully to fish the 60 and 70 fathom dropoffs around the Big Island for 'opakapaka, but I much prefer to fish the shallow water ledges between 25 and 30 fathoms. These waters abound in uku (grey snapper), kahala (amberjack), ulua (trevally), kaku (barracuda) and many other kinds of reef fish that provide continuous sport. The shallow water makes light tackle and small sinkers very practical, and my favorite rigs are 20-pound class spinning outfits with 2-ounce weights to carry the line to the bottom.

After finding a dropoff with a depth recorder (I like a ledge where the bottom falls abruptly for 30 feet or more), I anchor and begin to palu. I get the messy job while the rest of the family fishes. We generally work with four or five lines at once, each with two or more hooks.

By using a separate line for the palu bag and a much heavier weight (6 to 8 ounces), the palu is dispersed up-current of the other lines so that it attracts fish right to the hooks. I palu continuously until the fish begin biting, then drop a bag down only when no one is fighting a fish. Once the palu begins working, it is common for at least one line to be hooked up constantly.

As a matter of fact, there can be enough fish to be a nuisance. We get our best sport, for example, from ulua, uku, kahala and kaku. but some days the taape (blue lined snapper), pualu and other reef fish are so abundant they don't let the bigger fish get to the bait. On these days, we have to pick our bait accordingly.

Live baits of akule (big-eyed scad) are the best for the bigger fish and are, of course, left completely alone by the reef fish. When we can't get akule, we'll bait our big hooks with a small live reef fish hooked on the scene.

The best dead baits are strips cut from 'opelu (mackerel scad), but these soft baits are greedily eaten by pualu on some of our best reef grounds. One morning we boated over a hundred pounds of pualu (ranging from 4 to 10 pounds) on 'opelu and finally had to switch to a different bait just to keep from catching more. Squid works very well at such times not only because it is tougher and less easily stripped from the hooks, but also because the smaller fish aren't quite as fond of it.

For me, part of the fun of this type of action is the unpredictability of what you will find at the end of your line. On almost every trip, we've hooked at least one fish that has fought for over an hour, causing us to haul anchor and chase it, sometimes for miles. These have turned out to be kahala, ulua, giant barracuda and enormous grouper. On other occasions we've hooked sharks and huge rays with wing spans of four or more feet across.

The one thing we've never had is a boring day.

Downriggers!

Considering the opportunity, it's surprising how little fishing in Hawai'i is done with downriggers. The downrigger is a device for trolling a lure or bait under the surface. Some downriggers are capable of presenting a hook more than 200 feet down.

They are a nuisance, to be sure, but their potential outweighs their problems. Pacific Coast commercial salmon trollers would have to give up the sport were it not for downriggers. Their counterparts in the Great Lakes wouldn't think of fishing any other way.

Let's look at the equipment you'd need to get started and how to use it. We'll start with the downrigger, itself. Mine is a Penn Fathom-master downrigger, which has given me many years of good service, so I'll describe its features as part of the general story.

The downrigger has six main parts: a winch to store line, a metering device to tell how much line is out, a boom to hold the line away from the boat, a mounting base or bracket by which it is attached to the boat, a weight or planer for pulling the line into the depths and a release mechanism by which the fishing line is attached to the weight.

The winch should have a drag mechanism to release line if the weight gets snagged on the bottom. The downrigger line should be braided stainless steel wire, which gives strength and weight, preventing a large line belly. Not all downriggers have metering devices, but without one you have very little idea how deep your lure is. That's a real handicap because accurate depth is very important.

The length of the boom will depend on your boat and where the downrigger is mounted. My Penn Fathom-master came with two interchangeable booms of two feet and four feet in length. I use the shorter boom for fishing over the side and the longer one over the transom. This would vary from boat to boat, and many fishermen reverse the roles of the booms.

My Penn Fathom-master has a swivel mounting base. This allows me to swing the boom in parallel to the side for easy handling of the weight and perpendicular to the side for the best trolling position.

My trolling weight is a 10-pound cannon ball with a built-in release mechanism. Unlike cannon ball weights used in some fishing situations, this weight releases from the fishing line but remains attached to the downrigger line. In other words, I don't lose the weight on the strike.

When properly maintained, the Penn release mechanism does a fine job. You need to lubricate it before and after each day's use. It works by putting the pressure of a spring loaded piston on a plastic tab. The line is fed through a hole in the tab. On a strike, the tab is pulled free of the weight.

While fishing in the Great Lakes, I encountered a

different type of release mechanism that I like better. It's based on a spring clip attached to a round bead on the wire downrigger line. It seems to be more trouble free, requiring almost no maintenance. Best of all, you can attach several of these to one downrigger and fish more than one line at a time from the same downrigger.

Downrigger fishing requires a special rod. It should have a strong butt, reel seat and foregrip assembly. The rod blank itself should be very stiff in the butt section and much more flexible near the tip. This type of rod construction is very important because the rod should be flexed into a very deep bend when the downrigger is in trolling position.

The deep bend does several things. It keeps tension on the line, which minimizes the amount of belly in the trolling line. Also, the deep bend ensures a sharp upward jerk of the rod when the fish strikes. This jerk helps set the hook.

To maintain a bait or lure at any depth greater than 30 feet or so, you need to troll quite slowly. Downrigger fishing is rarely done at speeds faster than one or two knots. At faster speeds, you put too much strain on your gear. Worse yet, the weight swings up and away from the depth you think you are trolling at.

I find that even at two knots, my weight is positioned about 10-percent shallower in the water than my meter says it will be.

Lures or bait? I've used both successfully. Vibrating lures seem to be the best of the artificials. Swimming plugs and spoons do a very nice job on many kinds of bottom fish.

But I do prefer bait. I think that fish feeding in deep water rely more on smell than on sight. Perhaps my logic is flawed, but there is not as much light at, say, 100-to-150 feet down than there is at the surface. Still, I've caught salmon in the Great Lakes on spoons down 50 to 60 feet just before sunset. Take your choice.

I like to rig a filet from an 'opelu or akule when I can get them. Or bait up with a section of octopus leg or eel.

These baits get good strikes from a variety of amber-jack, ulua, aku, kaku and other species fished anywhere from 100 to 200 feet down in water that is roughly the same depth as your weight.

And those are precisely the depths I like to troll my downrigger rigs. An inescapable implication here is the need for a depth recorder. Without some means of accurately determining bottom depth, you'll be fishing outside the strike zone or hanging up on the bottom. I find that deep feeders don't like to chase their food up more than about 30 feet from the bottom. Unfortunately, our Hawaiian bottom zones vary more than 30 feet at the blink of an eye, or the wink of the orange light on your depth flasher.

I take that back, the depth variation is precisely the reason the fish are there; hence, it shouldn't be considered unfortunate at all. And, of course, since that's where the fish are, that's why you want to consider using a deep troller.

THE MAIN PARTS OF A DOWNRIGGER

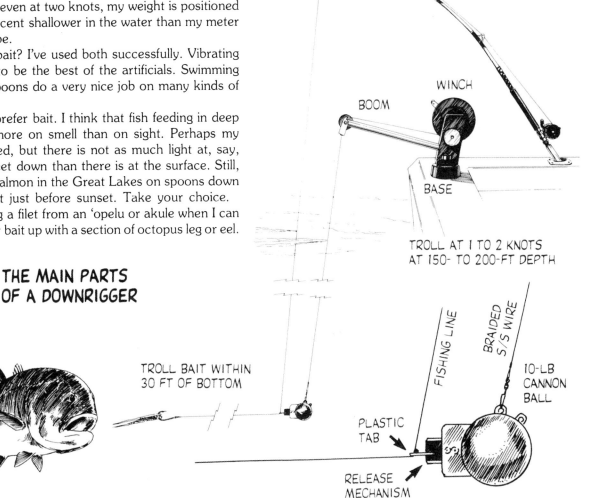

WINCH

BOOM

BASE

TROLL AT 1 TO 2 KNOTS AT 150- TO 200-FT DEPTH

TROLL BAIT WITHIN 30 FT OF BOTTOM

FISHING LINE

BRAIDED S/S WIRE

10-LB CANNON BALL

PLASTIC TAB

RELEASE MECHANISM

Big Game Basics

Baiting the Big Ones

Big offshore fish take big baits, and the unchallenged champion bait for marlin is a live aku.

Trolling with a live tuna or bonito is an extremely effective way of catching billfish, yellowfin tuna, big mahimahi and sharks.

Make no mistake, a live bait is not a dead bait rigged to look as though it might still have a little flavor left. It is an honest-to-goodness gill-pumping, tail-wagging, skin-shimmering bait fish ready to tantalize the palate of any predatory game fish across whose rapacious gaze it happens to quiver.

Baiting billfish is a method with a lot of plusses and only two minuses. The live bait is an almost irresistible target, meaning a sure strike once it is spotted by a fish on the prowl. Nearly every strike is a hookup since the bait is carefully fed to the marlin who gratefully gulps it down into the tender and vulnerable recesses of his mouth where a sharp hook point can find a sure hold. And it is very energy conservative, requiring less than half of the fuel consumption of the customary alternative: high-speed trolling with artificial lures.

The two minuses are, unfortunately, big ones. You can't fish a live bait unless you've got one (and they can sometimes be damned hard to come by). Furthermore, you cover very little oceanic territory at the slow trolling speed needed to keep your bait acting naturally. Add them up and they mean that your bait and your billfish can only come together under the ideal circumstances of a bait school near a marlin grounds.

Marlin hang around bait schools so often, however, that you are probably on the right side of the odds if you get into the habit of trying a live bait any time and any place you can catch one.

Here's what you'll need and how you'll do it.

First you'll need a rig to catch the bait. The proper bait will be either an aku, a kawakawa or a small ahi. It can be any size up to a practical limit of about 10 pounds. Marlin will attack much bigger baits, but the smaller tuna (and all three fish mentioned are of the tuna family) are more readily swallowed by the predators. After all, you do not want the marlin to slash the bait fish with its bill to stun it. You want that initial contact to be a determined chomp from the billfish's jaws.

Since you'll be fishing for small fish to be used as baits, your lure should be a small feather jig, or "king-king" as you'll often hear it called. The tiny quarter-ounce or less jigs are usually the best. Though they are often called feather lures, the modern trend is to dress them with soft plastic squids rather than chicken plummage. In fact, you may want to use only the squid, weighting it with a small egg sinker tucked inside the squid's head. Pick red, yellow or pink to start with. Usually the bait fish will snatch anything that comes by regardless of color.

The leader is more important than the color of the skirt in fooling bait fish. Always use a suji (monofilament) leader of 50-pound test or less. Make sure it is at least six feet long. In fact, you may find that the only way you can take bait from a finicky school full of apprehensive bait fish is by getting rid of the leader, snap and swivel entirely. To do that, you'll run the light monofilament trolling line right through the leader hole and tie the hook on the end.

Sure, there are days when you could catch aku on a cable leader as thick as a pencil, but why waste valuable fishing time discovering that today isn't one of those days?

The hook style you choose for the aku lure is also important. Pick a long shank hook with a short point. A stainless steel O'Shaughnessy style is good. You want to be able to remove that hook from the bait with a minimum amount of damage. The long shank gives you something easy to grab, and the short point can be readily extricated.

For catching bait, choose a rod heavy enough to horse the bait in but set the drag loose enough so that you don't break the bait's neck on the strike. An injured bait fish is useless because he won't swim right, won't live long and will attract sharks.

Long before you catch your bait, have your marlin trolling outfit ready. Don't rely on a rod already in use dragging a plug or jet. You'll waste too much time reeling it in, getting the lure off and the bait rig on. By that time your aku may be mortally injured, or will have shaken the short point hook.

Live bait fishing gives you considerable latitude in choosing the class of tackle to use. Because the trolling speed is slow and the bait is taken while the reel is set

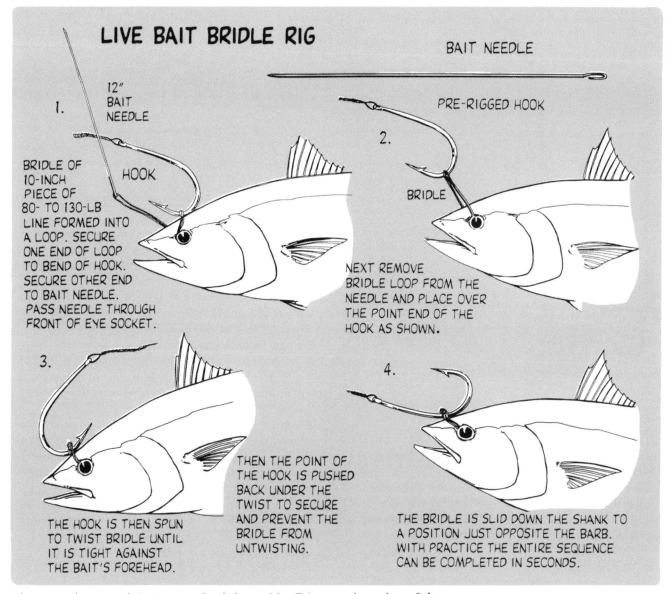

LIVE BAIT BRIDLE RIG

BAIT NEEDLE

1.
12"
BAIT
NEEDLE

HOOK

BRIDLE OF
10-INCH
PIECE OF
80- TO 130-LB
LINE FORMED INTO
A LOOP. SECURE
ONE END OF LOOP
TO BEND OF HOOK.
SECURE OTHER END
TO BAIT NEEDLE.
PASS NEEDLE THROUGH
FRONT OF EYE SOCKET.

PRE-RIGGED HOOK

2.

BRIDLE

NEXT REMOVE
BRIDLE LOOP FROM THE
NEEDLE AND PLACE OVER
THE POINT END OF THE
HOOK AS SHOWN.

3.

THE HOOK IS THEN SPUN
TO TWIST BRIDLE UNTIL
IT IS TIGHT AGAINST
THE BAIT'S FOREHEAD.

THEN THE POINT OF
THE HOOK IS PUSHED
BACK UNDER THE
TWIST TO SECURE
AND PREVENT THE
BRIDLE FROM
UNTWISTING.

4.

THE BRIDLE IS SLID DOWN THE SHANK TO
A POSITION JUST OPPOSITE THE BARB.
WITH PRACTICE THE ENTIRE SEQUENCE
CAN BE COMPLETED IN SECONDS.

almost at free spool, it is great for light tackle. Fifty-pound class makes this kind of fishing great sport and a satisfying challenge.

A 300-pound test, suji leader has many advantages for bait trolling. Its low visibility means a less suspicious presentation to the fish. It is tough enough to keep a marlin from whittling it down to the breaking point, but it will not resist the teeth of a shark, thus getting you out of an unwanted battle. Leader length should be several feet short of the IGFA allowances. This allows for the stretch of the nylon while still giving you an expanded leader short of the illegal limit in case your catch is world record sized.

The hook you pick depends on the size of the bait. Choose one roughly the depth of the bait's head. That gives you the biggest hook the marlin will swallow without suspicion, since the hook turns and lies against the bait's head when the marlin is gulping it down. And you want the biggest hook possible to insure a solid anchor

for a long fight.

Make a bridle by tying a 10-inch piece of 80- to 130-pound test line into a loop. One end of the loop should be secured to the bend of the hook, the other to the eye of a specially prepared bait needle. One side of the eye of the needle should have been filed through so that the loop can be slipped on and off easily.

The stage is set; get ready for the action.

You've found an aku school and are trolling through it. Your marlin rod is already in the holder with the reel set on free spool and ratchet engaged to keep the spool from over-running. The leader is held in coils by a rubber band that can be pulled free in an instant.

The aku hits. Cut back on the engine speed while a crew member works the aku in as quickly as possible. Lift the aku out of the water with the line. Don't gaff him (obviously), don't net him (you'll waste time untangling him), and don't bounce him on the deck or against the gunnels.

Adjust the boat's speed to 2 knots.

Flip the bait over on his back in the palm of your hand immediately. Cover his eyes. Blinded and on his back he will instantly go into a trance. Push the bait needle through the eye socket at the front edge of the eyeball. This won't hurt him. Draw the bridle loop through and disengage it. Drop the free end of the loop back over the hook bend and turn the hook to twist the bridle until the twists are tight against the bait's head. Then slip the point of the hook through the bridle right next to the head. Twisting the bridle and passing the hook back through it is really an optional step. Its purpose is to hold the hook in a better striking position and prevent the point from digging back into the bait when a marlin swallows it.

Return the bait to the water immediately. If you have done your preparation correctly, less than 10 seconds have elapsed since the bait was pulled from the water.

Be prepared for a strike immediately. Often a billfish will follow your hooked bait right to the stern, will be agitated by its disappearance and startled into action by its return.

Peel off line until the bait is back at least 100 feet in the wake. The actual distance will vary from boat to boat. With experience you'll learn what is best for yours. Grab the line carefully with your fingers while controlling the running spool with the other hand.

It is crucial that enough drag be maintained on the reel spool to prevent it from over-running on a strike,

but only this much. You want the billfish to feel no tension while accepting the bait.

Lever action drag reels are by far the best. In a pinch, a star drag reel will do, but you must set it at striking drag and rely entirely on the clicker to control the turning drum because the reel must be kept in free spool.

Keep the line pinched with your fingers and pull off an additional 30 feet of line to act as a dropback. This line is best left to trail in the wake in a large loop.

You are now in position waiting for the strike. Your boat is moving at about 2 knots, just enough to allow the bait to swim naturally. Actually, it swims in a constant state of tension with just enough fear showing to signal the attacking instinct in a predator.

Your first sign of a strike will be a dramatic increase in the bait's panic level. You'll feel him jerk his head to tug at the line in your fingers. He may actually dash to the surface and break water. At the very least, his steady swimming rhythm will become a rapid tattoo of quick beats.

Now you feel the strong tug of the big fish snatching the bait in his jaws. Let go immediately and yell for the skipper to cut back the engines to dead slow.

The trailing loop of the line will allow the marlin to swallow the bait without the alarming pull of the line in the water.

Immediately, tend to the reel. Guide the spool with your thumb to make sure it does not backlash. Many marlin will move off with the bait in a short and leisurely run that is little more than a follow-through of their striking charge. Then they'll stop. At the instant the marlin stops, stop the boat.

He is now turning the bait in his mouth so that it can be swallowed head first. The reel is barely turning.

Perhaps 10 seconds have elapsed, more or less, but don't count them; they do not matter. You will not strike the fish until he tells you to. His signal that he is ready to start the fight is his second run. With the bait swallowed, he moves. You move. Simultaneously, you gun the boat forward and engage the reel drag. The rod is still in the holder to take the full force of the strike. The boat is moving away from the fish in case he has circled toward it.

The hook stabs. The fight is on. Good luck!

Twenty Tricks for Trolling Live Bait

1. Count on having a hard time catching bait. True, there are times when aku will strike at anything that moves (more often, early in the morning before the fishing fleet has had a chance to chase them and make them wary). But more than likely, your search for bait will be a series of fast hops from bait school to breaking bait school as you wait until some less wary aku get overeager.

2. Troll your aku jigs on light line (sometimes you'll have to go as light as 10- to 15-pound test) with no swivel or leader. Put your lures at least 50 yards back. At times you may have to run them out 100 or more yards.

3. Though scientists say that aku are color blind, your best choice of an aku lure is pink. You'll get strikes on other colors, but not when they won't hit pink. In other words, if they are going to strike anything, they'll strike pink.

4. Pearl head trolling jigs are often your best choice, but it's good to run a pearl head and a metal head. The metal heads tend to stay under a little better, giving them the advantage at times.

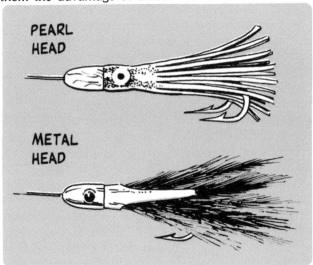

5. Rig your aku lures with a double hook. When bait is easy to get, flatten one barb to make the lure easy to remove for baiting. When bait is hard to get, keep the barbs up so you won't lose the one bait you've taken after two hours of trying.

6. If a barbed hook won't release, snip it off and leave it in the bait's jaw. It'll hurt him less than all of your struggling to get it free.

7. To rig your aku for baiting, use an open throat hook — the kind with the point parallel to the shank. The point is usually in a better striking orientation than the point on hooks that are curved in.

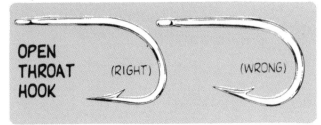

8. Don't trust a rubber band to hold your bait line. The rubber band will work right about half the time, breaking and releasing the bait when a marlin or tuna grabs it. It won't always break on a bill strike, leaving a suspicious marlin to swim away looking for another meal. It won't break on an ono strike, leaving you to go on thinking you are trolling a live bait when you are really just dragging a chunk of meat.

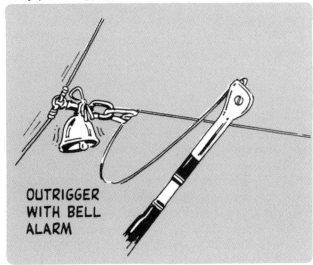

9. If you want to use a rubber band, try hanging a bell on the snap to which the rubber band is attached. An excited bait, panicked by the sight of an approaching billfish, will usually set the bell to jingling.

10. Use a strong bridle that won't break easily when a fish strikes. A bridle that has been used a few times may be too frayed to hold a big aku.

11. If you feel the rap-rap-rap of an ono strike, you can often catch the ono by being alert and ready. Back the boat down while someone reels in the line. You want to keep the chopped up bait near the surface and near the spot where the ono hit. When you spot the bait you'll frequently see the ono nearby, making passes back and forth as it decides whether to take another bite. Pull the aku from the water and immediately slice off some filets, tossing them back in as you slice them off. When the ono starts feeding on the pieces, impale a hunk on a hook with a wire leader and toss it to the fish. You'll frequently get him.

12. If you feel the bait get very excited, hang onto the line until you actually feel the strike. Letting the line go before the strike allows the aku to swim away with your slack line, leaving you light against the fish when he hits.

13. Strike the fish by driving the boat forward while the rod remains in the holder. Engage the drag to provide the striking tension. Running the boat forward puts you ahead of a fish that is swimming in the same direction as the boat.

14. Trolling the bait at the surface is only one of two ways to fish a live aku. The other is to send it down to the depths. A strong aku will usually want to power dive down as deep as it can go if it is given a free line. Once you bridle your bait, leave your reel in free spool, keep the boat stationary and let him go. Generally, the aku will swim down 60 to 100 fathoms. Let him plunge until he stops.

15. Once down, your aku will live for 10 minutes or more, but rarely more than a half hour. As long as your aku lives, he will continue to pull the line tightly downward. Once dead, you'll know it because you feel very little resistance. A live aku is much better than a dead one, but a dead one deep still draws strikes.

16. Be alert for a strike while your aku is swimming down. Billfish and tuna are found at many different depths, and they will often intercept a bait while it tries to jet down through their feeding level. You'll be warned of some impending action by your bait. If it speeds up dramatically, it's being chased.

17. If you have enough hands aboard your boat to do this effectively, try fishing two baits. One should be fished short, perhaps no more than 20 or 30 yards behind the boat. The other should be run out long, 100 or more yards back. It's not so much the distance from the boat that matters, it's the depth the aku will swim. The longer line bait will be able to use the extra line and the angle from the boat to swim deeper. The short line bait tends to get the marlin whose curiosity is piqued by the boat itself. Billfish do like to check out these intruders to their domain.

18. Akule can be bridled in exactly the same way that an aku can. Though the akule will not last as long, it will swim strongly for an hour or more at the same trolling pace as an aku. Because of its relatively small size compared to an aku, the akule is usually engulfed by a big fish with the first grab.

Even mahimahi will suck in the akule without hesitation. We fish them without dropback (unless they are the biggest of full-sized akule) and keep the drag brake set at "strike."

We get foiled by ono, which tend to whack the bait like a meat cleaver and leave us trolling the head. But that's the same thing that happens whether you fish the bait with a dropback or with the line running straight from the tip. Greedy ono will swallow the bait whole enough times to keep us believing we have a good chance at hooking them. If ono are our chief target, however, we switch to 'opelu and a double-hook rig — but more about that later.

Bridle an akule with lighter string and a smaller, lighter hook than you use for aku. The lighter terminal tackle is easier on the bait, though he'll get red in the face from the strain of the towing line anyway. Red in the face? I'm not sure what causes it, but the tissues in front of the eyes and around the mouth definitely do flush red. This color change as well as the panicky action of the bait probably excite game fish that might not otherwise be on the feed.

19. For short strikers like ono (fish that grab the bait by the middle rather than trying to swallow it whole) you are better off baiting with 'opelu and rigging a tail hook.

The technique is interesting and a bit tricky. To do it, you need a hook on a light stainless steel leader about half as long as the bait's body. And you'll need your bait needle.

Here's how you do it (and be sure to do it quickly, even if this means developing your skill by practicing on a dead bait).

Slip your bait needle under the skin of the bait about one-third of the way forward from the tail. Just break the skin, don't push the needle into the muscle. Now slide the needle forward, again being careful to slide the needle along just under the skin. You want the needle to slip along between the skin and the muscle without damaging muscle tissue and without breaking the skin.

When you do it right, you'll raise a mound under the skin and you'll be able to see the needle.

Now hook the eye of the needle to the loop in the leader and draw the leader up through the bait.

The point of the bait needle should emerge just behind the head on a line with the top of the gill. This can be a region of tough skin, as the bait generally has its heaviest scales just behind the head.

The eye of the leader should be even with the eye of the bait. The eye of the hook should be pushed under the skin so that the skin can hold the hook rigid.

Now push your main hook into the loop of the leader and then into the sinus cavity just in front of the bait's eye. The hook point should pass through the bait's head and out the other side.

If you do it quickly and correctly, the bait will swim strongly for an hour or more. Frankly, I've never really tested the rig to see how long the bait can swim before dying — every time I've done this I've had a strike within a half-hour.

Generally, the fish I've caught on this rig have been hooked either with the head hook or with both hooks.

As with the bridled akule, I fish this rig with no dropback and the reel set at striking drag.

20. Frigate mackerel are a bait fish that looks very much like an immature aku or kawakawa. As a matter of fact, fishermen often mistakenly call these "oi oi" and

describe them as young kawakawa. I've never seen any Hawaiian reference that used the term "oi oi"; hence, I have no idea of what that word really is supposed to mean. The actual Hawaiian term for frigate mackerel is keʻo keʻo, and every fish I've ever heard called an "oi oi"

has been a keʻo keʻo. I'd be glad to be enlightened by any reader who knows the story.

Fish the keʻo keʻo just the way you would an aku or kawakawa. Some of the biggest marlin ever caught in Hawaiʻi have been lured by this bright slim bait fish.

LIVE ʻOPELU RIG

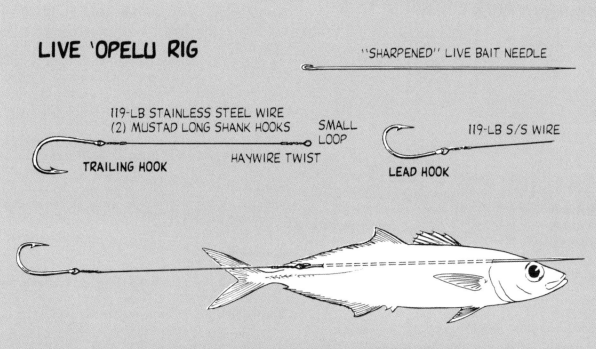

STEP 1   HOOK TRAILING LEADER LOOP IN EYE OF NEEDLE AND PENETRATE THE SKIN NEAR THE BAIT'S TAIL. RUN NEEDLE JUST UNDER SKIN, COMING OUT JUST BEHIND GILL PLATE.

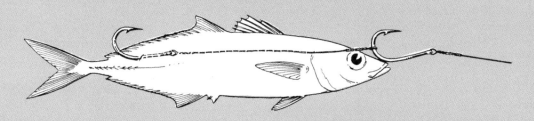

STEP 2   PUT LOOP OF TRAILING HOOK LEADER OVER POINT OF LEAD HOOK AS ILLUSTRATED.

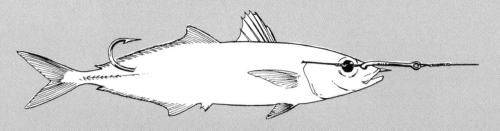

STEP 3   FINAL STEP IS TO PUT LEAD HOOK THROUGH NOSTRIL. ATTACH LEADER WITH SWIVEL TO MAINLINE AND GET BAIT INTO THE WATER QUICKLY.

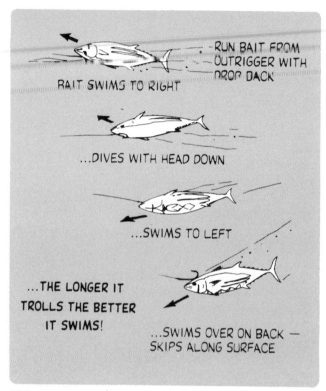

RUN BAIT FROM OUTRIGGER WITH DROP BACK

BAIT SWIMS TO RIGHT

...DIVES WITH HEAD DOWN

...SWIMS TO LEFT

...THE LONGER IT TROLLS THE BETTER IT SWIMS!

...SWIMS OVER ON BACK — SKIPS ALONG SURFACE

Rigging a Swimmer Bait

Few fishermen troll rigged dead baits in Hawai'i, preferring instead to hunt big game fish at high speed and lure them into striking artificial baits that resemble nothing they've ever eaten before. Lures, however, do make great sense here, where game fish are scattered and fishermen grope for them blindly. Hawai'i's fishermen rarely find fish; rather, they wander the sea until the fish finds them — a situation for which lure fishing is clearly the best possible choice. Yet, under the right circumstances, a rigged bait can be the deadliest of lures.

Rigged baits are a very successful choice around FADs, breaking schools of bait, and any other well-defined areas that have proved productive over and over. Rob Englehard, the skipper who showed me this rig, uses the rigged bait as a teaser when he's trolling a live aku on the marlin grounds off Keahole Point. He's had marlin rise to the rigged bait despite the fact that a live aku was swimming no more than 50 feet away.

Any fish that will eat a live aku will gobble a dead one if presented right. The steps shown here describe how to rig, Australian-style, an aku, kawakawa, ke'o ke'o or ahi. When trolled at 3 to 5 knots from an outrigger, the rigged bait will swim from side to side, splash, wriggle and thrash the surface with an exciting and provocative action.

Rob was introduced to this rig while on the "traveling deckhand circuit" — learning his trade by crewing on boats off the fabled billfishing ports of Australia and New Zealand.

Step 1. Tie a strong bridle (80-pound test dacron or stronger) securely to the shank of an 11/0 hook. Tie the bridle tightly because you don't want it to slip down to the bend. For the same reason, choose a tinned hook rather than a stainless steel hook — the latter is too slippery.

Step 2. Now, open your bait along the belly. Don't cut forward of the chest fins. You want the throat latch to stay secure so the bait doesn't pull apart from the strain of towing. Remove the entrails and the gills. The guts and gills are the first parts of the fish to be invaded by bacteria, and you want a bait that will last several days. According to Rob, rigged baits are better on the second or third day of use because they are softer, looser and more flexible in their action. He's caught fish on kawakawa that had turned white from being trolled in the sea for days.

Step 3. Pierce the bait's head along its center line with a bait sewing needle. The needle should enter at a point behind the vertical line passing through the eye. The further back the bridle is attached, the deeper the bait will swim. Run the needle out through the center of the cheek plate. Use the needle to pull one end of the bridle through the bait's head. Then do the same thing on the other side of the head.

Step 4. Pull the bridle ends through tightly to snug the hook up firmly against the bait's head. Tie the bridle ends under the bait's chin. The bridle not only tows the bait but also holds the gills shut.

Step 5. Sew the mouth shut by stitching up through the lower jaw and out one side of the bait's nose. Do the same thing on the other side of the head.

Step 6. Snug knots are needed to hold the mouth securely shut, maintaining the bait's streamlined shape.

Step 7. Sew the belly shut with a shoelace stitch.

Step 7a. Now flex the body from side to side to loosen the backbone.

Step 8. The bait should be towed at a high angle from the tip of an outrigger. A clothespin-type of release will hold it well, yet will let it go easily on a strike. Be sure to leave a loop of line for a tension-free drop back.

At first, the bait may not swim well, but the longer it stays in the water, the better it will swim.

When working well, the bait will lay on its left side and swim to the right, then dive with its head down for a few seconds of wiggle. From there it will work its way over onto its right side and swim to the left. Occasionally it will turn over on its back and skip along the surface with an occasional jump.

Don't freeze your baits but keep them on ice overnight between uses. Or prepare them ahead of time (as much as a day or two) before you need them. An iced brine soak will help toughen the skin to help the bait withstand the constant flow of water as it is towed.

Try it. When you watch its action, you'll be convinced that you've discovered another good way to catch big fish.

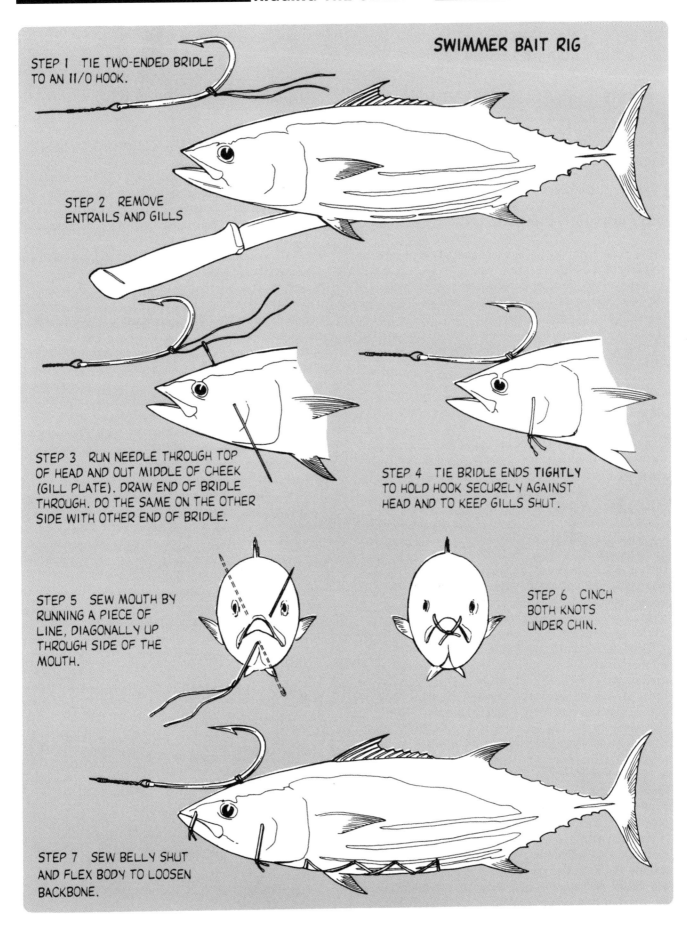

SWIMMER BAIT RIG

STEP 1   TIE TWO-ENDED BRIDLE TO AN 11/0 HOOK.

STEP 2   REMOVE ENTRAILS AND GILLS

STEP 3   RUN NEEDLE THROUGH TOP OF HEAD AND OUT MIDDLE OF CHEEK (GILL PLATE). DRAW END OF BRIDLE THROUGH. DO THE SAME ON THE OTHER SIDE WITH OTHER END OF BRIDLE.

STEP 4   TIE BRIDLE ENDS **TIGHTLY** TO HOLD HOOK SECURELY AGAINST HEAD AND TO KEEP GILLS SHUT.

STEP 5   SEW MOUTH BY RUNNING A PIECE OF LINE, DIAGONALLY UP THROUGH SIDE OF THE MOUTH.

STEP 6   CINCH BOTH KNOTS UNDER CHIN.

STEP 7   SEW BELLY SHUT AND FLEX BODY TO LOOSEN BACKBONE.

Plastic Resin Trolling Lures

How to Mold and Pour Your Own Resin Trolling Lures

Trolling lures with heads cast from plastic resins are expensive to buy, yet relatively simple to make. The initial investment in materials is little more than the cost of one or two lures. After the purchase of materials to make a mold and the subsequent cost of resin, catalyst and tubing, the only real investment is time. So little skill is required that professional lures can be made by anyone, regardless of how fumble-fingered he or she may be.

Before you can make a lure, you must have a mold. But before you can make a mold you must have a lure to copy.

Borrowing someone's proven "killer" is the easiest way to obtain a lure. However, you could start by molding a cylindrical chunk of plastic in a piece of PVC pipe and then turning the plastic on a lathe to get the lure shape you want. The latter path is really for the experimenter who wants to invent his own shape. Logic favors the man who copies a lure that has already shown its worth.

Let's call the lure you will be copying the "master." Prepare your master by following several steps. First file a small notch in the base of the master, at the exact top (or bottom) of the lure. This notch will form a nib of rubber in the mold opening. The nib will help you line up inserts. Second, polish the master with fiberglass polish to get the smoothest surface possible. Then coat your master with a good fiberglass wax. The wax will help you release the master from the mold.

Continue preparing the master for molding by cutting a 1-inch piece of tubing of the diameter you will be using for the lures you will cast. Some tackle stores carry brass tubing of the right diameter. Otherwise, buy copper fuel line tubing from a car mechanic. You want the tubing to become an extension of the inside pipe. The extension should stick out the front end of the master. Cut one end of the extension at the same angle as the face of the master. Attach the extension to the master by shaping a ½-inch sliver of wood so that it jams tight in the opening of the tube, holding the extension pipe to the lure by friction.

Pick a cardboard orange juice concentrate can of a diameter that will leave at least a ¼-inch of space all around the lure when it is placed inside. Actually, you are better off with a ½-inch or more surrounding the master, but this will require more molding rubber. The concentrate can should be at least an inch longer than the lure. If it isn't, tape two cans together, knocking out both ends of the can that is the extender.

From a roll of two-sided carpet tape, cut a circle the same diameter as the rear of the lure. Affix it to the lure, and use it to attach the lure to the base of the juice can.

Set the can down on its base with the open end up.

Prepare a quantity of molding rubber by mixing catalyst with liquid rubber. Follow the directions on the package for the right proportions. Mix thoroughly. The rubber compound should say "RTV" on the package. These initials stand for "room temperature vulcanizing," which means the rubber will harden with no other influence but the catalyst.

Pour the molding rubber into the concentrate can. Do it slowly to allow bubbles to escape. Fill the can beyond the top of the lure by at least a half inch. A full inch is better.

Now, let the rubber set completely. Don't try to remove the master until the rubber is thoroughly hardened. Soft rubber scores easily.

After the rubber hardens completely, it will adhere slightly to the surface of the lure. Tear off the cardboard form and loosen the lure by rolling the mold in your hands, putting pressure on the sides. After a few moments, the ripple of rubber along the surface of the master will help release it.

Depending on the characteristics of the rubber you have chosen, you may or may not be able to withdraw the master from the mold even after the rubber is released.

If not, make a cut partway down the side of the mold. By opening this cut carefully, you should be able to free the master. Actually, you will be repeating this process every time you mold a lure and then withdraw it from the mold. Give the mold some additional time to harden inside, now that the cavity is exposed to the air.

You are now ready to begin making lures. Start simply. The simplest lure to make is a one-pour, one-cast, solid pearl lure.

Here's how you do it. Into a wax paper cup, pour enough casting resin to fill the mold. Mix a few drops of "pearl essence" resin coloration, stirring as you go. Keep adding the pearl essence until you get the color and texture you want. Now add a few drops of catalyst for each ounce of resin.

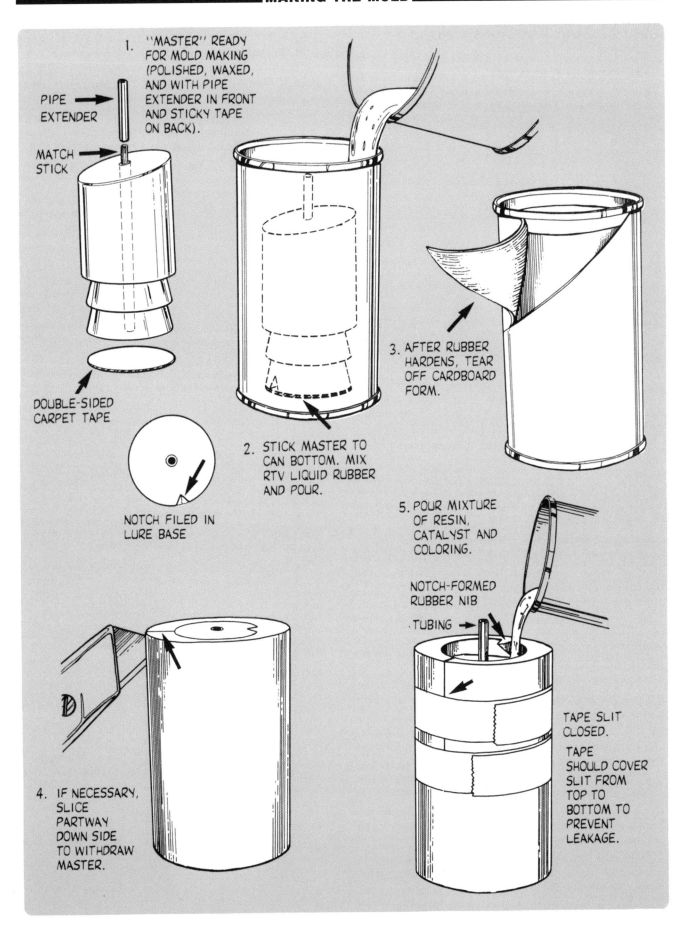

1. "MASTER" READY FOR MOLD MAKING (POLISHED, WAXED, AND WITH PIPE EXTENDER IN FRONT AND STICKY TAPE ON BACK).

PIPE EXTENDER

MATCH STICK

DOUBLE-SIDED CARPET TAPE

NOTCH FILED IN LURE BASE

2. STICK MASTER TO CAN BOTTOM. MIX RTV LIQUID RUBBER AND POUR.

3. AFTER RUBBER HARDENS, TEAR OFF CARDBOARD FORM.

4. IF NECESSARY, SLICE PARTWAY DOWN SIDE TO WITHDRAW MASTER.

5. POUR MIXTURE OF RESIN, CATALYST AND COLORING.

NOTCH-FORMED RUBBER NIB

TUBING

TAPE SLIT CLOSED.

TAPE SHOULD COVER SLIT FROM TOP TO BOTTOM TO PREVENT LEAKAGE.

Lure-Making Materials Price List

1 pound Silastic E RTV silicone mold rubber (enough for 1 medium-sized lure mold and 1 insert mold — each mold makes an unlimited number of lures).	$20.00

The following quantities are enough to make at least 10 lures:

1 quart resin (casting resin)	$ 6.00
1 two-ounce bottle of catalyst	1.30
1 ½-ounce bottle of colored dye (blue)*	1.00
1 ½-ounce bottle of pearl essence*	2.50
4 feet of 3/16" copper fuel line tubing	2.00
20 buttons for eyes	2.00
3 sheets of wet sandpaper (180, 400, 600 grit)	1.00
1 pint rubbing compound	2.50

Total for 10 lures $18.30

Comparison price: $15 to $25 per finished lure at tackle shops.
*Minimum quantities for 10 lures but will make many more.

The proper formula will take some experimentation since it will vary according to your environmental conditions, especially air temperature and humidity.

Close the split in the mold by wrapping it with masking tape. Use only as much pressure on the tape as needed to hold the split together. Too much pressure will deform the mold and change the shape of the lure.

Cut a piece of tubing a few inches longer than the lure. If the tube is not straight, manipulate it until it is. Insert it into the tube holder (formed in the mold by the extension pipe). If the tube is straight, the tubing should emerge from the mold at the exact center of the opening at the pouring end.

Fill the mold with the mixed casting resin. Let the resin harden for 12 hours. Don't get impatient and withdraw the lure too soon.

When the lure is withdrawn from the mold, it will be covered with a gummy film.

After pulling your lure from the mold, the first job is to cut off the pipe extensions protruding from the front and back. Do this with a sharp-toothed hacksaw, being careful not to nick or mar the front face of the lure. Once the extensions are cut off, smooth the raw ends of the pipe with a half-round file, again, being careful not to alter the lure face.

The sawing and filing process will create a burr inside the pipe. This burr will scar monofilament leader. Remove the burr by inserting the point of a large hook and reeming the pipe end.

Now, let's turn that gummy surface into a hard polish. Scrape the sticky stuff off with the blade of a utility knife. You'll learn to do this quickly after a few attempts. Scrape lengthwise using quick strokes and

very little pressure — you don't want the blade to bite into the surface.

Removing the sticky stuff from the front face is a bit tougher since the face may be concave and it has the metal end of the pipe in its middle. Some lure makers just scrape the face carefully. Others wipe the face with a rag moistened in acetone.

Scrape until you are down to hard plastic — that's actually just removing a thin coating of unhardened resin.

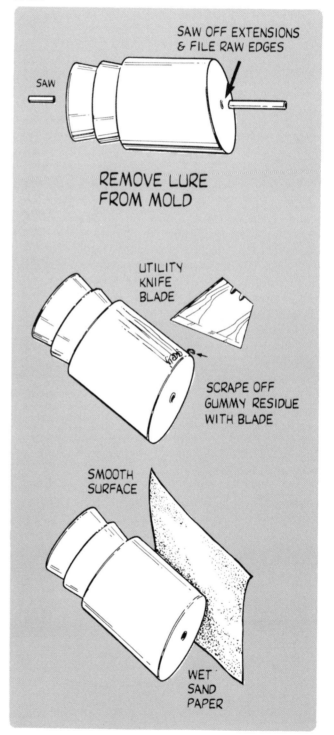

SAW OFF EXTENSIONS & FILE RAW EDGES

SAW

REMOVE LURE FROM MOLD

UTILITY KNIFE BLADE

SCRAPE OFF GUMMY RESIDUE WITH BLADE

SMOOTH SURFACE

WET SAND PAPER

To polish the surface, you'll need three grades of wet-or-dry sandpaper, a fine grit polishing compound (such as rubbing compound for automobile surfaces or fiberglass polish) and a final rub with fiberglass wax.

Start with 180 grit wet sandpaper, rinsing the residue of plastic powder from the sandpaper every few strokes. Then go to 250 grit and finally 400 grit. By now, the surface will look slick when wet, but don't let that appearance fool you. You'll need a final rubdown with polishing compound for a lasting luster.

Tie on a skirt, string some hooks on a leader and you are ready to troll.

The directions so far have given you a plain, simple, unadorned head of one color — white pearl. Without question, that's a great lure, but you can make more elaborate versions quite easily.

Let's look at some embellishments.

Modification #1. Other colors. When you mix in the pearl essence, add a few drops of resin coloration along with it. Pink is popular. So is blue. Add chartreuse for a wild-looking lure. Same with orange.

Modification #2. Eyes. For eyes, buy brightly colored buttons. I like the kind that are solid (no thread holes) with a rounded top and step for sewing to clothing. Cut off the stem. Cut a small circle of black tape for the pupil of the eye.

You want your eyes to be embedded in the plastic inside the lure. Here's how. After you've molded your solid color head and before you polish it, saw off a sliver of plastic down each side. You can remove the whole side or just cut away the plastic partway down.

Attach the eye in proper position with a small piece of double-sided carpet tape. The tape is just there to hold the eye in place till the plastic hardens. In the finished lure, the eye will be completely encased in plastic.

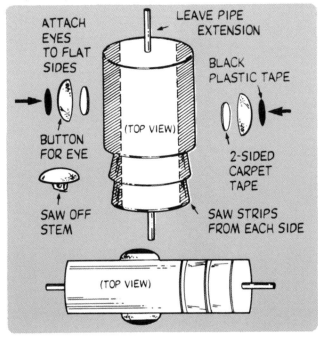

ATTACH EYES TO FLAT SIDES

BUTTON FOR EYE

SAW OFF STEM

LEAVE PIPE EXTENSION

(TOP VIEW)

BLACK PLASTIC TAPE

2-SIDED CARPET TAPE

SAW STRIPS FROM EACH SIDE

(TOP VIEW)

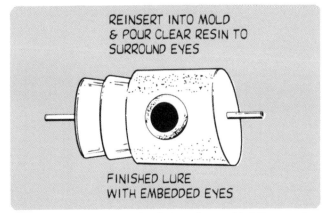

REINSERT INTO MOLD & POUR CLEAR RESIN TO SURROUND EYES

FINISHED LURE WITH EMBEDDED EYES

Next, insert the lure back into the mold. Mix up a few ounces of clear plastic catalyzed resin. Pour the liquid into the mold, down each side to fill up the space formed when you cut away the plastic. Let this plastic harden and you will have a lure with eyes embedded inside the plastic.

Modification #3. A contrasting stripe. Since bait fish have dark backs and light bellies, fishermen like to try to imitate this living pattern by making the top of the lure head a contrasting color. Remove the lure from the mold; saw off a sliver down the top; reinsert the lure into the mold; mix colored catalyzed resin; pour and set.

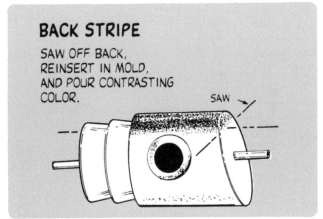

BACK STRIPE

SAW OFF BACK, REINSERT IN MOLD, AND POUR CONTRASTING COLOR.

SAW

Modification #4. Reflecting inserts. To do this we go back to step one, the bare leader tube. To the tube, attach two strips of mirrored glass. Attach them by first wrapping the tube with a turn of double-sided carpet tape. The mirrored strips can easily be cut from a discarded mirror.

Though mirror glass is a traditional choice, I prefer to make mirrored inserts from other materials, because the sharp edges of the glass tend to cause the casting resin to crack when it hardens. Strips cut from polished metal are good, because their edges can be smoothed with sandpaper to minimize their cracking effect on the plastic.

I've had success with inserts cut from stiff cardboard, faced with reflective foil. For more professional looking results, I've cut the strips from any thin, rigid plastic and faced the plastic with foil.

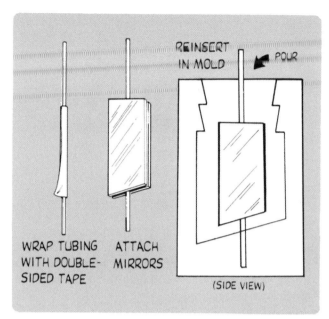

WRAP TUBING WITH DOUBLE-SIDED TAPE

ATTACH MIRRORS

REINSERT IN MOLD

POUR

(SIDE VIEW)

Attach the reflective insert as already described. Position it inside the mold. Tape the mold shut so it won't leak. Mix clear, catalyzed resin with a tint of color (I like a strong shade of blue) and pour. The insert allows you to make a fancy-looking lure with one pour.

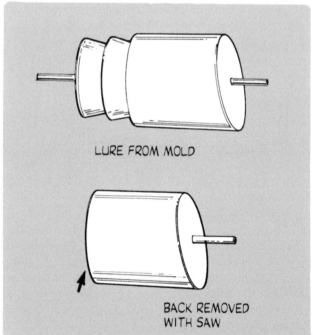

LURE FROM MOLD

BACK REMOVED WITH SAW

Modification #5. Shaped inserts. These are my favorites. The insert is shaped approximately like a fish head. Exact fish shape is not important, but a decent replica is relatively easy to make.

For shaped inserts, you'll need to make a special insert mold. First, make an insert master. Do this by molding a lure shape in your lure mold around a piece of tubing. Withdraw the lure and cut off the back behind the head and even with the ridge used to tie on the skirt. Now, saw strips off the sides and file the remaining

piece until it is shaped like a popsicle, leaving the pipe extension intact. When you've shaped this the way you want your insert to be, follow the steps for making a mold as illustrated at the beginning of this section. No need to slit this mold. It is very easy to withdraw the master and any inserts molded from it.

Shaped inserts can be decorated with various colored metallic glitter sparkles, wrapped in aluminum tape, molded in attractive colors or painted in appropriate patterns.

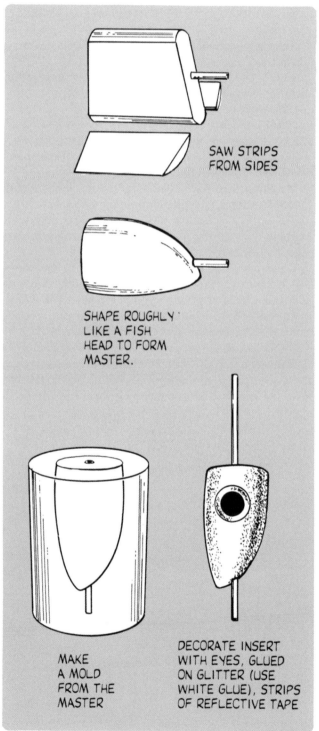

SAW STRIPS FROM SIDES

SHAPE ROUGHLY LIKE A FISH HEAD TO FORM MASTER.

MAKE A MOLD FROM THE MASTER

DECORATE INSERT WITH EYES, GLUED ON GLITTER (USE WHITE GLUE), STRIPS OF REFLECTIVE TAPE

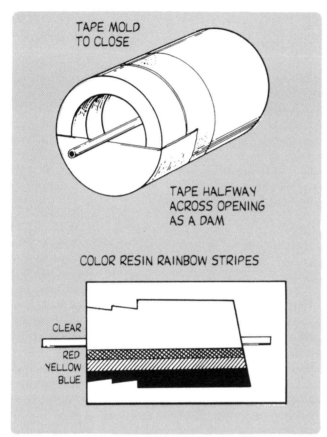

TAPE MOLD
TO CLOSE

TAPE HALFWAY
ACROSS OPENING
AS A DAM

COLOR RESIN RAINBOW STRIPES

CLEAR
RED
YELLOW
BLUE

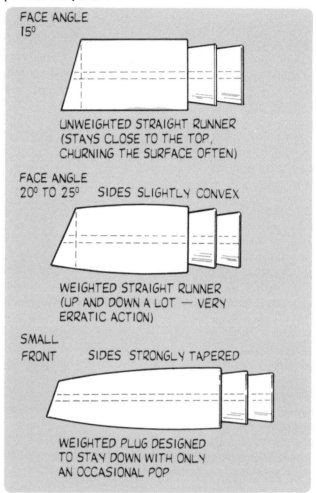

FACE ANGLE
15°

UNWEIGHTED STRAIGHT RUNNER
(STAYS CLOSE TO THE TOP,
CHURNING THE SURFACE OFTEN)

FACE ANGLE
20° TO 25°   SIDES SLIGHTLY CONVEX

WEIGHTED STRAIGHT RUNNER
(UP AND DOWN A LOT — VERY
ERRATIC ACTION)

SMALL
FRONT   SIDES STRONGLY TAPERED

WEIGHTED PLUG DESIGNED
TO STAY DOWN WITH ONLY
AN OCCASIONAL POP

Modification #6. Rainbow stripes. First, make a reflective insert and position it in the mold on its tube. Then dam half of the mold opening with masking tape. Mix a tablespoon or so of blue catalyzed resin, strongly tinted. Pour this in the mold and lay it on its side, using the dam to keep the liquid resin from spilling out the opening. After the blue has hardened, make a batch of yellow catalyzed resin and pour it into the mold, again laying the mold on its side until hard. Do the same with red resin.

At this point, you have three stripes of color, with blends along the boundaries, giving you all of the colors of the rainbow. Stand the mold up and finish the lure with a pour of untinted resin. The finished product will be a masterpiece of the lure-maker's art.

This is one man's approach to lure-making, based on methods taught to me by charter boat captain Zander Budge, to whom thanks goes for these and thousands of other fishing tips.

Getting the Lead In, and Other Lure-Making Tricks

You add lead to make a lure that either dives deeper or stays deeper when it tracks, and there is a marked difference between the two actions. Some anglers want a very active lure that thrashes around with a highly erratic action. With some adjustments to the lure, the addition of a lead insert will make the lure do this. Others want a lure that plows along a few feet down,

staying below the base of the waves where it remains continuously visible. Such lures are often heavily weighted with very little plastic except what is needed to provide shape and color.

The best example of the former is the weighted straight-runner or "Henry Chee" style lure. The straight-runner is usually a straight-sided cylinder with a round, flat face, cut at a modified angle. It's leader hole is dead center. If you just add lead to a standard straight-runner with no other modifications, it tends to die. The lead depresses the action and you end up with a lure than tends to stay down.

If you compensate for the lead by widening the angle, you get an active lure that thrashes around on the surface, then plows deep, works quickly back and forth from side to side and darts back to the surface.

It'll do all that if you are very careful when you cut the angle. If the angle is too steep or not true from side to side or the insert is not centered, the lure will tend to corkscrew through the water.

You can avoid worrying about this by only adding lead to a lure copied from one that has a lead insert. In other words, for lures to be ballasted, make your original mold from a weighted lure with the desired action.

(ABOVE) KONA CLONE STYLE HEAD
WITH OFF CENTER LEADER HOLE,
SHARP ANGLE, FLATTENED LEAD
INSERT

Lures with off-center leader holes are extremely difficult to ballast correctly, and I've seen very few of them that were successful. The Kona Clone, made by Sevenstrand is one of the few exceptions. Its success may be due to the precision of its molding process, both in ensuring the symmetry of the shape and scoop as well as the vertical orientation of the lead insert.

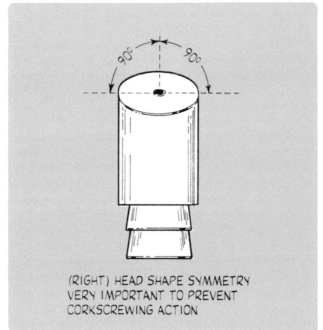

(RIGHT) HEAD SHAPE SYMMETRY
VERY IMPORTANT TO PREVENT
CORKSCREWING ACTION

Symmetry of the head shape, by the way, can be very critical. Skipper Bart Miller insists on it. The line of lures he sells under his trademark are turned on a lathe to make sure they cleave the water evenly with the same flow on all sides. Bart told me that he doesn't trust rubber molds because they deflect in the molding process, producing lures that are mishapen, even if only so slightly that the imperfections are not detectable without measuring.

With all of those cautions, here are some ballasting suggestions:

1. When molding an opaque solid color lure with centered leader hole, simply slip a net sinker over the leader tube, squeeze it to hold it in place and pour the lure. The only way you'll be able to tell the difference between this and an unweighted lure is by heft of it and by the slightly increased angle of the face. The sinker won't show through the pearl coloration.

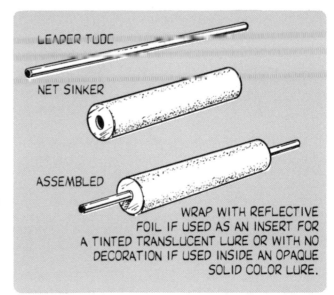

LEADER TUBE

NET SINKER

ASSEMBLED

WRAP WITH REFLECTIVE
FOIL IF USED AS AN INSERT FOR
A TINTED TRANSLUCENT LURE OR WITH NO
DECORATION IF USED INSIDE AN OPAQUE
SOLID COLOR LURE.

Since the net sinker is roughly symmetrical itself, you don't even really need to worry about its position on the tube — but the tube needs to be kept in the center of the lure whether the lead is used or not.

2. For a colored transparent lure, the insert will show and the lead can be a factor in making an attractive lure. Make the insert by using lead strips. These can be purchased already shaped or you can hammer them out of lead pieces. Since I am both lazy and afraid to pour molten lead, I'm happy to hammer flat strips out of net sinkers. A few quick blows flatten them and a few more spread them as I work the lead into strips of ⅛th-inch width. Then I shape the strips with metal shears.

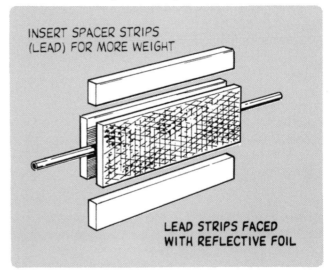

INSERT SPACER STRIPS
(LEAD) FOR MORE WEIGHT

LEAD STRIPS FACED
WITH REFLECTIVE FOIL

Using double-sided carpet tape, I attach the strips to either side of an insert and face them with reflective foil. The finished insert looks great.

For a little more weight, I add spacer strips of lead the same width as the tube. These are positioned on either side of the tube and between the lead sides. It's hard to explain, but the diagram shows how easily this can be done.

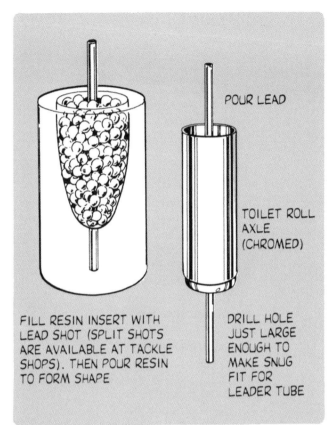

FILL RESIN INSERT WITH LEAD SHOT (SPLIT SHOTS ARE AVAILABLE AT TACKLE SHOPS). THEN POUR RESIN TO FORM SHAPE

POUR LEAD

TOILET ROLL AXLE (CHROMED)

DRILL HOLE JUST LARGE ENOUGH TO MAKE SNUG FIT FOR LEADER TUBE

inside to push them apart and force the ends into the openings of a toilet paper holder. Take one section, cut it to the right length and drill an opening in the closed end. The hole should be just big enough to admit your leader tube with a snug fit.

Prop the chromed piece and pour it full of lead. This gives you a shiny insert on its own, but you may wish to add to the glitter by wrapping it with reflective tape.

Such a heavy insert is often best with a lure you wish to run deep and stay deep. These have tapered front bodies ending in small diameter flat noses cut at very little angle.

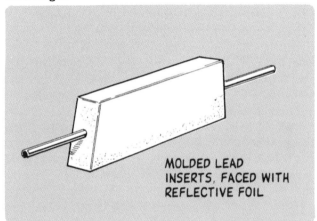

MOLDED LEAD INSERTS, FACED WITH REFLECTIVE FOIL

3. Still without needing to melt lead, you can add a great deal of weight to a lure using your resin insert mold and a handful of lead shot. Stick the leader tube into the resin insert mold (the one previously referred to as the "popsicle mold"). Fill the mold with shot. Then pour catalyzed resin to hold the lead in shape. Finish the head-shaped insert with reflective tape or coat it with glue sprinkled heavily with silver glitter.

One commercial lure company from Louisiana (the makers of the "Yapp" trolling lures) covers their inserts with brightly colored and highly reflective sequins (dressmakers' stuff).

4. To make an insert for a fat lure, get a chrome-plated toilet roll axle — the kind that has two sections, each closed on one end, which fit together with a spring

5. Finally, you can make your own inserts of any shape you wish by molding them from melted lead. Make the original out of poured resin, because the plastic is relatively easy to cut and shape. Then make your insert mold out of a type of rubber designed for metal casting. Many types of jig lures are now being made in such molds, and the rubber is just as easy to work with as the molding rubber for casting resin.

Good lead inserts for small lures can be fish shaped and spray painted. Others are flattened trapezoids, coated with reflective tape or faced with shell strips.

With experience you will graduate to more professional pourings and castings, but these suggestions will make you lures that catch many fish while you perfect your techniques.

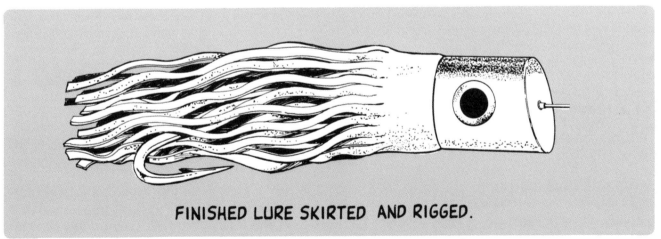

FINISHED LURE SKIRTED AND RIGGED.

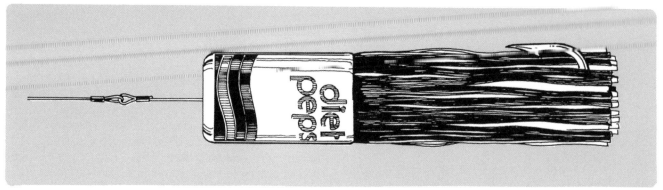

Big Game Trolling with Lures

Hawai'i is the birthplace of the big game trolling plug, a lure that honors its origins with the name "Konahead." The circumstances have to be right to spark any creation, and Hawai'i's clear waters, invaded annually by big, aggressive fish, are home to an imaginative group of fishermen with centuries of experience as lure makers. Though modern lures look nothing like the artificial pearl shell creations that skipped across Hawaiian seas behind outrigger crews before Captain Cook, they follow the tradition as surely as they follow the fisherman who believes in their magic.

Today's colorful plastic trolling plugs and metal jet lures evolved from cruder counterparts carved from wood, molded from lead or hybridized from other materials. Just a generation ago one of the most successful forerunners of today's trolling lures was a modified section of a chrome bathroom fixture.

The earliest of the plastic big game plugs was the "straight-runner," a lure as often as not molded inside a jelly glass jar to rough out its shape. After the glass was broken away, the craftsman cut an angle in the face for action and a ridge around the back to hang a skirt. A final polish, the addition of hooks and leader and the finished product was ready to plough the fertile ridges of the marlin grounds.

Today, the straight-runner is no longer made the same way, but it is still the standard by which all other big game lures are judged.

What's the best action for a marlin trolling lure? Answers vary from skipper to bluewater skipper. If your choice is anywhere in the frantic dimension of darting, vibrating and plunging hyperactivity, you won't like "straight-runners," but if your action standard is measured in marlin strikes, you'll make sure you always have a straight-runner humming along behind your boat.

What's a straight-runner? Imagine an artificial bait with no fishier shape than a beer can. As a matter of fact, consider just that: a straight-sided, flat-faced, poptop cylinder dressed with a flexible wrap-around skirt of fringe hanging off one end. That image is the picture of your basic straight-runner.

Let me quickly add, we aren't talking about a lure that is actually made from a beer can. Though straight-runners made from beer cans have been very successful, most are a bit more sophisticated looking. Professional lure makers cast them in solid plastic, formed around an insert that is fish-shaped, tantalizingly tinted with carefully chosen colors or embedded with flashy mirrors; yet, no matter how disguised, the straight-runner clearly doesn't imitate a bait fish or squid.

The very name is a misnomer. The straight-runner doesn't really run straight. Its action is a matter of degree when compared with the more active Konahead type of plugs. The latter generally have a steeply-slanted front face, scooped for a better grab of the water and with a center hole set off to the side. This specially designed head is constantly thrusting out to one side or the other, yanking the lure from side to side, plunging it down and then darting it upward.

The straight-runner doesn't charge back and forth. Rather, it shifts gracefully like an agile halfback successfully outwitting a succession of rampaging tacklers. Yes, it moves from side to side. Yes, it drops and returns to the surface for a quick splash. These are all movements that interest hungry marlin. Especially beguiling is that splashing lunge along the surface, during which the lure makes a bubble that breaks underwater in a long spurt of white foam and, presumably, produces an attractive sound.

Does a straight-runner really make noise? It's hard to imagine that any resisting object being pulled through the water could *not* make some sort of sound — and the flat face of a straight-runner is definitely a resisting object. In fact, noise could prove to be its most important attribute. After all, a lure slipping through the water without setting up vibrations would probably go unnoticed or, even if noticed, draw no particular response from a marlin. For example, I doubt that the streamlined leadheaded trolling jig would ever be able to match the marlin catch rate of any form of big game plug, whether it be a straight-runner or any other form of Konahead.

Straight-runners derive their action from a face that is either perfectly square with the sides or from one that features only a very slight angle (perhaps as little as 15 degrees from the perpendicular).

Perhaps the tamest of these is the straight-runner with a perpendicular face and dead center leader hole. No matter how the lure revolves on its leader, it basically attacks the water at the same angle. The lure's action is entirely the result of trying to force its flat face through a resisting sea. Moldcraft, a manufacturer of soft plastic trolling lures, calls its version the "wide-range softhead" because its action automatically adjusts to a wide range of trolling speeds from 2 to 20 knots. Fished off Cozumel, Mexico, in the spring of 1981, the Moldcraft wide-ranger was credited with a clean sweep of billfish for one angler in 12 hours of fishing: a sailfish, white marlin, blue marlin and broadbill swordfish.

One Hawai'i lure manufacturer molds his right-angled plugs with the leader hole off center, then drills six holes through the body from front to back in an attempt to imitate the sonic effect of "jet" type trolling lures. I've got one that raised two blue marlin in the first two days I used it. It features a quicker shift than other square-headed plugs.

I've also experienced great success with straight-runners that have angled heads. These tend to swing across a wider path than do the "bottle bottoms," yet they are not as erratic as the Konaheads. At one point, these were called "pusher plugs" because their flat faces shoved the water aside, perhaps creating a pressure wave in the process.

When the angle of the face increases much beyond 15 degrees and the leader hole remains at dead center, the action of the lure abruptly changes. It can no longer turn downward to grab the water and dive, but just seems to flop helplessly along the surface in a very unappealing style.

Honolulu lure maker Joe Yee has managed to shave away a few extra degrees of angle on his straight-runners by molding the heads around a lead insert. The extra weight gives the lure the ballast it needs to get back underwater, and the lure literally explodes along the surface as the weight tries to drown the lure against the struggling slanted edge. This lure won the Henry Chee Memorial Award in the 1978 Hawaiian International Billfish Tournament for skipper Jack Ross.

Interestingly enough, if you go back through the records of tournament fishing in Hawai'i, you will find that straight-runners have figured high in the scoring for

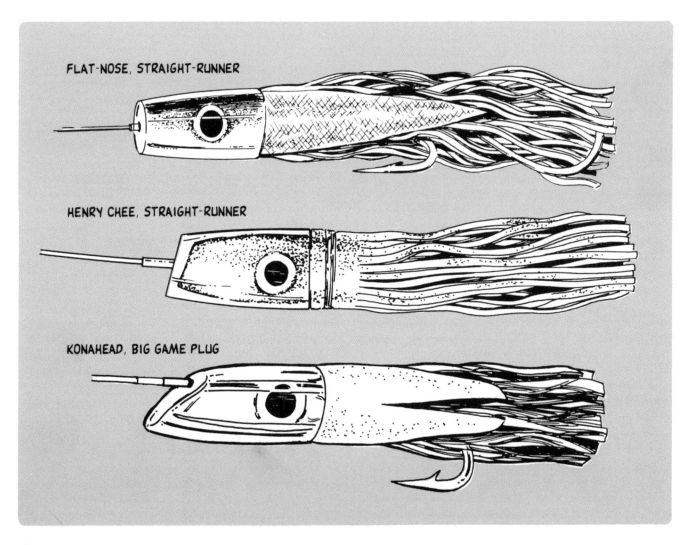

FLAT-NOSE, STRAIGHT-RUNNER

HENRY CHEE, STRAIGHT-RUNNER

KONAHEAD, BIG GAME PLUG

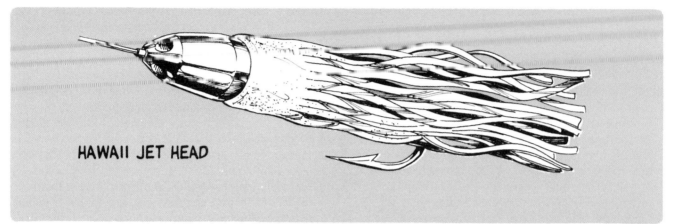

HAWAII JET HEAD

as long as there has been tournament trolling. That may surprise you if you are new to lure trolling for big game, as fishermen who have only recently "discovered" the straight-runner tend to regard it as a "new" development. A recent article in a national fishing magazine refers to the success of straight-runners as a threat to the "traditional" Konaheads. Hawai'i's fishermen chuckled over that. Straight-runners were very popular with the pioneering trollers of Hawai'i. Henry Chee, a Kona charter boat fisherman back in the days when the Kona fleet numbered just two or three boats, developed and used straight-runners with so much success that they are still known as "Henry Chee" lures by Hawai'i's veteran anglers.

Lumping Hawaiian big game trolling plugs together as "Konaheads" suggests a uniformity not matched by reality. These lures come in as many different sizes, shapes, colors and actions as there are lure makers. Fishermen today continuously experiment in the tradition of their ancestors, producing new designs, patterns and styles in a constant search for the lure that marlin find irresistable.

"Of course we experiment," says Jack Ross. "If good fishermen didn't experiment, we'd still be using fishhooks made of bone and lines of grass fibers."

Crowding the Konaheads and the straight-runners for places in the wakes of Hawai'i's fishing fleet are the rocket-nosed "jet" lures.

Jet contrails are now as common a sight in Hawai'i's seas as they are in Hawai'i's skies. The streamlined multi-hued fishing lures with the aerodynamic nose cones are now among the most popular attractors tracking the wakes of the big game fishing fleet. For some fishermen the jet lure has eliminated the plastic trolling plug, but even the anglers who still have faith in Konaheads cover their bets by pulling a brace of jets as alternative offerings.

Why this surge of interest in the chrome lures with the built-in whistle? For the best of all possible reasons, they catch fish when others don't.

Fishermen, being patient romantics with a lot of time on their hands between strikes, are known for the mystiques they spin out in their misspent imaginations to convince themselves that they have more working in their favor than just the simple fact that fish get hungry.

The jet, with its chameleon ability to change colors according to the angler's whim (and pocketbook), its enigmatic cluster of intake ports, and its ability to hide all degrees of ballasting, lends itself to legends.

What color are they hitting today? Don't broadcast it over the CB. Just tell me in code. Last week it was "killer," today it's "convincer," but if not, we've got 75 more combinations to choose from.

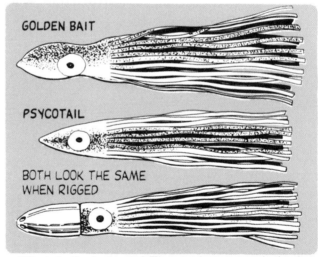

GOLDEN BAIT

PSYCOTAIL

BOTH LOOK THE SAME WHEN RIGGED

What do the holes do? They make a special whistling sound. No, they make bubbles. That's not right either; the water flow just makes the skirt act better. Hell, they don't do a thing because I've got one so full of lead no drop of water could ever squirt through and it's my best one. Take your choice.

How much lead is enough? They're great the way they are, but be sure to have a few in each color with graduated loads just in case.

See what I mean? Anglers don't agree on jets just because they don't like to agree on anything. Agreement merely means you aren't really doing anything better than anyone else, and what good fisherman could stand to believe that?

Everyone has to have a baseline to start with, even if as a take-off point for his own evolving technique. Here is that baseline.

There are many different kinds of jets. I have 14 types in my tackle box, and I'm sure I have not exhausted all of the possibilities. What they have in common is their metal heads, circular in cross-section, and their central passages running the length of the lure from intake ports at the nose to relief vents opening into the skirt. There are many variations in size, silhouette and substance. The standard jets have tapered noses, but one version is made with a slanted front end and still another has a concave face. The tapered jets track straight; the slanted ones are a bit more erratic, changing directon and occasionally splashing if run on a short line.

Some of the best of the jets have never been sold over a tackle shop counter. My top producer is one cut from a bar of stainless steel. Though it has the exact specifications of the original pot metal heads poured by the late Kona lure-maker K.O. Dean, this one takes five fish for every one the standard lure hooks. Another good one is no longer on the market: a chrome tube filled with lead except for the central passages.

Weighting may be the whole story. I confess that I prefer to get as much weight into the lure as I can. My feeling is that the jet works best when it is running deep in the wake. A few tackle stores provide special lead slugs molded to fit inside the jet head and ported to continue the central passages right through the lead. One of these slugs continues past the stern of the head and flares out to make a second stem for a second skirt; it also makes the jet a deep plowing enticer.

Don't despair if you can't find the special inserts. Buy a batch of egg sinkers. Pick a size about half the diameter of the interior cavity of the head. You can string a few over your leader, and they'll give added weight without choking off the flow.

The leader? There would never be any competition if it weren't for the presence of those lure-thieving ono. Only the ono can cut a heavy nylon leader, so you should use wire whenever you are fishing near enough to shore to make an ono strike likely. You'll land many ono on nylon, of course, but you'll also lose enough lures in the process to make you feel it just isn't worth it.

Off the ono grounds, always use mono leaders. Your chief quarry for the jet lure is the ahi, the fish with the best eyesight in the ocean. Mono will catch him when wire just makes him nod knowingly. Pick the heaviest mono leader that will pass through the leader hole.

The tail? Your choices range in price from strips cut off your shower curtain to molded plastic squids at four

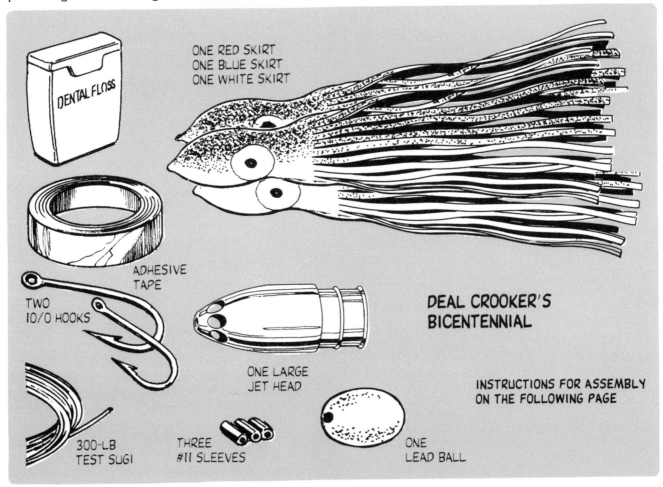

ONE RED SKIRT
ONE BLUE SKIRT
ONE WHITE SKIRT

DENTAL FLOSS

ADHESIVE TAPE

TWO 10/0 HOOKS

ONE LARGE JET HEAD

DEAL CROOKER'S BICENTENNIAL

INSTRUCTIONS FOR ASSEMBLY ON THE FOLLOWING PAGE

300-LB TEST SUGI

THREE #11 SLEEVES

ONE LEAD BALL

bucks a head. Two or more squids are needed to make the most effective skirts. Cut off the closed end of the skirt just far enough back to make an opening that will fit over the lure stem. Tie on the underskirt facing in the direction it will stream when in use. Tie on the overskirt in reverse and pull it down over the underskirt so that it is right side out. Now protect your investment with a few wraps of Monel wire to make sure one sharp tooth does not steal two expensive squids.

Or, three expensive squids, because one of the most famous of the jet lure dressings is the tri-colored "bicentennial."

Like Farrah Fawcett-Majors, this alluring creation would probably just be another pretty thing were it not for a lot of publicity. In 1976, America's bicentennial year, every red, white and blue lure was referred to by some fisherman or other as "bicentennial" whether it was a plug, a jig or a jet. But, that beloved fisherman Deal Crooker came up with his own version. Since Deal was a man whose mere presence created powerful vibrations, whether his voice was reverberating over the heads of hundreds at a cocktail party or thousands over the CB airways, the bicentennial pattern became the most famous of possible jet lure dressings. (Just think what Deal could have done for Farrah).

Deal's directions for skirting a bicentennial are shown.

The accompanying illustrations should be enough to show you the details on how to rig the bicentennial.

(1) Cut the white squid above the eyes. Put liquid detergent on the jet head so that the squid skirt will slide easily over the head. Tie on with dental floss.

(2) Using the detergent, slip the pink squid over the lead ball.

(3) With more detergent, slide the blue squid over the pink squid.

(4) Cut the sugi leader at a sharp angle to form a point and insert into the hole of the lead ball. Poke the point of the sugi through the heads of the pink and blue squids.

(5) Insert the sugi into the middle hole of the jet head, and your bait is ready to have the hooks attached.

You'll also see in my tackle box a wide assortment of skirts cut out of sheet materials. These are the least expensive skirts of all which is especially important if ono are your quarry. Golden Baits makes sheet plastic in the same colors and the same materials as its squids. This material seems to be just a little thicker and tougher than the molded squid, hence it lasts longer. A sheet costs very little more than one big squid, and from it I can cut the equivalent in lure tails for about four lures.

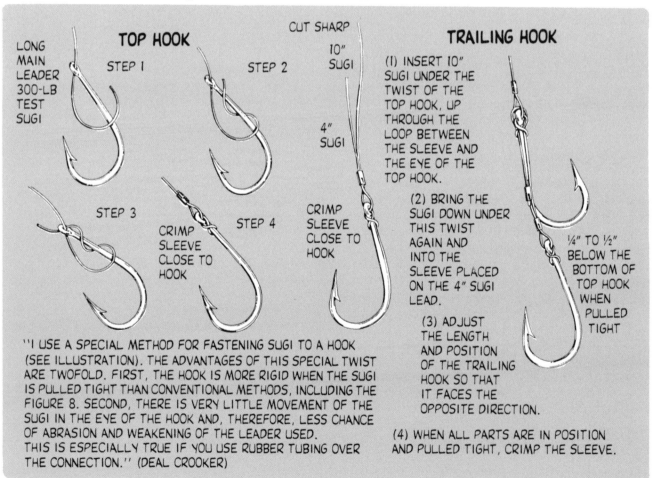

TOP HOOK

LONG MAIN LEADER 300-LB TEST SUGI

STEP 1

STEP 2

CUT SHARP

10" SUGI

4" SUGI

STEP 3

CRIMP SLEEVE CLOSE TO HOOK

STEP 4

CRIMP SLEEVE CLOSE TO HOOK

TRAILING HOOK

(1) INSERT 10" SUGI UNDER THE TWIST OF THE TOP HOOK, UP THROUGH THE LOOP BETWEEN THE SLEEVE AND THE EYE OF THE TOP HOOK.

(2) BRING THE SUGI DOWN UNDER THIS TWIST AGAIN AND INTO THE SLEEVE PLACED ON THE 4" SUGI LEAD.

(3) ADJUST THE LENGTH AND POSITION OF THE TRAILING HOOK SO THAT IT FACES THE OPPOSITE DIRECTION.

¼" TO ½" BELOW THE BOTTOM OF TOP HOOK WHEN PULLED TIGHT

"I USE A SPECIAL METHOD FOR FASTENING SUGI TO A HOOK (SEE ILLUSTRATION). THE ADVANTAGES OF THIS SPECIAL TWIST ARE TWOFOLD. FIRST, THE HOOK IS MORE RIGID WHEN THE SUGI IS PULLED TIGHT THAN CONVENTIONAL METHODS, INCLUDING THE FIGURE 8. SECOND, THERE IS VERY LITTLE MOVEMENT OF THE SUGI IN THE EYE OF THE HOOK AND, THEREFORE, LESS CHANCE OF ABRASION AND WEAKENING OF THE LEADER USED. THIS IS ESPECIALLY TRUE IF YOU USE RUBBER TUBING OVER THE CONNECTION." (DEAL CROOKER)

(4) WHEN ALL PARTS ARE IN POSITION AND PULLED TIGHT, CRIMP THE SLEEVE.

When I dress my lures using sheet material, I usually put on a white squid as the underskirt and cut a matched pair of panels for either side of the lure for the overskirt.

Other sheet material is stuff I've cannabalized from upholstery shops. Such material tends to be stiffer and much less flexible, but it comes in colors that are just as attractive. Lures dressed this way do catch their share of fish. Indeed, for many years they were the standard dressings for offshore fishing baits. Those were the years when fishermen looked with disfavor on the molded plastic squid and wondered why anybody would spend the extra money for them! You can dress a lot of lures for a buck when you cut your own out of upholstery plastic.

Where in the wake should you troll jets? I've taken fish spitting-distance off the stern, but have had my best luck with a lure run just behind the spot where the white turbulence from the prop clears out to blue water. I've also had success with a heavy lure dragged a hundred yards back. A word of caution. Make sure the angles of the lines from rod tip to lure leave a good deal of vertical spread or you will have the fish that hit the short lines cut the long lines by accident on the strike. Ono do this with their teeth. Ahi do it with their fins.

How fast should you troll a jet? Probably not slower than seven knots. The lure has no action of its own and relies on speed to enhance its attractiveness.

Yet, a few seasons ago, skipper Jerome Judd on the Kona boat *JUN KEN PO* brought a black marlin back to port that had struck a lure that was traveling just about as slowly as a lure can go without turning into an anchor. The *JUN KEN PO* had stopped to fight an aku to be rigged as live bait. The battle, boating and rigging took longer than usual because Capt. Judd was alone without a crew. While the boat was nearly stopped, the jet lures on the outriggers settled into the depths. That's where one deep-swimming black marlin found them angling downward.

At the other end of the spectrum, you should not go so fast that the lure regularly breaks water. Some will argue this point, but a jet is most effective running below the surface. Breaking lures will catch fish, the Konaheads prove this everyday, but you troll the jet as an alternative to the breaking lure.

What makes a fish strike a lure? No matter how well designed it is, it cannot be an exact replica of real fish food. If a natural appearance was the final criteria a fish used in deciding whether or not to strike, we'd all be fishing with fresh natural baits and never use a lure.

Fishing scientists and scientific fishermen have advanced many theories and combinations of theories to explain the striking instinct.

Curiosity is part of it. Exotic colors, unusual whirling parts, strange noises, all contribute to stimulating the curiosity of a predator. That's when he's in the mood to be stimulated. What may be seductive sometimes will spook the same fish at others.

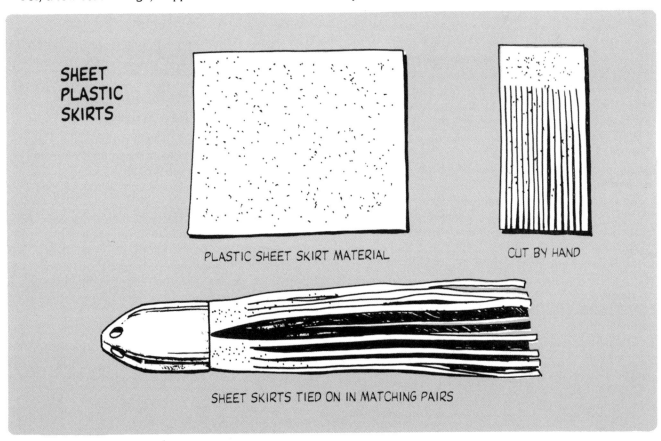

SHEET PLASTIC SKIRTS

PLASTIC SHEET SKIRT MATERIAL

CUT BY HAND

SHEET SKIRTS TIED ON IN MATCHING PAIRS

The instinct to attack an intruder may excite a fish to charge a large noisy lure chugging along in a challenging manner. The lure appears aggressive, the fish responds to the invasion of his domain.

Occasionally, a fish is stimulated to strike by the feeding action of others. One fish will leave a school to attack a trolled lure. The others watch the strike as they hold back; then all hell breaks loose as all the lines are hit simultaneously.

But no matter how else you choose to look at it, the prime instinct is food. Fish are not always hungry, to be sure. They do show definite feeding periods, as well as other times when even the easiest meal won't rate a nibble. The ocean is not an easy place to make a living, even for a fish, and he cannot pass up very many of the opportunities available for feeding his belly.

Which is the better lure for the Pacific blue marlin, plug or jet? Or is neither as good as a live bait?

According to a survey of 121 Pacific blue marlin, it is no contest. They overwhelmingly preferred the plastic plug, with the live bait a distant second and the metal jet trailing way behind.

So the survey says. But, you ask, how do you survey the tastes of a horde of uncooperative marlin?

Well, you don't survey the uncooperative ones, just the ones that oblige themselves by getting caught. And these 121 obliging fish were the ones that tested the offerings of the contestants in the 1980 Hawaiian International Billfish Tournament (HIBT) and the Hawaiian Billfish Tournament (HBT) held the week before.

Of the 100 marlin taken in the HIBT, 78 were caught on plugs. Likewise, 14 of the 21 marlin caught in the HBT went for the action of the plastic trolling plugs that originated and evolved here in Hawai'i.

Twenty-seven of these willing 121 gobbled up live baits. Only eight marlin in the two tournaments combined fell victim to their preference for jets.

Well, you say, the jet is really the better lure for ahi. Perhaps, but the ahi didn't think so during these two fish fights. Nineteen ahi obliged. Nine ate plugs. Eight ate live baits. Two (only two!) hammered metal.

But there is always an unknown factor to prevent such statistics from being 100 percent reliable. That factor is what fishing scientists call "effort."

You catch fish on what you use. You don't catch them on what you don't use. If the majority of fishermen troll plugs, then the majority of fish will be caught on plugs.

And that is probably what happened. It's a chicken and egg situation. If you believe plugs work better than jets for marlin, you'll fish plugs rather than jets in billfish tournaments. Then when you catch your marlin on a plug, it reinforces your prejudice.

Despite that note of caution, the figures do suggest that the good old plastic Hawaiian marlin plug is a very fine lure for hooking marlin.

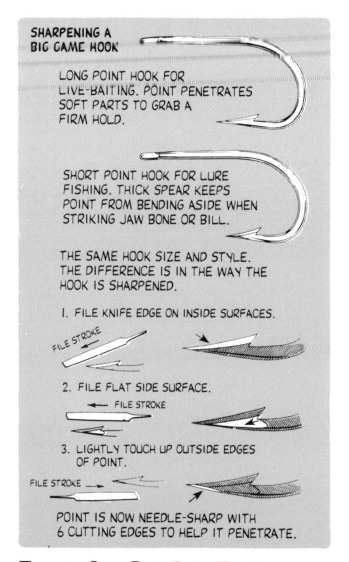

SHARPENING A BIG GAME HOOK

LONG POINT HOOK FOR LIVE-BAITING. POINT PENETRATES SOFT PARTS TO GRAB A FIRM HOLD.

SHORT POINT HOOK FOR LURE FISHING. THICK SPEAR KEEPS POINT FROM BENDING ASIDE WHEN STRIKING JAW BONE OR BILL.

THE SAME HOOK SIZE AND STYLE. THE DIFFERENCE IS IN THE WAY THE HOOK IS SHARPENED.

1. FILE KNIFE EDGE ON INSIDE SURFACES.

FILE STROKE

2. FILE FLAT SIDE SURFACE.

FILE STROKE

3. LIGHTLY TOUCH UP OUTSIDE EDGES OF POINT.

FILE STROKE

POINT IS NOW NEEDLE-SHARP WITH 6 CUTTING EDGES TO HELP IT PENETRATE.

Twenty-One Details in Rigging Big Game Trolling Lures

1. Use fresh line. Store it away from the deteriorating effects of sun and heat (except, of course, when you are actually using it). Examine it often for chafing. Discard end sections as soon as they show the first signs of abrasion.

2. Use a double line. Carefully tie your double with a proven knot like the bimini twist (practice until you can tie it perfectly). Serve the knot with waxed dental floss to protect it from damage of bumping back and forth through the guides. Use one knot for one fish (cut off and discard your double after a long fight with a strong fish).

3. Make sure your double line meets International Game Fish Association specifications on length allowance. It takes no more effort but may put you in the record books. (See current IGFA specifications in item 12.)

4. Tie your double to your swivel with a clinch knot, drawing it up tightly without bruising by lubricating the

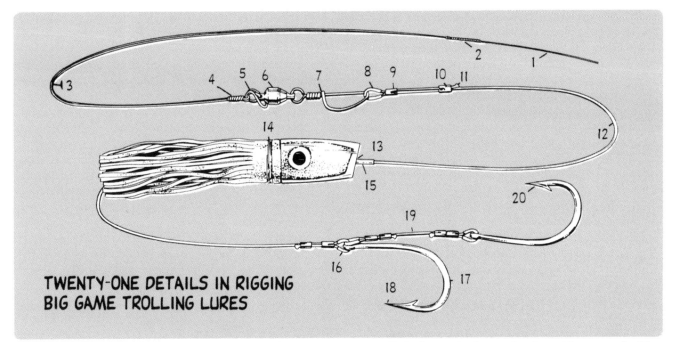

TWENTY-ONE DETAILS IN RIGGING
BIG GAME TROLLING LURES

line with saliva so the knot slides together easily when being formed.

5. Slip the swivel through the end loop of your clinch knot to prevent the end from backing out from the constant strain of a long bout with a strong fish.

6. Be sure your barrel swivel is strong enough. Pick the right size, one that will match or exceed the strength of your leader. Bigger swivels are better. They prevent the leader from slipping through the mate's hand during gaffing. (If the mate touches the line rather than the leader, even accidently, the fish will be disqualified for record consideration — and even for entry in many major angling tournaments.) It should, of course, be a ball-bearing swivel for maximum control over line twist and should be oiled regularly to keep it turning easily. Twisted lines break at less than their rated strength.

7. Check your snap to ensure that it has been closed securely and won't open under strain.

8. When forming your end loop, slip a section of plastic tubing over your leader as chafing gear. This prevents abrasion and cushions the cutting effect of the wire snap on the leader.

9. Crimp your sleeves with as much force as you can muster, bracing one handle of your crimping tool against a firm surface as you squeeze.

10. Use a second sleeve for extra holding power. Some fishermen crimp their second sleeve a foot down from the end loop. This keeps the lure from sliding all the way back to the snap, which leaves your line vulnerable if a second sharp-toothed fish grabs the lure when it trails behind the fish you are fighting. Some fishermen feel that a foot is not enough insurance. They crimp a sleeve in the middle of the leader so the lure stops halfway.

11. Ball the end of your leader with a match. The extra thickness keeps the end from snaking back through the sleeve under heavy and prolonged strain.

12. Use a clear, hard-surfaced monofilament leader of 300-pound test or more. Be sure it fits with current IGFA specifications on length of leader and double line (combined length of leader and double cannot exceed 40 feet with the leader limited to 30 feet). Allow yourself a few feet of margin for stretch (say, 18 feet of double and 18 feet of leader). Monofilament stretches out on a long fight and keeps its stretch for quite some time afterward — long enough to disqualify a record or tournament catch.

13. Ream out the central tubing of the lure to smooth it so the lure won't chew through the leader.

14. Overwrap your skirt with Monel wire. This prevents a sharp-toothed striking fish from taking the skirt undetected, leaving you trolling only the lure head.

15. More plastic tubing for chafing gear. This tube should be about an inch longer than the length of the lure. It fits inside the leader tube to act as a bearing surface, protecting the leader from the constant attack of an active lure.

16. More tubing for chafing gear on all end loops. Use chafing gear here even if you use cable leaders instead of nylon. In use, wire leaders will saw through hook eyes, especially if electrolysis occurs.

17. Choose hooks with the correct gap size. The hook should be big enough to allow the lure head to fit inside the gap, guaranteeing that the point will always be able to protrude from the skirt.

18. File your hook points until they are too dangerous to handle. No hook is sharp enough the way it comes from the box. Stroke it carefully with a fine-toothed metal file until you've got a point that refuses to

slide across your fingernail without digging in. Work on the knife edge along the inside of the point so that it is sharp enough to slice bone. You want a point so sharp it can be driven through a marlin bill (and you'll hook some of your marlin in just that way)

19. Make your trailing leader the right length. It must be long enough so that the two hooks don't overlap and short enough so some part of the trailing hook is hidden by the lure skirt. Both are IGFA regulations.

20. The point of your tail hook should face in a different direction from the lead hook, giving you a second direction of attack.

21. Tape the hook section until it is rigid. Overwrap all connections with plastic tape from the shank of the trailing hook up through the sleeves of the main leader. Rigidity will result in more hookups and fewer foul-ups. The latter result when the trailing hook flops over the main leader. Foul-ups happen from the normal action of the lure, but they can also occur when a fish strikes and misses the hook. Once the hooks are tangled, they aren't free to catch a fish on the second pass.

Hooking a marlin is like latching onto an express train. Marlin have so much power that they will find a way to pull your tackle apart if you have left them some way. That's why most successful big game fishermen are nearly paranoid in their attention to detail. In a world where every marlin is out to outwit you, paranoia about your equipment makes good sense for a few cents.

Braking and Breaking

You've hooked a good fish. He runs long and hard. Then your line breaks. What do you blame it on?

Assuming your line is fresh and undamaged and you've tied good knots, you've got to blame it on your drag setting.

You'll hear a lot of bad advice on how to set your drag, probably more bad advice than good.

Why so much bad advice? Because many fishermen, even some of the most experienced, don't recognize that there are three independent factors affecting the amount of resistance your tackle applies to a running fish. Three factors, not just the most obvious one.

These three factors are (1) the internal braking system inside your reel — called the "drag," (2) the amount of line on your reel and (3) the resistance of the water to your line.

Let's take the last one first, because it is the one most often ignored. Spool a thousand yards of 50-pound test line out in your wake, tie the line off on a cleat and then speed your boat up to 20 knots. Before you hit that speed, the line will break from water resistance alone. Now turn that image around in your mind. Imagine a marlin streaking away from you at 20 knots with a thousand yards of line in tow. He'll break that line even if your reel is on free spool with no drag from the reel at

all. It is the resistance of the line, itself, that accounts for the fact that a line breaks off at the swivel end and not at the reel end when you fight a fish.

Take that image a little further and you'll realize that what a fish fights against is the pull of the line in the water. He's not really fighting the pull of the reel, the rod, the angler or the boat. Not, that is, until he's within a few hundred yards of the boat and the skin friction on the line is negligible.

Now, for just a bit more thought on this factor, consider what happens when the line is pulled sideways in the water. If a fish has curved around and looped a belly in the line, he's increased the water friction by pulling the line sideways.

So, the first rule: line friction alone can create enough drag to break the line regardless of the drag setting of the reel. The more line in the water, the more water resistance and the lighter your drag should be set.

Now for factor two, the law of diminishing line. This can be hard to picture, but apply a little mental muscle and you'll get it. Believe me, it's worthwhile. Imagine that your line is pulling on a lever. The fulcrum is the center of your reel spool. The lever is an imaginary line drawn from the center of the spool to the point at which the line pulls free of the spool. The lever is at its longest when the reel is full. The lever continuously shortens as line leaves the reel and the spool diameter shrinks.

When the lever is long (the spool is full) the line pulls off easily. As the lever shortens (line leaves the reel) the line requires more and more force to make the spool turn despite the fact that your braking mechanism is at the same setting. According to the manufacturers of the Everol reel, your drag triples as your spool reaches half empty.

Imagine then that a fish has run off 500 yards of line on the strike. Resistance from the reel is far greater than your initial drag setting. Resistance from the friction of the line in the water is enormous. That fish is pulling against a tremendous amount of braking effect, more, perhaps, than you realized when you set the drag in the first place.

Factor two actually comes into play before the strike. When do you set your drag? Obviously, you do it before you release your line and run the lures back to trolling distance. Think about that a minute. You set your drag the way you want it. Then you release, say, a hundred yards of line for your long outrigger. That hundred yards has diminished your spool size and increased your striking drag.

But all of these variables are under the control of your first factor, the braking mechanism built into your reel.

Your drag should be adjustable from free spool right through to full lock up. Setting your striking drag should only be done after weighing the factors already noted. To give yourself the greatest margin for error, set your striking drag between one-fourth and one-fifth of the breaking strength of the line. Don't trust to arm-pull-judgment. Run the line through the guides. Attach a spring scale to the swivel and pull until the line releases from the reel. The scale reading will tell you your breaking strain.

Most important of all, as line disappears from the reel, go against your instinct. Your great urge, when you see the line shooting off the reel, will be to tighten the drag. The laws of mechanics and hydraulics are already doing this for you more rapidly than you realize. As a matter of fact, be prepared to back off. Some skippers back almost off to free-spool when their reel reaches half empty. Believe me, you aren't giving the fish a break. You are just making sure your line doesn't get a break.

Rigging Up and Out

The outrigger is a fundamental tool for all three types of big game trolling. It helps the troller present lures, live baits and skip baits. Each type of presentation requires a slightly different type of rigging, but one combination of arrangements will allow the troller to fish all three ways.

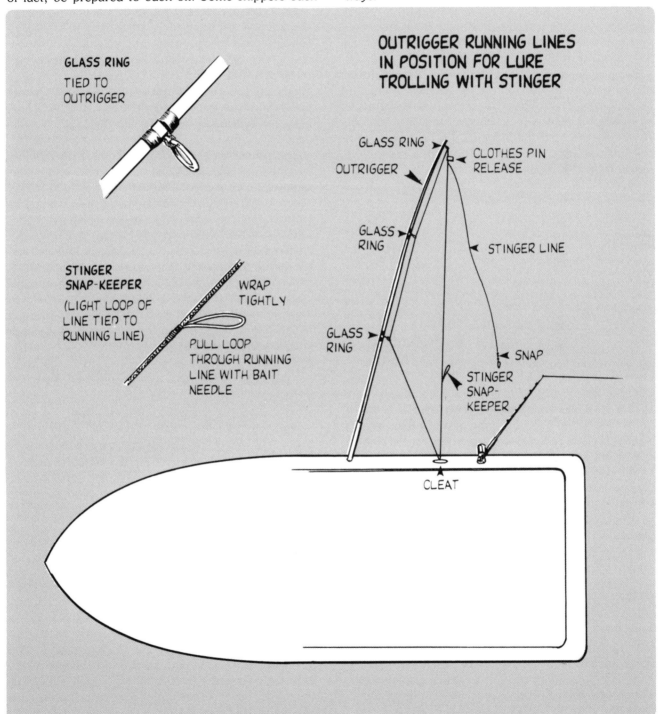

GLASS RING
TIED TO
OUTRIGGER

STINGER
SNAP-KEEPER
(LIGHT LOOP OF
LINE TIED TO
RUNNING LINE)

WRAP
TIGHTLY

PULL LOOP
THROUGH RUNNING
LINE WITH BAIT
NEEDLE

OUTRIGGER RUNNING LINES
IN POSITION FOR LURE
TROLLING WITH STINGER

GLASS RING
OUTRIGGER
CLOTHES PIN
RELEASE
GLASS
RING
STINGER LINE
GLASS
RING
SNAP
STINGER
SNAP-
KEEPER
CLEAT

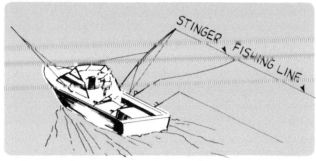

Lure trolling requires a "stinger" line to eliminate any slack line on the strike. When a fish crashes a trolling lure, you want the line to remain tight at all times, preventing the fish from letting go when he learns that the lure is out to hurt him, not feed him.

Skipping dead baits, like trolling with lures, requires a high angle presentation to keep the line out of the water and to lift the bait to keep it sliding across the surface. However, the difference is that the dead bait must be released gently and the line must be kept slack for a brief period to avoid scaring the fish away by the unnatural feel of tension pulling on the bait.

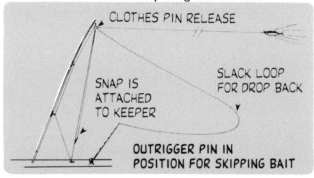

Live-bait fishing requires a slack line drop back, but it also is aided by a rigging that allows the angler to visualize what the bait is doing. The angler needs to be able to tell if his bait is swimming normally; he needs to be alerted by the nervous action of a bait that is being tracked by a predator; and he needs to be able to release the bait at the right moment.

The rig we'll describe here serves all three methods extremely well. It incorporates a stinger line for lure trolling, a clothes pin release for live baiting and skipping baits, and a running line to adjust the position of the clothes pin and provide a means for clearing the outrigger of the occasional tangle that messes up the system.

The accompanying diagrams best show how the arrangement is set up. The running line should be a strong, tightly braided nylon cord. "Solid braid nylon" in 350-pound test or greater is a good choice. The outrigger should be set up with three or more glass rings; these are available at the larger boat supply stores. You need rings with an inner diameter of a ½-inch or more to accept the stinger line snap and to allow the running line to move easily.

The clothes pin release is a standard fitting and is available at boat supply stores. Commercially made releases are molded from plastic, but some anglers have had success making their own from hardwood. you can adjust the tension of the pin by adding or removing heavy rubber bands cut from bicycle inner tubes.

In position for trolling with lures, the release is run up to the tip of the outrigger. The snap, usually held in a keeper loop, should be within easy reach of the fisherman standing at the gunnel. The snap should be small enough to pass through the glass rings.

Give careful consideration to the release trajectory of the outrigger pin when a fish strikes. The snap will shoot forward when the rubber band breaks away. On some boats, depending on how high the flying bridge is in relation to the tip of the outrigger, the path of the stinger line snap could make the crew a target. On most boats, however, the outrigger tips are either sufficiently high or sufficiently wide to eliminate any possible danger.

The rubber band from the outrigger snap should be wrapped very tightly around the trolling line to prevent slippage. You want the rubber band to hold the line securely but to be cut almost immediately when a fish strikes.

The rod being serviced by the outrigger should be positioned in a holder that is far enough forward along the gunnel to allow the deckhand to reach the tip easily, making the tying and untying of the stinger line convenient. Once the rubber band is wrapped and the loops are secured by the snap, the deckhand should release a few yards of line from the reel, swinging the stinger line into trolling position.

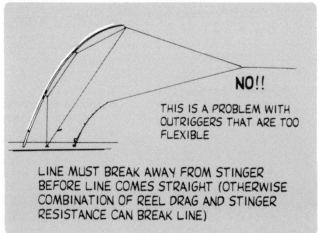

Beware of a fatal mistake that sometimes happens with "soft" outriggers. You don't want the outrigger to bend down so much that the trolling line straightens out before the rubber band is cut. Should that happen, you'll be doubling up the tension on the line at that exact point and the trolling line will break rather than the rubber band. To prevent this, shorten the stinger or brace the outrigger.

For live-bait fishing, the stinger line is no longer used. Attach the snap to the keeper, and pull the running line down until the clothes pin release is within reach. Then attach the baited trolling line to the clothes pin. You must ward off the abrasive effect of the pin's surface. The quickest and simplest way is to tear off a strip of newspaper, wrap it around the line a dozen times, bend the wrapped section back on itself like a hairpin and clamp the papered section of line in the jaws of the pin.

Some professional skippers prepare their lines by serving the point of attachment with a 2- or 3-inch section of waxed floss wraps. These floss wraps serve three purposes: they mark the line so the skipper knows he's got the right amount trailing behind the boat; they provide the attachment point with some bulk, making the line easier to hold in the jaws of the pin; and they, of course, protect the line.

When live-bait fishing, the release pin should be run back up the outrigger only part way. It should be at a point where it can be easily watched by the deckhand. What the crew will see when the bait fish is swimming contentedly is a slight but steady jiggling of the release in sympathetic vibration with the steady beat of the bait's tail. When a marlin approaches the bait, the bait will panic and try to escape. The release pin will begin to dance quite actively. Then, of course, as the big fish snatches the bait, the release will let the line go.

The illustrated rigger arrangement is one of many possible setups, but one of the very few that does all three jobs well.

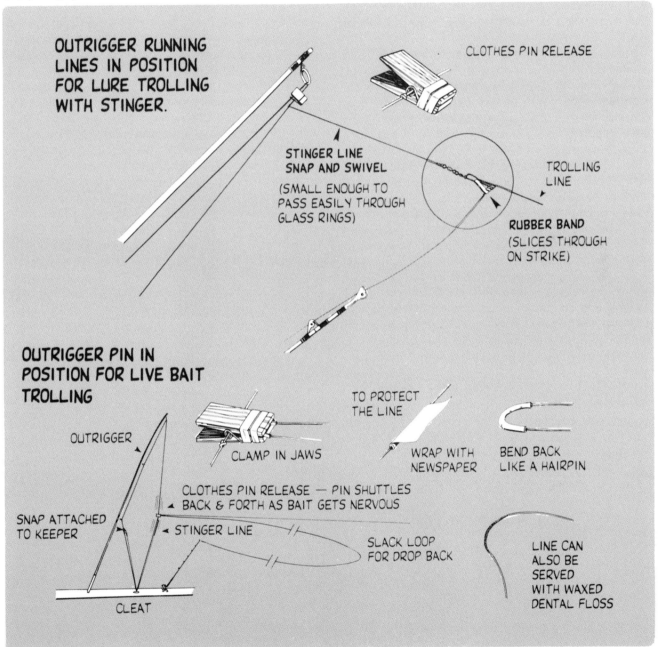

OUTRIGGER RUNNING LINES IN POSITION FOR LURE TROLLING WITH STINGER.

CLOTHES PIN RELEASE

STINGER LINE SNAP AND SWIVEL

(SMALL ENOUGH TO PASS EASILY THROUGH GLASS RINGS)

TROLLING LINE

RUBBER BAND (SLICES THROUGH ON STRIKE)

OUTRIGGER PIN IN POSITION FOR LIVE BAIT TROLLING

OUTRIGGER

CLAMP IN JAWS

TO PROTECT THE LINE

WRAP WITH NEWSPAPER

BEND BACK LIKE A HAIRPIN

CLOTHES PIN RELEASE — PIN SHUTTLES BACK & FORTH AS BAIT GETS NERVOUS

SNAP ATTACHED TO KEEPER

STINGER LINE

SLACK LOOP FOR DROP BACK

LINE CAN ALSO BE SERVED WITH WAXED DENTAL FLOSS

CLEAT

Fishing the FADS

Tips for Fishing the Buoys

Operating from the knowledge that free-drifting objects — like logs and other debris — attract and hold schools of tuna, mahimahi and other offshore game fish, the Honolulu Laboratory of the National Marine Fisheries Service set out in 1977 to determine if anchored objects could do the same. Their first efforts were enormously successful as the placement of six "fish-aggregating devices" attracted huge schools of fish.

Within months, catch reports from sport and commercial fishermen showed remarkable results. During this pioneering period, commercial boats reported a one-month total of 400,000 pounds of aku and ahi taken on 52 visits to the FADs. Sport fishing boats reported as much as 400 pounds of mahimahi boated on a single visit. The buoys were here to stay.

At this writing, the Division of Aquatic Resources of Hawai'i's Department of Land and Natural Resources has assumed the responsibility for a fish aggregating system of 26 buoys with plans to add that many more.

The buoys have opened up possibilities for every kind of sport fishing from whipping with light spinning gear to trolling live bait for the largest game fish in the sea. Tomo Rogers, for example, used a live bait hooked at one of the Kona buoys to entice a 1,450-pound blue marlin for a charterer aboard the *KONA SEAFARI*. This was the largest marlin ever caught on 80-pound test line. Many other anglers enjoy days of sport with ultra-light tackle to catch fish the size of Tomo's bait.

Tips on How to Fish the "FAD" Buoys

Sometimes, you can catch all the fish you want by trolling back and forth past the buoy. Sometimes, the only way you can catch fish is by jigging. Sometimes, you can only catch fish with bait. And sometimes, there are no fish at the buoy at all and no way to catch them.

Here are some tips on how to catch fish around the FADs, if the fish are there, of course.

1. Aku are usually very easy to catch when they are gathered at the buoys. No matter how fussy they are in other places, we find they bite a trolled "king-king" eagerly, even when we use heavy monofilament leaders of 50- or 80-pound test. At the buoys we like to use the heavier leaders if we can. The stong nylon makes it easier for us to get the aku in quickly if porpoise are around snatching hooked fish. Sometimes, however, there are so many boats annoying the aku with their

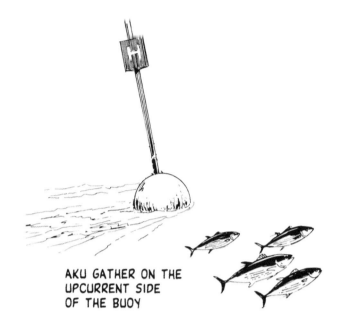

AKU GATHER ON THE UPCURRENT SIDE OF THE BUOY

commotion that these small tuna get very selective about what they will bite.

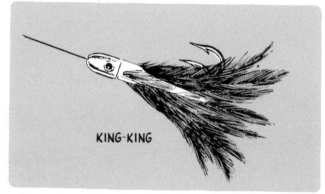

KING-KING

Once in a while, the aku feed so greedily that you can catch them on chunks of bait with a handline. By scattering chopped squid, 'opelu and even chunks of other aku into the water, you can occasionally provoke a feeding frenzy. I've actually seen fishermen scoop free-swimming aku from the water in hand nets when the hungry fish have dashed to the surface next to the boat to snatch a tossed bit of food.

Aku tend to gather on the upcurrent side of the buoy or right next to it. When the aku are there, you'll see them splashing the surface as they feed.

2. The most common buoy fish is usually a type of yellowfin tuna known as the "bigeye" tuna. These gather at the surface on the down-current side and are caught by trolling the buoy's wake. They hit small aku lures, but they also take bigger feathers. They are rarely fussy about leaders and will strike lures that have heavy nylon rigging of 80- and 100-pound test. Some fishermen who don't want aku but do want bigeye purposely choose bigger lures and heavier leaders to chase the aku away.

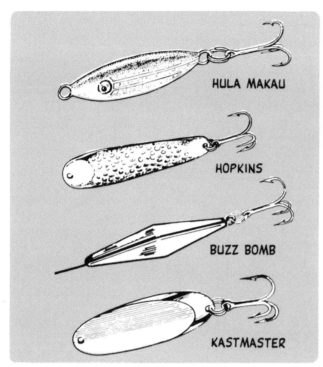

HULA MAKAU

HOPKINS

BUZZ BOMB

KASTMASTER

Even when you can't catch these yellowfins at the surface, you can usually get them down deeper, 30 to 300 or more feet down. That's when spinning tackle is great fun. Quick-sinking metal lures, like spoons and jigs, are the best producers. We try to match the size of the lure to the size of the fish, but the bigger tuna will sometimes snatch the small jigs and all we can do is hang on until the reel is stripped.

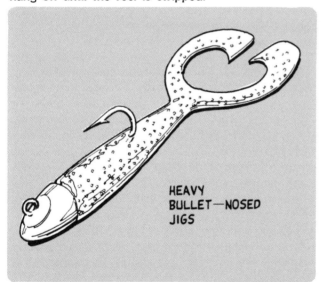

HEAVY BULLET—NOSED JIGS

The bigger bigeyes tend to hang out farther below the surface, though they will occasionally make sorties to the top to feed. Mostly, though, you must be prepared to drop your lure down 20 to 50 fathoms. Letting 4-ounce jigs plummet to 50 fathoms has produced tuna of 50 to 70 pounds for us. When these bigger fish are around and feeding, we switch over to the 4/0 and 6/0 trolling reels to jig with.

3. Mahimahi are the glamour fish of the buoys, but they do not congregate in numbers as large as the schools of bigeye and aku. The first boat to make a pass at the buoy may be lucky enough to catch a mahimahi or two on standard trolling lures, but these brightly colored acrobats quickly wise up.

We've had our most consistent success with mahimahi by trolling live bait or fresh dead bait. Mahimahi feed eagerly on keʻo keʻo, a small tuna-like fish known as the frigate mackerel. These slim, bright bait fish look like young kawakawa, for which they are often mistaken. When the keʻo keʻo hang around the buoys, many kinds of big fish become suckers for a bridled bait trolled just fast enough to keep the bait swimming.

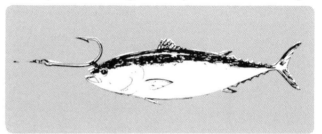

Mahimahi will also take trolled squid and ʻopelu rigged whole. When we've had no other kind of bait, we've cut strips from aku that were too big for the mahimahi to eat whole. These strips, hung from the hook on a trolling lure, have done the trick handily.

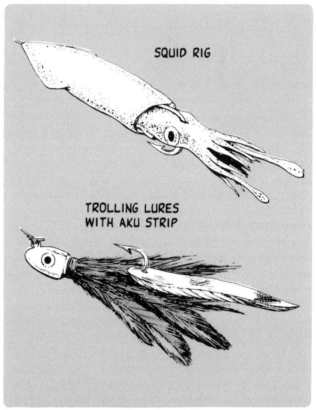

SQUID RIG

TROLLING LURES WITH AKU STRIP

Sometimes mahimahi will gobble a jig bouncing on spinning gear, but they are usually too smart to be fooled by deep-jigging.

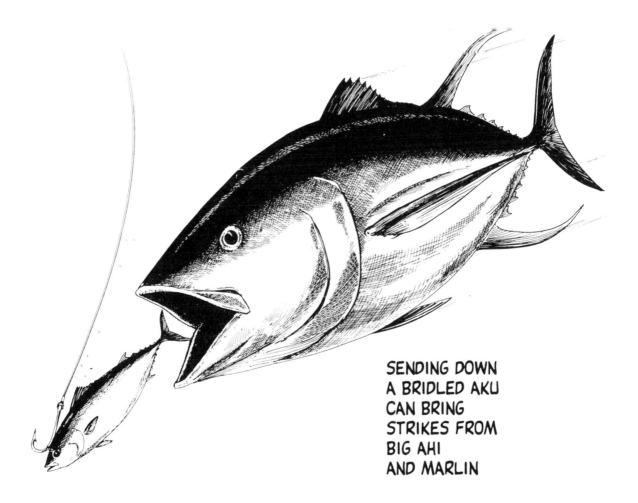

SENDING DOWN
A BRIDLED AKU
CAN BRING
STRIKES FROM
BIG AHI
AND MARLIN

4. Sending a bridled aku down into the depths while the boat is drifting is an excellent way of hooking big ahi and marlin. A bridled aku will usually swim straight down. Cruising ahi and marlin will snatch the bait on the way down.

If no fish tries to grab it while your bait is diving, you can still have luck when the aku stops. Generally, an aku will race down as much as 60 or 70 fathoms before it decides to quit. That's a good depth for a big ahi.

In the depths, the aku will stay alive for a short time, perhaps as much as a half hour if the aku is really strong to begin with. Drifting with a live aku swimming at the end of a deep line is an excellent fishing technique. Even after the aku dies, the fresh bait is still a very attractive target.

At times, many other types of fish gather at the buoys. FAD fishermen have caught ono, rainbow runner, kahala and even ulua. Occasionally, sharks take up residence around the FADs, and they can be a great nuisance. Generally, however, they stick fairly close to the buoy and can be avoided by dragging baits 40 or 50 yards away.

Despite the overall record of success, fishing around the buoys can be disappointing. For some reason, as yet unknown, the fish seem to disappear at times. At other times, they appear to become extremely selective. Dr. Richard Brock of the Hawaii Institute of Marine Biology has observed, by looking in on the buoy fish from below, some interesting behavior that may explain some empty fish boxes.

"While in the water, I have watched ahi, ono and aku either sound on the approach of a boat to a buoy or just not pay any attention to trolled lures or to bait going by. In general, mahimahi that I have watched underwater completely ignore the fisherman's 'tempting baits.' Almost every fishing line that I have seen underwater out in that clear oceanic water shows up like a sore thumb — especially when the sun reflects off of it. This is true not only for handlines but also for monofilament lines. It might be that the fish which have resided around the buoy for a while are smart and recognize boat motor sounds and lines as dangerous signs."

In fishing, nothing — not even the buoys — is a sure thing.

Safety: First and Always

Keeping Safe While Fishing

Safety in fishing is simply a matter of common sense; but as a sensible person once observed, "There is nothing so uncommon as common sense."

Because of the nature of fishing, small problems can eventually become big ones. A week-long fishing trip early in my fishing career is a good example. Our family had planned to spend the week camped out on the eastern end of Moloka'i to fish for papio, 'o'io and kaku. We picked our spot carefully, both for fishing potential and comfort. We brought along all of the right gear to make the trip a success. Yet it ended in agony and disappointment for me due to some simple hazards that could have been avoided if I had thought about them.

During the course of the week, I nicked my fingers repeatedly with the points of small hooks. At other times, I pulled on lines and leaders, either to break them or to tighten knots, and the lines cut into the creases in my fingers. Furthermore, in my enthusiasm over catches, I was not careful in handling spiny fish. As a result, my palms were poked by fins and scratched by gill plates, scutes and scales.

By the end of the week, my hands were swollen claws. I could neither open nor bend my fingers without discomfort. Finally, I could no longer fish, not because of any major catastrophe or injury but merely because of the accumulation of the many minor abuses. All could have been avoided with thought and care.

Here is a collection of tips on how to keep safe and comfortable while fishing.

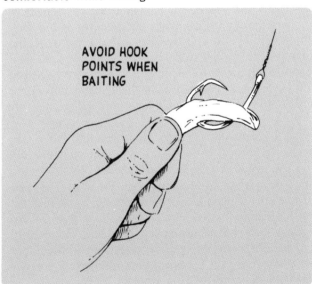

AVOID HOOK POINTS WHEN BAITING

1. Develop careful hook-handling skills.
Keep hook points from contacting your skin. Avoiding hook points is usually easy in ordinary hook handling, such as when tying knots and putting baits on hooks. Some fishermen always grip their hooks with pliers while pulling the knot tight, for example, thereby escaping the stab from a point that slips through the fingers unexpectedly. Baiting hooks, on the other hand, can present special problems for the unwary. The points of our Tankichi-style hooks always seem to emerge from a bait in an unexpected spot because the point is bent back toward the shank. The problem is increased with baits chosen for their toughness. Forcing a hook point through a tough bait sometimes results in a baited finger.

PULL KNOTS TIGHT WITH PLIERS

Avoiding hook points is often much more difficult during fishing operations. One of my friends says that she despises 'opelu fishing for that reason. She fishes for 'opelu at night with a light to attract schools of them. She fishes a line with several flies in hopes of catching three or four fish at once. If she is handlining several 'opelu to the surface and they start pulling hard at an unexpected moment, they sometimes slide the handline through her fingers and drag a hook into her hand.

And those are just problems with small hooks. Big game fishing hooks create far more serious problems. Several of my friends have had the terrifying experience of being impaled by a big game hook from a fishing lure while a second hook from the lure was holding onto a thrashing mahimahi. As a youngster, one of these men had been dragged across the deck by a big bull firmly attached to him by a hook through his heel. Another was yanked back and forth across his transom by a fish tethered to him by a hook through his forearm.

One of these cases was caused by a careless youngster blundering into the middle of the action, blinded by his enthusiasm to be part of the excitement. The other was caused by inattention at an important moment. Both could have been prevented by care and thought. Fishing is unforgiving of the careless and the thoughtless.

2. Wear proper protective clothing.

Protect your skin from sunburn. Though this may be less of a problem for local folks than for visitors, we all get sunburned at some time, and it is extremely painful.

Protect your eyes from glare and thrown objects. There have been many occasions when my sunglasses have prevented a major catastrophe. My glasses deflected the handle of the winch on my trailer when the winch slipped and whipped backward into my face. They warded off the hooks on a lure jerked out of the mouth of a big fish at gaff. They turned back the attack of a 2-ounce sinker yanked back into my face when my bail snapped shut on a cast. And they've done all that while patiently sifting out the harsher rays of the sun.

Protect your feet from encounters both expected and

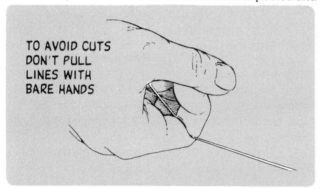

TO AVOID CUTS DON'T PULL LINES WITH BARE HANDS

unexpected. You expect to set your feet on sharp coral, spiny sea urchins or rough lava when you are whipping. Be prepared with tough-soled shoes with sturdy high tops up to your ankles. Good fishing shoes will also protect your feet from being mangled by gaffs, hooks, broken glass or any of the other unexpected objects you can expect to find at your feet sometime in your fishing career.

IF THE HOOK JERKS FREE, LURE WILL BE THROWN INTO YOUR FACE. SUNGLASSES WILL PROTECT YOUR EYES.

WHIPPING THE REEFS

3. Go carefully wherever you go.

Seldom do you ever need to rush into anything without thinking in fishing. And chances are, if you do feel the need to, you shouldn't anyway.

If you are working a shoreline from lava outcrops, plan your path carefully. Don't jump from place to place. Don't perch on precarious ledges. Think about yourself before you think about the fish.

If you are wading a reef, watch where you place your feet. You may step on a chunk of coral that turns or a moray that refuses to. Or, you may step on what looks like a limu-covered outcrop, only to find it is a limu-covered hole.

For added stability, many reef fishermen use a wading staff. A lightweight staff, slung from your shoulder or wrist with a loop of rope, can give you a rigid three-point stance as you explore an unfamiliar bottom. It can help you probe spots for safety before you set your feet on them. It can prevent you from falling when your feet slip.

4. Plan for an accident.

Have some elementary first aid equipment available in case of minor cuts and scrapes. The day I left my first aid kit at home was the day an ono whacked the back of my hand, laying it open neatly and decorating the deck with scarlet spatters. It was, however, a day when the ono were hitting repeatedly in pairs and triplets, so I just wrapped a rag around my hand to keep from having to look at the slice. You might say that the rag sufficed for first aid, but a bandage would have kept me in action for the rest of the day.

Tell someone where you are going and when you expect to return. Doing so means that someone will look for you if you do have an accident. Not only will they know when to start looking, but where, as well.

From this catalog of woes and dangers, you may get the impression that fishing is dangerous. It is for the careless. Careless fishermen don't last long. Some pay a very serious price for their carelessness. Others drop out along the way, taking up less dangerous pursuits like skydiving and race-car driving.

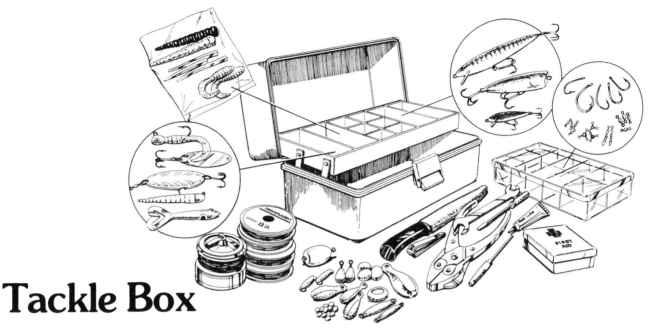

Tackle Box

Take Along What's Right for the Job

Fishermen seem to be evenly divided into those who carry too much tackle and those who don't bring along enough. Bring too little tackle and you are in danger of not having the proper equipment to do the job when conditions change. Bring along too much tackle and you may need a forklift just to carry your tackle box.

Not only is unused tackle a nuisance to lug around, it is also a nuisance to maintain. All that extra gear needs to be cleaned, sharpened, oiled and otherwise looked after and cared for. Usually, it is a lot of extra and unnecessary work.

The problem increases for the whipper, that highly mobile fisherman who searches shorelines, rock by rock, for the perfect cove to match his perfect cast. The whipper needs to be free of excess gear in order to keep his going easy. The problem is his wide-ranging explorations mean that he'll be too far from home or the friendly neighborhood tackle shop when a papio takes his last jig.

Each of us must find his or her own best compromise. Here's some help. Look over these suggestions to see how well equipped a whipper should be.

The tackle box. Pick a box no bigger than the smallest you need to hold the equipment you bring. In other words, the first step should be the last. If you get a tackle box that is too big, you probably will fill it up anyway, much to the regret of your sore shoulders.

You probably won't need more than one tray, so don't get a box with two. Most of your gear will need to be kept separated, but you can accomplish this with insertable boxes full of small compartments.

Your box lid should be watertight, of course. That means the lid should overlap the bottom section to make water run off rather than into the box. Also,

check the handle attachment. Try to find a box with a raised handle hinge. Boxes with handles that fit into a depression should be avoided. The water gathers in the well and soaks through any openings, dousing the contents. You can use a box with a handle well only if the handle hinge is completely watertight.

Box? Well, of course it could be a knapsack strapped to your shoulders. The backpack approach is really the one I favor for my own fishing. The gear is always with you. You don't need to back track to get it and shift it to the next spot.

Make sure your box has a sturdy, rust-proof closure with a safety catch. The latter can be any of a variety of gimmicks that will keep the lid from springing open if the latch is accidently disengaged. The best catches require two steps to open: the first step loosens the catch; the second disengages it.

The bottom compartment needs to be roomy enough for a variety of gear of odd sizes and shapes. Pad the bottom with towelling. The pad not only absorbs moisture, but also protects your gear and keeps it from shifting.

Now, let's stock the box. Get a clear plastic box with numerous small compartments. It must fit conveniently into the bottom. The box should have enough compartments to carry an assortment of hooks and swivels. The hooks should include several sizes of limerick style hooks (sizes 6 and 8 being most useful), several sizes of Tankichi-style hooks, and either some of the O'Doul or tarpon-style hooks. The sizes you pack will be determined by your type of fishing. The swivels should include two-way and three-way types.

Next, into the bottom compartment, go the leader and extra line spools. Stock a second line spool that fits your reel. It should be filled with a different pound test line than the spool on your reel. This gives you extra versatility if your action changes. You may, for example, want to whip with small jigs on 6-pound line, then switch to larger plugs on 12-pound test. Obviously, changing the line is very inconvenient. Changing a pre-wound spool, on the other hand, takes only seconds. Occasionally, your reel will be stripped by a big fish or roughed up with heavy use. An extra spool of line will put you back in business. Also, bring along spools of leader material. Unlike monofilament line, which is quite limber, good leader material tends to be harder and stiffer. Pack leaders in an assortment of sizes. My box carries leaders testing 2, 4, 8, 12, 20 and 30 pounds breaking strength.

The bottom compartment is also home to an assortment of light sinkers. I have coin sinkers, bank sinkers, ring sinkers and split shots. The coins and rings are ½-ounce, ¾-ounce and 1-ounce sizes. The bank sinkers are 1½-, 2- and 3-ounce weights. I only carry one size of shot, since shot weights are easy to adjust by adding or removing shots. The weights are kept in cloth bags which keep them from rolling around and banging into other gear.

Finishing out the gear, in the bottom compartment are my tools. I carry Sportmate pliers, chromed nail clippers (for snipping lines and leaders), a hook sharpener and a bait knife. Again, these have their own sheaths for protection.

Now, let's stock the tray sections. In one section, I house an assortment of jigs. Whipping jigs are quite small and my carry-along collection contains ⅛-, ¼- and ½-ounce sizes. Other sections are home to spoons (mostly Kastmasters, crocodiles and fiord spoons), curly tails (to match the jigs — and kept in plastic pouches which keep them from softening the paint on other lures or melting the tackle box), minnow strips (likewise encased in protective material) and plugs (poppers and swimmers).

Also, carry a minimum of reel fixing gear. I carry a screwdriver and a wrench to tighten up parts that loosen from use. Some reels (even relatively good ones) always seem to be coming apart from normal casting and cranking. It's always good to keep checking and tightening your reel. I also carry critical spare parts for the reel. These include a spare bail spring, an extra bail nut and some extra drag washers. I also carry a tube of reel lube, though I try to keep my reels greased and maintained through home care. Reels well-cared for at home need little attention when they are supposedly working to earn their keep.

And that's it.

Of course, there have been times when I've wished I had an extra thinga-ma-jig when I've run out, but only rarely have I wanted anything that I don't normally carry.

Virtues of Sport Fish

Playing Favorites

Playing favorites, that's what fishing is all about, whether you are playing your favorite game fish on the end of your line or playing that popular parlor (or bar-room?) game: "What's your favorite fish?"

Right from the earliest days when the first ancient angler discovered that a trout looked different, fought different and tasted different from a sunfish, fishermen have formed ranks to debate the virtues of the different sport fish.

Fishermen tend to like what they like. They don't reason their way to a preference, but let's try to reverse that a bit and think our way through the matter.

We'll begin by looking at some criteria, some of the factors that might affect your decision.

1. Striking thrill. Who could dispute that the glamour of marlin fishing comes partly from the spectacle of a marlin's strike? The thrilling sight and power of a giant game fish flashing out of the sea and lashing out at a fast-trolled lure, that's magnificence, poetry and power all at once.

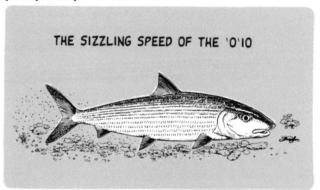

THE SIZZLING SPEED OF THE 'O'IO

But, on the other hand, consider the suspenseful "strike" of an 'o'io. The subtle touch of the bait tele-graphed gently through the rod tip to the hand of the poised and hopeful angler. The agonizing wait as the expectant fisherman wills himself to be still and the fish to be confident. The sizzling speed and surging force of the first run are spectacular, but they are clearly the aftermath of a "strike" that plays on a different set of emotions than does the marlin's unbridled fury. But the thrill is no less, however different it might be.

2. Strength and endurance. A game fish should be a formidable adversary. It should do more than merely protest your efforts to reel it in. It should test your tackle to the maximum and find reserves of energy and stamina to match your skill, patience and technique.

Yet, on the other hand, this endurance test can be carried to ridiculous extremes. A visiting friend once described a battle he had with a bluefin tuna off Nova Scotia during which he was pulled from the chair and bashed against the gunnels, breaking two ribs and a finger in the process and bruising himself so badly he spent the remainder of his vacation in bed — all this after three hours of physical strain comparable in excitement to that of coal-shoveling.

Yes, you do want to live to fight another day. And, in fact, you do want the fight to be short enough that you can fight another fish or two. It is, after all, the whole process of fishing — from strike to gaff — that is fun, and the more repetitions of this cycle, the more fun.

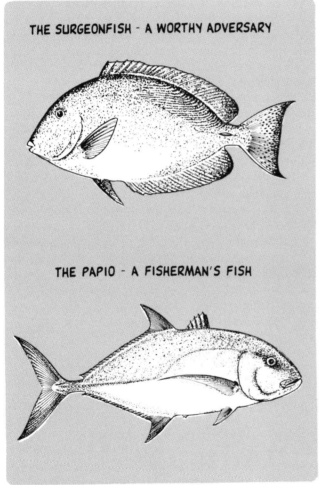

THE SURGEONFISH - A WORTHY ADVERSARY

THE PAPIO - A FISHERMAN'S FISH

3. Beauty. You want a fish that looks good, like a worthy adversary should. Consider, for example, that a pualu (that flat-sided gray and yellow surgeonfish) fights very much the same as a papio of similar size. As a matter of fact, some light-tackle fishermen aren't able to tell which of the two they've hooked until they've pulled the fish to within eyesight.

There may be little difference between the two as far as the fight, but the papio is certainly a better fish in appearance.

Yet, "beauty" is really quite subjective, isn't it? It is surprising what those who love us are willing to overlook. 'O'io fishermen, for example, give little thought to their quarry's weak jaw and distinctly unhandsome rubbery nose. And, despite how beautiful I think the mahimahi is, I can't look at one without remembering the comment a German guest on my boat made as I brought his first mahimahi aboard. "What an ugly fish," he said. The mahi's strangely shaped head and decidedly unfish-like colors had turned him off.

And then there is the butterfly fish. After all, despite its unquestioned beauty, it is unquestionably not anyone's favorite sport fish.

4. Edible quality. Probably not a factor at all. Marlin, for example, are just barely edible. Sure, some of you will disagree with that assessment, but just go down to the dock and ask any marlin fisherman how much he gets for his billfish when he sells them and what kinds of foods they get used for.

Furthermore, in those areas of the world where the bonefish (our 'o'io) is considered the ultimate game fish, the overwhelming majority are released because they are judged inedible.

5. Matching tackle. To enjoy catching a fish, you've got to enjoy the heft and feel of the kind of tackle used to catch them. If you don't like to strain against a harness in a fighting chair, braced against the pull of a 130-pound class tackle, you aren't going to like bluefin tuna fishing. If heavy surf-casting gear just throws your back out of whack, you'll never be a slide-bait fisherman. If, on the other hand, the rhythmic flex and turn of light spinning gear satisfies your spirit, you are going to enjoy any kind of fish you can catch that way.

6. Fishing conditions. No kind of offshore game fish will ever become your favorite if setting foot on deck automatically brings on waves of seasickness. No ulua will ever thrill you if your idea of a good bed is soft and warm rather than salty and rocky. Yet, there are plenty of people for whom the pitch and roll of the sea are the rhythms of their souls, and there are others for whom the crash of the surf on a moonlit shoreline is the primitive call of unshackled joy.

7. Availability. Fishermen tend to fish for whatever they can catch. Let's face it, if the rainbow trout was the pinnacle of fishing achievement for me, I'd be living in New Zealand and not Hawai'i.

Yet, a fish can be too available. Someone described his idea of hell as being consigned to fishing in a spot where he caught a fish on every cast.

So what does it all add up to? The variables are all too many and the ranges too wide to give simple equations with ready-made solutions. Thank goodness fishing is like that.

The best answer I've ever heard was from the fisherman who told me that his favorite fish was always the one he had on the line at the time. When you think about it, that's the way it really should be.

Hawaii's Game Fish

Where and How to Catch Them

"If you want to catch a good fish, you gotta know him by his first name." The man who said those words to me many years ago was a Canadian fishing guide with a weathered face full of creases and a head full of knowledge about the habits of fish. What he meant was that fish don't grow big by being dumb and fishermen don't catch them unless they are as smart as the fish. Not just intelligent, mind you; the fisherman has to know everything he can about what the fish like and don't like, where the fish hide and hunt, and, most of all, what it takes to fool them.

Let's study some of Hawai'i's fish. We'll look at information about where to find them and how to catch them.

And we are going to include some information you may be tempted to skip over. We're going to include some special information about their names. You see, the facts we are going to give you are just the start of your study. As you read more about fish and fishing, you will find the same fish called by many names. These names change from place to place. For example, an 'o'io in Hawai'i is a bonefish in Florida, a bananafish in the Bahamas and a macabi in South America. Even more confusing, a grey snapper in Hawai'i is nothing at all like a grey snapper in the Caribbean.

The only name that doesn't change from place to place is the scientific name. The scientific name is Latin and has two parts. The first part tells the group or "genus" the fish belongs to. The second part tells which member of the genus the fish is — this is the "species" name.

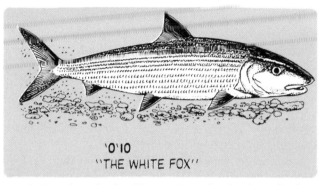

'O'IO
"THE WHITE FOX"

sandy beaches. It also likes to hunt for food on the flats between shore and the outer edges of the reef. The 'o'io lives in deep water outside the reef, and swims through channels in the reef. It feeds in the deeper sections of the channels at low tide and moves up onto the reef as the tide rises. During high tide it pokes around the reef flats looking for shrimp, crabs, small fish and any other small creatures not quick enough to get out of its way. With its tough, rounded nose, it pokes around in the sand and grubs out food that tries to hide by burrowing in the bottom. With its hard, rounded "teeth," it crushes shells and grinds its food. These "teeth" are like cobblestones, paving the inside of the mouth.

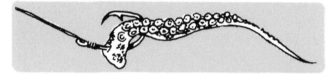

I have caught 'o'io on shrimp, strips of squid, slices of octopus, whole sand turtles, shelled hermit crabs, and strips cut from aku, kawakawa, 'opelu and akule. Squid and octopus are very good baits because they are tough enough to stay on the hook for long casts. Shrimp is also a good bait, but it is easily chewed off by small fish.

When bait fishing for 'o'io, I use a size-18 Tankichi hook on a 15-inch leader of clear 30-pound test nylon monofilament. The leader is attached to the line at a swivel. I use the lightest sinker that will cast the bait to the spot and hold it on the bottom.

'O'io
Bonefish

The 'o'io is *Albula* (genus) *vulpes* (species) no matter where it is found in the world. Scientists, by the way, have a bit of fun when they make up these Latin names. *Albula vulpes* means "the white fox," a good name for a fish that is quick and crafty and so perfectly pale that it seems to disappear in the water.

So let's begin our study of fish right there, with the disappearing bonefish, 'o'io *(Albula vulpes)*.
The bonefish is a swift, tough fighter. It likes to feed in the clear water at the outer edges of the surfline along

'Omilu and Papio
Bluefin Trevally

'Omilu or bluefin trevally has the Latin name *Caranx melampygus. Caranx* tells you that this fish belongs to the jack family, which includes all of the ulua, trevallys, jack crevalles, amber jacks, rainbow runners and scads (including 'opelu and akule). Of these, the most common one caught near shore in Hawai'i is the 'omilu. The typical size is about 1 to 3 pounds (the size-range Hawai'i's fishermen call "papio"). Papio is the name used for any ulua under 10 pounds.

This fish is neon blue along its back with dark spots

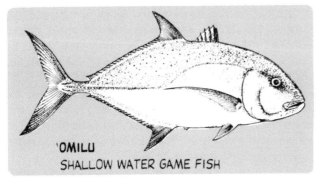

'OMILU
SHALLOW WATER GAME FISH

and golden flecks along back and sides. When caught over sandy bottoms, its color is lighter and silvery. Over coral and lava bottoms, the 'omilu can be extremely dark with black blotches over much of its body. It can change color from light to dark very rapidly. A bright silver 'omilu can rush at a lure and turn black the instant it strikes.

'Omilu can be caught in the same places and with the same baits and rigs already described for 'o'io. One excellent bait should be added to the list. Any small fish rigged to stay alive will catch 'omilu, but the very best live bait is the small goatfish called 'oama. These young weke are so appealing to 'omilu that they are even good as dead bait. Rigged with two hooks in tandem (one through the lips, the other thorough the tail) they are excellent baits trolled slowly in shallow water.

The 'omilu likes a moving bait better than a still bait. For this reason, many fishermen cast their bait, let it sink to the bottom, then draw it forward a foot or two every 10 to 20 seconds. The movement catches the papio's eye. The smell and taste makes him an offer he can't refuse.

Because any 'omilu likes an active lunch, lure fishing is an excellent way to get him to strike. Small jigs (especially with a strip of squid for taste), popping plugs, darting plugs, swimming plugs and small spoons are all great attractors. Sometimes they work best when fished fast, racing erratically across the surface. At other times a jerky jigging action is the best. To do this, jerk the lure forward with the rod tip and then let it rest for a second. This gives it an injured and panicked look. Fish that eat other fish seem to get excited when their prey is excited.

The 'omilu strikes with a rush and is in full flight by the time the fisherman realizes he's hooked a fish.

The 'omilu uses its flat sides, its powerful head and its well-muscled body to put up a long, strong fight. Because of the way it strikes, fights and tastes, the 'omilu is Hawai'i's best-loved, shallow-water game fish.

Bob a Jig!

The jig-and-bobber combination is a good starting point for papio fishing. And there are lots of reasons why.

The best is that a jig bouncing along behind a gurgling bobber will make papio bite when nothing else will even catch their eye.

The commotion made by the bobber attracts their attention. It is noisy as it chugs along, churning up bubbles; it's big enough to be seen from long distances; and, it jumps back and forth from side to side with a lot of action.

Even though the bobber is too big for most papio to try to eat, its crazy motion and glug-glugging sound drive them wild.

Fish are curious. They want to know what's happening. They like to explore strange things they've never seen before. And since a fish doesn't have fingers, it tests things by biting them.

Fish are aggressive, especially papio. They like to chase things. They are bullies. Like dogs that snarl and bark at cars, papio like to threaten invaders to their home waters. They don't have fists to punch with or arms to wrestle with, but they do have strong jaws to snap and grab with.

Fish are hungry. Well, almost always. Sometimes, even when their stomachs are empty, they aren't in the mood to eat. Other times, even when their stomachs are full, they keep right on swallowing. But lots of the time, when they see something that looks good to eat, they try to eat it.

Curiosity, hunger and aggression, for a big fish with a big mouth and tough ideas in his head, that's enough for a fight. And if you're lucky, that fight will be with you.

So how do you get lucky?

Choose the right jig and the right bobber.

The choice of a bobber is pretty easy. I like an egg-shaped bobber and pick a size that has the right amount of weight for casting. The size depends on the rod, reel and line I use.

My favorite bobbers are about 2 inches long and 1¼ inches wide. They look just like eggs, except that the fat end is flattened.

Sticking out of the flat end is a screw eye, the place you tie both your line and the end of the jig leader.

The flat spot makes a gurgling noise when you pull the bobber through the water.

The other end (the round end) is almost pointed. It makes a streamlined shape that travels through the air easily. That means your casts will be longer.

I color my bobbers with bright orange paint. The bright colored bobber is easy to see from a long way off. It stands out against the blue water and against the white tops of choppy waves.

What jig is right?

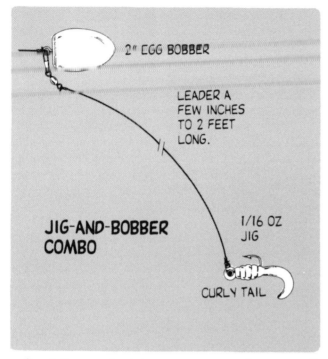

2" EGG BOBBER

LEADER A
FEW INCHES
TO 2 FEET
LONG.

JIG-AND-BOBBER
COMBO

1/16 OZ
JIG

CURLY TAIL

Small jigs are best because most papio are small. They usually weigh less than a pound. Even small jigs will catch big papio. I've caught 6-pound papio on jigs as small as 1/16th of an ounce. That's my favorite size jig. (And it's my favorite size papio, though I'm not often that lucky.)

Sometimes I use even smaller jigs. I brought back a 1/64th of an ounce jig from the mainland. It's so tiny it will fit entirely (tail and all) on a nickel. In freshwater ponds, I used it to catch small bass, sunfish and crappies. And, there on the mainland, I even fished it with a bobber.

Here in Hawai'i, this same tiny jig has caught me many kinds of small reef fish besides papio. It is great for moano and moano kea (goatfish).

I like to use bucktail jigs with tails made from the hairs of a deer's tail. But I like jigs with plastic tails even better.

My favorites are the curly tails. These soft plastic tails curl like the letter "c." When you pull them through the water, they wiggle like little fish. The slightest movement makes them look like they are alive.

White is my favorite color. But sometimes clear plastic is best. Lots of small sea creatures have clear bodies. You can see right through small fish and shrimp; the clear plastic tail looks just like these tiny creatures.

And sometimes I like very dark colors — like purple and black.

How far away from the bobber should the jig be?

That's hard to answer. One of my friends uses a very short leader only a few inches long. The jig stays so close to the bobber that it looks like it is trying to hide behind it. I've seen papio shove the bobber out of the way to try to grab the jig.

Another friend keeps his jig 15 inches behind the bobber. He catches papio that swim along beside the bobber for a short distance. Then they stop to let the bobber escape. When the jig bounces by a second later, they pounce on it without thinking.

Still another friend makes his leader 2 feet long. He likes to put a piece of bait on the jig's hook. (He uses shrimp when he can get it, but he'll settle for squid.) The longer leader catches papio that aren't as easily fooled.

Why not just use the jig alone?

Jigs are good lures to use by themselves without the bobber. But the bobber makes them special.

We already explained how the bobber helps attract papio.

The bobber also helps you to cast much farther. It is much heavier than the jig alone. You should be able to cast your bobber five times further than you can cast the jig without it.

The bobber keeps the jig away from the bottom. Since the jig stays up near the surface, it can't sink down to the coral and get stuck.

The bobber keeps the hook point riding up. This helps you hook the fish.

The bobber gives the jig a special action. When you jerk the bobber, the jig hops almost straight up toward the surface. Then it drops almost straight down.

To help this special action, always tie the jig on with a loop. Don't tie it on with a clinch knot.

The bobber helps you keep a hooked papio from diving down into the rocks. No matter where he goes, he must pull the bobber behind him. Since the bobber floats, it pulls the papio back toward the surface when he tries to dive down into the coral.

How do you use the jig-and-bobber?

Throw it out as far as you can and reel it back to you steadily. Twitch the tip of your rod in short jerks as you reel.

You know you've got the right action when the bobber dances along without hopping out of the water and when the jig darts up and drops back. You know you've got the right action when the bobber disappears as a papio tries to pull the rod right out of your hands.

Other Papio Methods

Papio fight hard, can be caught without a lot of fancy equipment, are available along the shoreline and are good to eat. They are common enough to give you a good chance at catching them, but they are not too common to be a challenge. You know you've done something special when you've hooked and landed one.

Actually, in some seasons, in some places and with some methods, you can catch quite a few of them at once. Your best chance at catching papio is by trolling near shore with a small boat.

We'll describe how to troll sheltered shallows for papio. The information comes from a dozen of my friends who are in their early teens and fish for papio from small boats of their own. One has a 14-foot aluminum skiff with a 25 hp outboard; another has a homemade outrigger canoe made of plywood; a third owns a small, fiberglass skiff powered by a 15 hp outboard; and a fourth fishes from little more than a rowing dinghy.

All of these boats have one thing in common, a second source of power if the motor quits. And in all cases, that second source of power is arm muscle. All of these boats are easily driven by paddles or oars.

My young friends troll for papio at nothing more than paddling or rowing speed, using live or fresh-dead bait. They prefer live 'oama or halalu if they can get it. If not, they troll whole, fresh 'oama (first choice) or whole, fresh halalu. In desperation, they use thawed strips of squid.

Catching 'oama is a large part of the fun. Our fishing areas here on the Big Island are a little different from the typical 'oama spots with shallow sandy beaches found on the other islands. Our fishing methods, therefore, are a little different and worth mentioning. We usually fish from docks or seawalls, so we must use longer than normal fishing rods and we must spot the 'oama along the bottom or we are wasting our time. A lot of our fishing is confined to harbors and other man-made calm spots. In other places, the sea rolls right up on the beaches or bangs into rocky cliffs.

The long pole, 12 feet or so of bamboo, means you must always be ready and quick. You drop in a bit of shrimp on a tiny hook, watch the school converge on it and snap the rod tip up quickly just before the 'oama touches the bait. By the time the snap is transmitted to the hook, the 'oama has just sucked the bait in. If you wait until you see or feel the bite, the 'oama has already felt the hook and leader and has spit it back out.

Okay, you've got your bait. Now, you need to know one more skill before you can troll it. You need to know how to tie a snell knot.

Follow the steps shown and you will need no other directions.

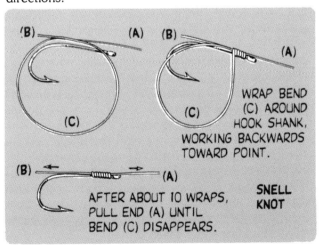

WRAP BEND (C) AROUND HOOK SHANK, WORKING BACKWARDS TOWARD POINT.

AFTER ABOUT 10 WRAPS, PULL END (A) UNTIL BEND (C) DISAPPEARS.

SNELL KNOT

There are many uses for the snell knot, but here its job is to make a rig with a sliding front hook. You need to be able to slide that hook to adjust your rig to the length of the bait. Most of your fish will be hooked on the trailing hook, but even those snagged on the front sliding hook will be held firmly. There is enough friction inside the tight snell to set the hook, and the front hook will not be able to slide back off the line past the rear hook.

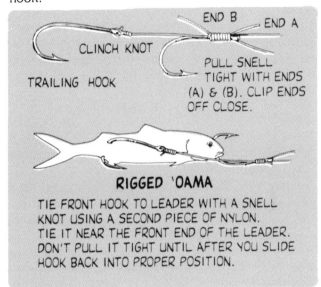

CLINCH KNOT

TRAILING HOOK

END B   END A

PULL SNELL TIGHT WITH ENDS (A) & (B). CLIP ENDS OFF CLOSE.

RIGGED 'OAMA

TIE FRONT HOOK TO LEADER WITH A SNELL KNOT USING A SECOND PIECE OF NYLON. TIE IT NEAR THE FRONT END OF THE LEADER. DON'T PULL IT TIGHT UNTIL AFTER YOU SLIDE HOOK BACK INTO PROPER POSITION.

I prefer to make my trolling rigs with clear, hard, 30-pound test nylon. Sometimes, I use lighter leaders if the fish seem to be spooky and shy away from the bait because they can see the leader. If, however, you do use lighter leader, you will lose many big fish and will be cut off immediately when a barracuda or big stickfish strikes.

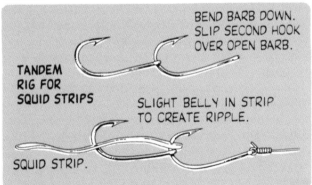

TANDEM RIG FOR SQUID STRIPS

BEND BARB DOWN. SLIP SECOND HOOK OVER OPEN BARB.

SLIGHT BELLY IN STRIP TO CREATE RIPPLE.

SQUID STRIP.

If trolling squid strips, use a tandem rig with the eye of the rear hook slipped over the point of the front hook. You'll need to press the barb of the front hook down gently with pliers to get it through the hook eye of the rear hook, and you'll have to lift the barb back up again with a knife blade to keep the rear hook from sliding back off. When hooking on a strip of squid, always leave just a little bit of slack in the section between the hook points. This loose section starts a ripple that shimmies along the full length of the strip.

I like to troll with a 4- to 6-foot leader. The leader is attached to a rigged sinker that pulls the bait underwater. The size of the sinker depends on the size of the bait, the depth of the water and the thickness of the trolling line. One-half to one-ounce sinkers are usually best.

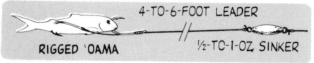

4-TO-6-FOOT LEADER

RIGGED 'OAMA   ½-TO-1-OZ SINKER

Don't troll more lines than you have fishermen to handle them. There are two reasons for this. First, when you do find papio, you'll hit several at once, sometimes hooking up on all lines. These papio will dive right down into the rocks and coral unless you've got someone working the rod to keep the fish up. Second, your lines will drop down and tangle in the bottom when you stop the boat to fight a fish. Remember, you are

fishing in relatively shallow water, from 5 to 20 feet deep on the average.

Don't set your lines too far back. Papio seem to be attracted by the propeller and are willing to strike at lines between 15 and 50 feet behind the boat. That's a lot closer than lines trolled for big game fish.

When you hook a papio, keep the boat moving ahead slowly until all of the empty lines have been reeled in. That's when I like to stop the boat and keep it just a battle between me and the fish, with no help from boat or motor.

Finish the fight with a landing net. Many papio are lost when fishermen try to lift them out of the water with a line that is attached to the fish by just a tiny bite of a small hook. Push the landing net down into the water and lead the papio over it. Even if the fish does get off the hook, it'll drop right down into the net.

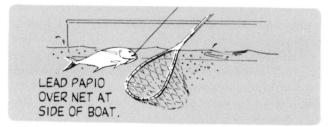

LEAD PAPIO OVER NET AT SIDE OF BOAT.

Lift that net, and Hawai'i's most popular light-tackle champion is all yours!

Kaku

Barracuda

I always think of barracuda as the wolves of the sea. Their long, narrow tapered heads are wolf-like. Their mouths are set in an expression that looks like the start of a snarl. Their large pointed teeth reach out to rip and slash. They sometimes roam singly, but frequently hunt in packs.

Like fearless, lazy dogs, they sun themselves in safety as they hang motionless in the stillness of shallow bays and harbors. But at the end of a fishing line, their dogged fight feels like the battle of an angry canine against the pull of an unwanted leash.

So vicious are the barracuda that they will eat any other fish, including their own young. Furthermore, they grow big enough to challenge just about any other type of fish except for sharks and billfish. The biggest barracuda are longer than a man is tall. These big ones, 6 feet long, live in deep water offshore. The smaller ones live in shallow water where they are a great game fish for whipping with light spinning tackle.

Whether small or large, the true name of Hawai'i's barracuda is "the great barracuda." This name is used to point out the difference between this, the biggest type of barracuda, and the many other kinds found in

other places. The Hawaiian name is kaku, and the scientific name is *Sphyraena barracuda*.

Kaku can be caught using any kind of fishing method used in Hawai'i. Whippers catch them on small jigs, spoons and plugs. Dunkers catch them on strips of squid, octopus, 'opelu, kawakawa, akule and many other kinds of fish flesh, including frozen smelt from the supermarket. Slide-bait fishermen catch huge barracuda at night on large sections of eel, octopus and whole live fish. Drift fishermen catch big offshore barracuda on live bait fish suspended from floats. Trollers catch them on whole kawakawa and aku fished alive. Bottom fishermen catch barracuda on whole fish of many kinds or on chunks cut from any tasty seafood. Even lure trollers occasionally catch barracuda on jets, leadheads and big game plugs.

But the best method of all uses a small live 'opelu or akule trolled slowly in water 40 to 100 feet deep.

Whatever fishing method you use, you'll need to use a wire leader. The barracuda's sharp teeth knife through nylon leaders in one bite, unless you are lucky enough to catch the hook in the front of the jaw — where the teeth can't reach it.

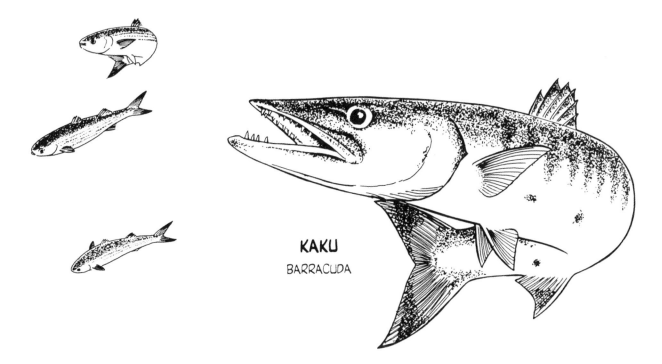

KAKU
BARRACUDA

Barracuda seem to have a strong "gaming instinct." They are attracted by action that isn't normal. For example, if you watch a barracuda in shallow water, you will often see many small fish swimming nearby. These fish seem to be in no danger at all as long as they act normal. If one acts unusual, the barracuda will spring to life and pounce on it.

I've proved this to myself several times by dipping up small bait fish from one spot, carrying them in a pail over to a spot where a barracuda was resting and then tossing the bait fish into the water near the barracuda. Because the bait fish were frightened from being dipped up, they acted panicky when tossed into the water. Their frantic darting always caused the barracuda to strike almost instantly. That's good for a fisherman to know. Making your bait or lure act erratic is a good way to get more strikes.

Handle barracuda carefully, even when you think they are dead. Barracuda are hard to kill and will sometimes "come to life" when you think they are dead. even when you know they are dead, you have to be careful. Kaku teeth are just as sharp when the fish is dead as they are when it's alive.

Small barracuda are great fun on very light tackle. Some of Hawai'i's fishermen have had great success fishing for small kaku with tiny homemade jigs. These are made with a split shot for the head, the tips of several feathers for a tail and a feather wrapped around the hook for a bushy body.

Hawai'i light-tackle fisherman Ernest Theodore calls them "mini-hotshots" and finds them to be perfect for his ultra-light tackle. He fishes the mini-hotshots on 1-pound test line with no wire leader. Though he loses a lot of fish, he feels that the small lures and invisible leader bring him many more strikes than he'd get on wire.

Ernie fishes the mini-hotshot with a fast retrieve that brings exciting strikes. According to Ernie, the only hard part in catching a kaku on ultra-light is the run right after the strike.

"The kaku hits very fast and hard, then streaks through the water with lightning speed — sometimes snapping your line right away," he says. "If you can stop the kaku on the first run, you'll have a chance at landing him. He'll tire out fast after his second run, and then you can fight him thrashing and jumping in the water."

Ultra-light is definitely not for all kaku, especially the bigger ones. Ernie confines his miniature feather jigs to shallow water with his average kaku catch weighing between 1 and 2 pounds.

If you'd like to try your own mini-hotshots, we've included Ernie's directions for making them.

Hawai'i's barracuda are great table food, which is a surprise to many fishermen who have caught them in other places around the world.

In many warm seas of the world, barracuda are poisonous, but not in Hawai'i. Fileted and pan-fried, barracuda makes a perfect end to a great fishing trip.

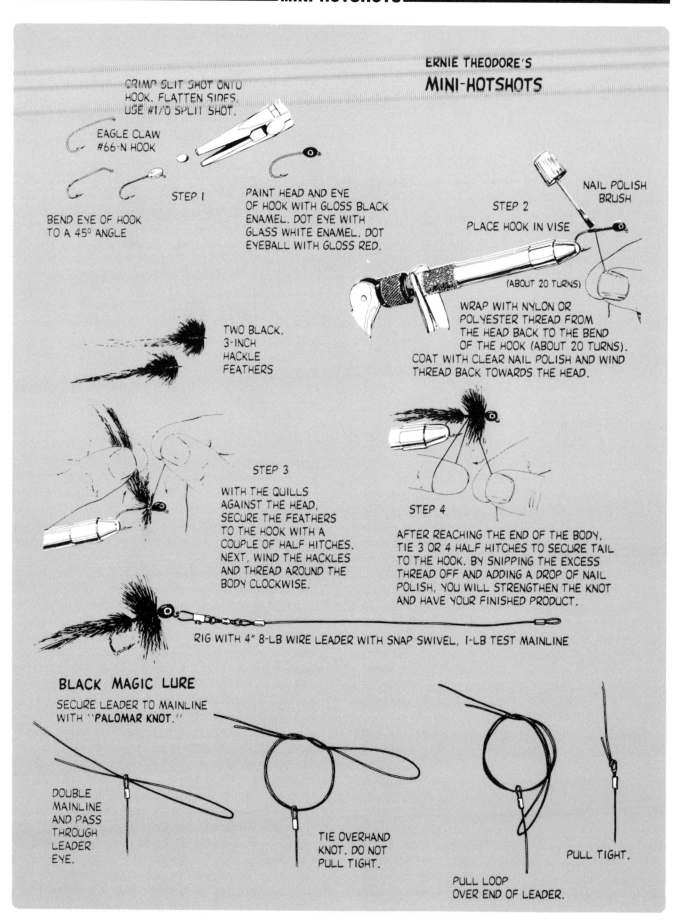

ERNIE THEODORE'S
MINI-HOTSHOTS

CRIMP SLIT SHOT ONTO HOOK. FLATTEN SIDES. USE #1/0 SPLIT SHOT.

EAGLE CLAW #66-N HOOK

STEP 1

BEND EYE OF HOOK TO A 45° ANGLE

PAINT HEAD AND EYE OF HOOK WITH GLOSS BLACK ENAMEL. DOT EYE WITH GLASS WHITE ENAMEL. DOT EYEBALL WITH GLOSS RED.

NAIL POLISH BRUSH

STEP 2
PLACE HOOK IN VISE

(ABOUT 20 TURNS)

WRAP WITH NYLON OR POLYESTER THREAD FROM THE HEAD BACK TO THE BEND OF THE HOOK (ABOUT 20 TURNS). COAT WITH CLEAR NAIL POLISH AND WIND THREAD BACK TOWARDS THE HEAD.

TWO BLACK, 3-INCH HACKLE FEATHERS

STEP 3

WITH THE QUILLS AGAINST THE HEAD, SECURE THE FEATHERS TO THE HOOK WITH A COUPLE OF HALF HITCHES. NEXT, WIND THE HACKLES AND THREAD AROUND THE BODY CLOCKWISE.

STEP 4

AFTER REACHING THE END OF THE BODY, TIE 3 OR 4 HALF HITCHES TO SECURE TAIL TO THE HOOK. BY SNIPPING THE EXCESS THREAD OFF AND ADDING A DROP OF NAIL POLISH, YOU WILL STRENGTHEN THE KNOT AND HAVE YOUR FINISHED PRODUCT.

RIG WITH 4" 8-LB WIRE LEADER WITH SNAP SWIVEL, 1-LB TEST MAINLINE

BLACK MAGIC LURE

SECURE LEADER TO MAINLINE WITH "PALOMAR KNOT."

DOUBLE MAINLINE AND PASS THROUGH LEADER EYE.

TIE OVERHAND KNOT. DO NOT PULL TIGHT.

PULL LOOP OVER END OF LEADER.

PULL TIGHT.

La-i

Leather-Skin Jack

Another game fish favorite is the la-i, or leather-skin jack *(Scombroides sancti-petri)*. This bright silver fish is an exciting fighter because it strikes a lure at high speed and leaps like a tarpon. It is hard to hook because its jaws are very narrow and tough. The la-i feeds right at the surface and will only strike lures or baits that travel within an inch or two of the top.

Unlike the kaku, which is happy to lie around lazily soaking up the sun, the la-i is a very nervous and energetic fish. If you are lucky enough to spot a school of la-i, you'll see them darting quickly back and forth before fleeing to a new area. Not only is it their quick movements that make them hard to spot, but also their color. Their bright sides are like mirrors that reflect the sea around them. When they move through the water, it looks like the water itself is moving.

Because they are so slender and flat-sided, the very biggest of the la-i still don't weigh very much. Adult la-i may reach 25 to 30 inches in length, but even these fish may weigh no more than a few pounds at the most.

La-i feed on any small creatures that live in or near the surface. They gather in the sheltered waters of bays and harbors, but they can also be seen in deep water along calm coastlines.

They are not very tasty to eat, and there is very little meat on the typical 10- to 15-inch la-i. But because of their skin, they are still a catch that is highly prized by fishermen. The tough leathery skin makes a good dressing for fishing lures. The skin dries without rotting and becomes soft and flexible again when it is put back into saltwater.

Big game fishermen use the skin to dress jets, marlin plugs and leadheaded jigs. Whippers cut the la-i skin into very thin strips, which they tie to tiny jigs.

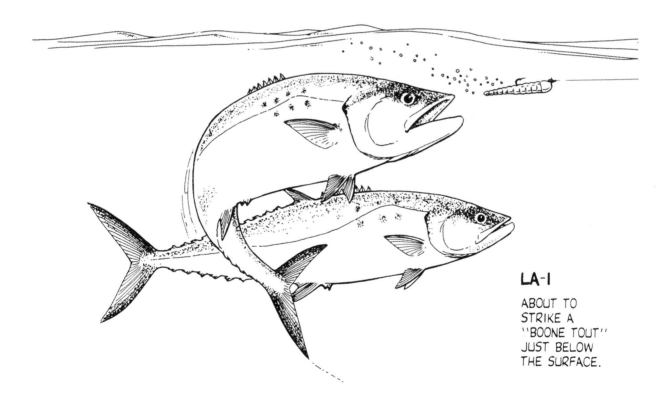

LA-I
ABOUT TO
STRIKE A
"BOONE TOUT"
JUST BELOW
THE SURFACE.

Weke and 'Oama

Yellow or Samoan Goatfish

You don't have to work overtime to catch weke. They are found in calm waters over sandy bottoms in most places throughout Hawai'i. Look for them in shallow harbors and in sandy channels cut through coral reefs.

Weke travel in schools, so once you find one you'll catch several. The very first time I ever went fishing for weke, my partner and I caught over 30 of them, each weighing about a pound.

They don't look much like game fish. They have a pale pastel tan color that matches the sandy bottom of their home. They have a set of chin whiskers for probing the bottom. They have a pair of large and frightened-looking eyes that should remind you that they scare easily.

But looks are misleading. The weke is a tough fish and a good fighter. It runs hard when it is hooked and fights strong right up until you net it.

To catch it, you must use small hooks and very light leaders. You must use a size 6, 8 or 10 limerick hook (the larger numbers are smaller sizes). You should use no more than a 2- or 4-pound test leader. The small hook and light leader force you to play the fish gently.

Heavy leaders scare weke. They feed on small shrimp with clear bodies so their eyes are trained to spot things that are supposed to be transparent. Nylon leaders are much thicker and more visible than the legs of a tiny shrimp. That's why you must use the thinnest leaders that are still strong enough to keep from breaking.

Weke nibble on small baits. They don't open their mouths wide and gulp their food greedily. That's why you must use a small hook. The weke should not feel the hook while he is tasting the bait. If he does, he'll drop it before you even know he has picked it up.

The best rig is a simple one. Tie your line to a small swivel. Then tie the swivel to a 15- to 18-inch leader with the hook at the other end. Tie a dropper loop to the swivel and add a ½-ounce or ¾-ounce sinker.

Use shrimp for bait. Use live 'opae (small grass shrimp) if you can get them and keep them alive. A dead 'opae is almost as good. Or use a small piece broken off a frozen shrimp. The piece should be about the size of a green pea. The hook should run through the bait, turn and run back through. It should be almost completely hidden. Only the point should stick out.

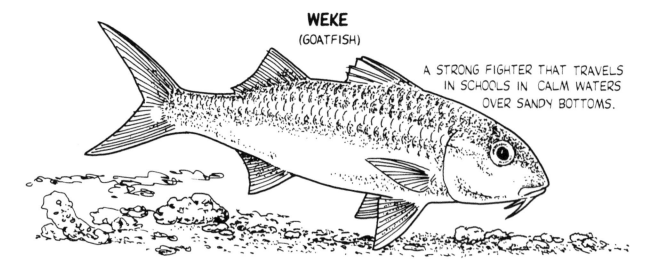

WEKE
(GOATFISH)

A STRONG FIGHTER THAT TRAVELS
IN SCHOOLS IN CALM WATERS
OVER SANDY BOTTOMS.

Cast your bait past the spot where you expect the weke to be. Let the sinker settle to the bottom. When it hits bottom, reel a few turns to straighten the leader. Keep the line tight against the sinker and watch the rod tip for the slightest movement. To catch weke you must train your nerves to react instantly to the merest twitch.

If you feel no bite in 30 to 60 seconds, slowly crank in a few more turns of line. This will move the bait to a new location. The new spot may have weke. The movement may attract a weke's attention.

Until you get the hang of it, you will lose a lot of bait to weke. They'll nibble it from your hook before you even realize they are there. That's a good reason to use very light spinning tackle. The lighter the tackle, the more the rod will twitch when the weke picks up the bait.

Keep moving your bait every minute or so until you have reeled it all the way in. If you have not gotten a bite in several casts, change to a new spot or cast to a new place.

Weke seem to bite better on certain tide conditions than on others. They like the bottom half of an incoming tide best. But this may be different in different places. Try different tide conditions until you find the one that works best for you. Weke also seem to like to feed in the very early morning and the last part of the day just before nightfall.

Weke are called "goatfish" because of their barbels (chin whiskers). When you get to be a really alert fisher-man, you will occasionally hook weke in the chin by the barbels instead of in the mouth. This may be because you can feel the bite while the weke is "tasting" the bait with his barbels.

The weke's scientific name is *Mulloidichthys samoensis*. This Latin name may not be of much use to you in hunting for information about weke in other places around the world. Hawai'i is the only place I know of where fishermen try to catch them.

Young weke are called 'oama (pronounced oh-ah-ma). These small fish are "a culinary delight," according to Hawaii Fishing News publisher Chuck Johnston.

Chuck's opinion is shared by thousands of other fishermen who anxiously await the month of August, which is the peak of the annual 'oama run on Hawai'i's sandy shorelines.

Chuck says, "There are several groups of anglers that benefit from the yearly swarms of 'oama that invade the shallow sand areas during the late summer."

The first he calls the "bamboo brigade," a colorful group seen standing waist-high in the ocean with a single pole in hand, a bright red dip net and, many times, a bright yellow bait bucket in tow.

"At the sight of several dozen anglers circling a school of these silvery fishes, one might first think it's a club outing or family gathering," Chuck says. "Chances are, though, most of the group are strangers who don't hesitate to wade out and join the fun."

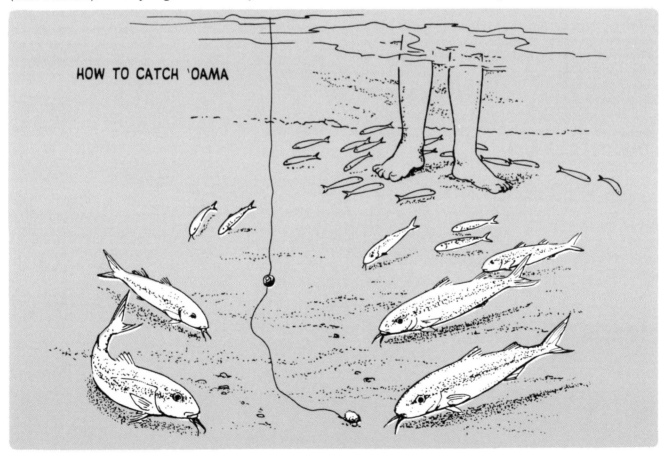

HOW TO CATCH 'OAMA

Chuck described 'oama fishing in an article for Hawaii Fishing News, and that description follows:

"The equipment you will need is inexpensive and basic: 1) a short bamboo or fiberglass pole; 2) 1 pound test monofilament line; 3) BB shots or split shots and 4) a small #18 Mustad hook. For bait you have a variety of choices: aku belly, frozen shrimp or bits of flesh from previously caught 'oama (probably the best). These little critters are not only carnivorous but also cannibalistic.

"As always happens, some members of the group will be pulling them in one after the other, while others appear to be under the hex of the kahuna (sorcerer). If you are one of those that just can't seem to get the technique, perhaps I can end your frustration. Try this sure-fire technique: Drop your baited hook to the bottom into the school and simply count off 1, 2, 3 seconds and set the hook with a quick jerk. You will be amazed, as will others, as you pull in one after the other. Oh yes, remember, the daily limit is 50 'oama per angler and the Department of Aquatic Resources has said they will be watching 'oama fishermen closely and enforcing bag limits.

"Once you've caught enough for dinner, just scale the fish and remove the entrails and gills, then dip into your favorite batter mix and fry with the heads on. California has their grunion, the Gulf states their smelt and Hawai'i has the 'oama. Delicious!"

The second group of anglers who await the 'oama consists of shore fishermen and for good reason. Man is not the only predator of the 'oama schools. Where you find the 'oama, you will find the larger reef dwellers such as the kaku, 'omilu and ulua.

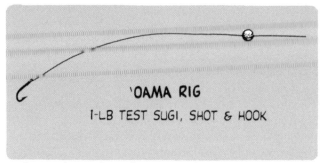

'OAMA RIG
I-LB TEST SUGI, SHOT & HOOK

A popular and productive method of shore fishing is to catch a bucketful of 'oama for bait. (The use of a small battery operated aerator will help keep them alive.) Then get out your medium spinning tackle (12- to 30-pound test line range) and go dunking with live bait.

We've illustrated two live bait rigs for those of you just getting started. Get a sand spike to hold your rod, hang a cowbell near the tip, and wait for the big strike.

The third group includes the small boat trollers. Trolling from small boats is a sport that has become increasingly popular in the last couple of years.

With the use of a 12- to 14-foot boat and a small outboard motor, this new breed of Hawai'i angler works in and out of the shallow reef areas, generally in waters from 4 feet to no more than 20 feet deep. The advantage over the dunking method is obvious. The angler can cover wide areas of the productive fishing grounds slow trolling with either live or previously frozen 'oama.

Tackle used ranges from ultra-light 2-pound test spinners to 20- and 30-pound test line spooled on conventional reels with short boat rods. The rig we've illustrated for trolling is the popular and productive type used by Charlie Teves.

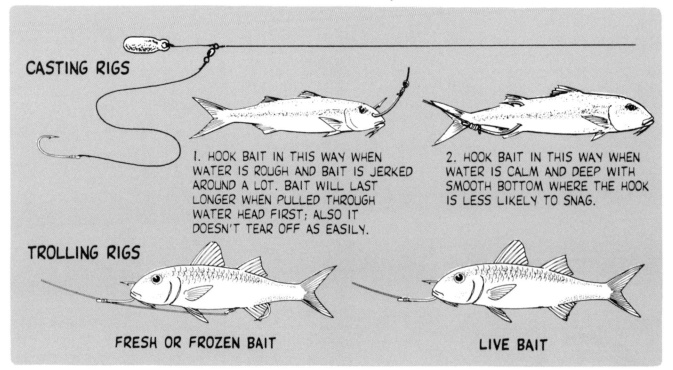

CASTING RIGS

1. HOOK BAIT IN THIS WAY WHEN WATER IS ROUGH AND BAIT IS JERKED AROUND A LOT. BAIT WILL LAST LONGER WHEN PULLED THROUGH WATER HEAD FIRST; ALSO IT DOESN'T TEAR OFF AS EASILY.

2. HOOK BAIT IN THIS WAY WHEN WATER IS CALM AND DEEP WITH SMOOTH BOTTOM WHERE THE HOOK IS LESS LIKELY TO SNAG.

TROLLING RIGS

FRESH OR FROZEN BAIT

LIVE BAIT

Weke-'ula

Red or Sacred Goatfish

The weke-'ula is the most sporting of Hawai'i's "red fish." Like the 'opakapaka and the onaga, the weke-'ula is a strong fighter and a beautifully colored catch. What makes the weke-'ula special for the sport fisherman is its feeding grounds. Schools of weke-'ula are found in waters that are shallow enough to allow fishermen to use light tackle to catch them.

Weke-'ula are members of the goatfish family. Hawaiian waters are home to three different goatfish that are very similar looking. Their bodies have the same shape, but they are differently colored and they live on the bottom at different depths.

In the shallowest waters, anywhere from a few feet down to about 20 feet, the sand-colored weke roam. Its only trace of color is a yellow stripe down its side. Some of these fish occasionally turn pink after they die, which makes fishermen think they are the real red weke.

In slightly deeper waters, ranging from 20 to about 100 feet, is a type of weke that is always red. It matches the sand-colored weke in nearly every way including its size. Both grow to be about a foot and a half long at their biggest. It also has a yellow stripe down its sides. The inside of its belly cavity is covered by a thin black skin.

The biggest of the weke, and the most highly prized for both eating and sport fishing, lives in the deepest water. You can catch it at depths between 100 and 300 feet. It can grow to be about 2 feet in length. It does not have a black lining to its belly cavity.

The two red weke are called weke-'ula because 'ula means "red." 'Ula also means "sacred," and weke were occasionally used by the Hawaiians in special religious rites. Even today, the beautiful red colors of the weke-'ula make them valuable additions to any ceremonial feast, such as parties at Christmas and New Year's.

With their comical "chin whiskers," weke-'ula present a humorous appearance. The whiskers, which are more accurately called "barbels," are very important to their way of life. The goatfish family uses barbels to test the sandy bottom for bits of food. They also tell the fisherman to fish close to the bottom to catch feeding weke-'ula.

The red weke feed best at night. Red makes good camouflage at night in the deep water, so the weke can feed safely. Many other kinds of bigger fish enjoy eating weke, and they need to take all the safety precautions they can.

Some weke-'ula can be caught in the daytime. The secret is to use very fresh bait. My greatest successes in daylight hours have been with baits caught the same day. Good baits include strips cut from the belly sections of kawakawa, aku, ahi, akule or 'opelu. Weke-'ula also like octopus and squid.

My favorite feeding ground for weke-'ula is about 240 feet down over a sandy bottom. The area has a few mounds of coral and sand to break up its level surface and provide a certain amount of safety. I have caught weke in shallower waters on the inside edge of this sandy area, but the baits get chewed up quickly by triggerfish.

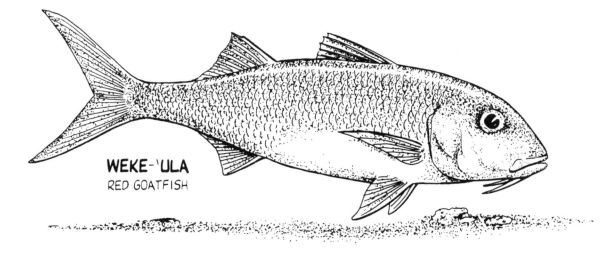

WEKE-'ULA
RED GOATFISH

To help start weke feeding, I use palu mixed with sand and lowered to the bottom in a bag. The sand helps keep the tasty bits of chum down near the bottom where the weke-'ula hunt for food. I lower the bag on its own special line, which is not armed with hooks for fishing. The palu is chopped aku, kawakawa, 'opelu or any other fish I can get.

Because of their vivid colors, weke remind you of the kind of goldfish you keep in an aquarium as a pet. This similarity adds to your surprise when you hook them. You don't expect such a tame-looking fish to fight so hard. They don't make long runs, pulling hundreds of yards of line off the reel like a classic game fish, but they do pull as hard as any other fish of their size.

Since they are strong fighters, I like to catch them on spinning tackle. My favorite sport rod is a spinning rod with 15-pound test line on a reel that holds about 250 yards of it. I fish from an anchored boat, which allows me to get to the bottom easily with only a few ounces of lead. The palu brings the weke-'ula to the hooks.

For sport fishing, I use only one hook when the fish are feeding well. That's the best way to enjoy the tussle. If you fish a line with several hooks, you can catch several weke-'ula at once. That, too, is a good sport, but it's not the same as a fight with a big weke-'ula alone. Most fishermen are more interested in getting a lot of them into the boat on a fishing trip because they are good-eating and have a high market price.

Small weke-'ula make great live baits for bigger fish, and some anglers rig an 8- to 10-inch weke-'ula and lower it almost to the bottom with a large hook through its back just behind the back fin. Live weke-'ula baits take kahala, ulua, uku and kaku.

Feeding in the same areas as the weke-'ula is another sporting catch for bottom fishermen, a type of ulua that lives only in the depths. Because it has thick and fleshy lips, this deepwater denizen *(Caranx cheilio)* is called the pig ulua (or sometimes the thick-lipped ulua). It seems to be a pig in its eating habits as well.

A National Marine Fisheries Service research assistant, Michael P. Seki, had the opportunity to examine the stomach contents of 64 pig ulua caught in the Northwestern Hawaiian Islands. Mixed in with a nutritious assortment of eels, flounders, groupers and pufferfish, the pig ulua stomachs contained rocks, shells and other bottom debris. Nature is seldom foolish. Those thick, tough lips clearly have an important job as these bottom foragers scavenge their way among the rocks and sand.

From my experience with an assortment of pig ulua ranging from 2 to 20 pounds, they are not only tough of lip, but tough as fighters and tough to eat. Though I've caught them on many different kinds of bait, my most successful bait seems to be fresh 'opelu strips.

Caught on the same spinning tackle I use for weke-'ula, the pig-lipped ulua is a stubborn fighter.

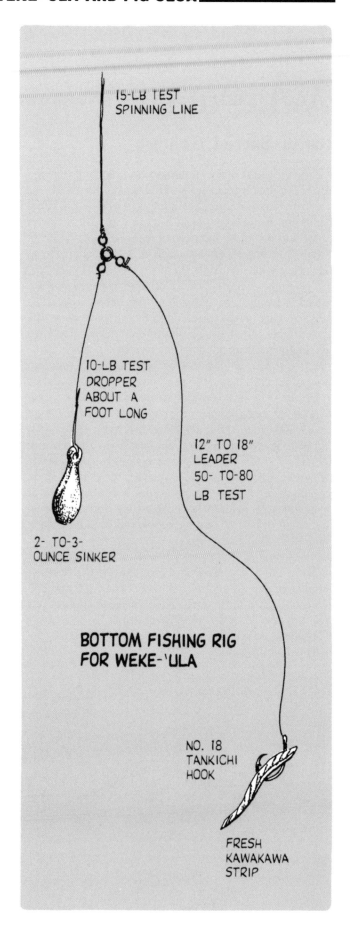

15-LB TEST SPINNING LINE

10-LB TEST DROPPER ABOUT A FOOT LONG

12" TO 18" LEADER 50- TO-80 LB TEST

2- TO-3- OUNCE SINKER

BOTTOM FISHING RIG FOR WEKE-'ULA

NO. 18 TANKICHI HOOK

FRESH KAWAKAWA STRIP

Awaawa

Ladyfish or Hawaiian Tarpon

The awaawa (or awa'aua) is well-known as a fighting fish in many places around the world. Long, slender and agile, this silvery fish shoots through the water like a torpedo.

What makes catching awaawa most exciting is their leaps and cartwheels. Their jumps are thrilling to watch. Part of the thrill is knowing that the jump is the fish's best chance to throw the hook. It is always a great satisfaction after each jump to feel the line draw tight again and know the fish is still hooked.

Sometimes the line does not draw tight even if the fish is still hooked. That's because a favorite trick of the awaawa is to turn and run straight at the fisherman. When the fish loops the line in this way, the line goes slack. With no tension on the line, the fish has an easier time working the hook free. The fisherman must reel as fast as he can to get the loose line back on the reel. Often, as soon as the line comes tight again, the awaawa will instantly leap. If you are not prepared for this trick, you will pull the hook free because the turning reel jerks the line too tight against the fish.

Awaawa have tender mouths, and the hook can tear free easily if the fish is hooked in the lips or at the outer edge of the jaw. All of these problems should be taken as warnings to fight the awaawa with a light drag and to always be alert and quick to respond to the fast changes the awaawa makes.

Though it is tender, the awaawa's mouth is big, and the fish does like to gulp its food. Awaawa will wolf down a bait lying on the bottom. They'll charge a bait or lure working along the surface. They'll strike a lure or bait jigged somewhere between the surface and the bottom. They like to feed in sheltered waters of bays, harbors and fish ponds. They'll eat anything small and tasty, including shrimp, small fish, squid and crabs.

Awaawa are found in most warm water seas around the world. To find out more about them in other places, look for the name "ladyfish" and the scientific name *Elops saurus*. The scientific name of Hawai'i's awaawa is *Elops hawaiensis*, but the fish does not seem to be different from its cousins in Florida or the Caribbean.

They may have once been very common in Hawai'i. They may still be common in some places. But in most of Hawai'i, they are now an unusual catch.

The biggest awaawa I ever caught, a tough 8-pounder, was hooked on a strip of squid dunked in a sandy Moloka'i channel. He was already halfway through his first spectacular cartwheel before the rod tip whipped over and we realized he was not just showing off for the tourists.

Some of the best action with awaawa comes just as nightfall shuts down the normal activity of small boat harbors. One such evening, as a group of us fished for hahalalu, we were startled by a series of big splashes at the mouth of a small inlet. Baiting up with live hahalalu, we got several strikes but no hookups. With no more live bait to use, Alex Budge switched over to a 3-ounce Kastmaster spoon and was soon hooked to a yard-long fish. In gathering darkness the fish's aerial display had all the magic of fireworks as the last of the sun's rays glinted off its flanks. But as with many leaping fish hooked on heavy lures, this one finally shook free.

The fisherman who catches an awaawa can feel a great sense of accomplishment. And, because they are rare (and not very good to eat), he or she can feel an even greater sense of satisfaction by releasing all awaawa unharmed. The best prizes are those you know you can keep on winning. After all, a catch that is only "once-in-a-lifetime" is really more sad than sensational.

AWAAWA

EXCELLENT LIGHT-TACKLE QUARRY THAT LEAPS REPEATEDLY.

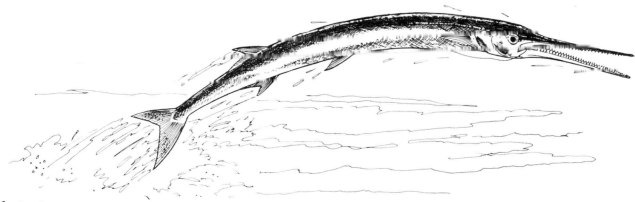

'Aha

Giant Needlefish

Another fish for the angler who wants to do battle with a leaper is the 'aha, or giant needlefish (Strongylura gigantea). It jumps repeatedly from the time it is hooked until it is landed. What's more, it gets big enough to put up a very strong fight on spinning tackle. I once caught an 'aha that was 49 inches long.

The giant needlefish is well named. It is long, slender, silver and pointed. Its upper jaw is like a marlin bill, and so is its lower. Together, they create an odd beak-like appearance. Both jaws are lined by rows of sharp teeth. The head of a needlefish is even more vicious-looking than the head of a barracuda. The barracuda, at least hides its teeth when it closes its mouth. The needlefish, on the other hand, never seems to close its mouth.

Its sharp teeth and long strong body make it dangerous to handle. The safest place to grab it is behind the head. But when you do, be prepared for the fish to lash its body from side to side. It's wise to use a glove, or at least a piece of cloth, when trying to hold the 'aha.

Those same long jaws make the 'aha hard to hook. When the needlefish attacks a bait, it grabs it with the middle of its beak. It clamps down on its food with its needle teeth and holds on for a few seconds before swallowing. You must wait until it swallows the bait before you can set the hook. If the needlefish feels the tension of the line, he'll just open his jaws and let go.

That's why fishing with bait is better than fishing with lures. The needlefish spits the lure out almost as soon as he strikes it. Its jaws are so bony and hard that the hook has a difficult time trying to penetrate. But lures are effective and fun to use for 'aha. I have caught them on small spoons and swimming plugs like the Rebels, Rapalas, Redfins and Sea Bees. The hooks must be extremely sharp and you must jerk the line to set the hook as soon as you feel the strike.

When you set the hook, the 'aha will instantly start leaping. You must play him with the lightest drag possible. Gentle pressure is the key. If you try to horse him in, you'll pull the hook loose. If you put too much pressure on him when he jumps, he'll jerk the hook free. The needlefish will teach you patience.

Hawai'i is home to several kinds of needlefish, but the biggest and gamiest one is the giant Stongylura gigantea, as it is known to scientists. Where it occurs in other places around the world, it is called the "houndfish."

You'll find the 'aha at the surface in deep channels when the current is flowing away from shore. These lazy giants like to cruise back and forth across the current while they wait for it to bring them some unsuspecting bite of food.

To fish for 'aha with lures, cast across the current and reel as fast as you can. The rapid movement of the lure will attract their attention. And the speed will also help you set the hook because the lure is already moving when the fish hits.

To fish with bait, use a slim wooden bobber as a casting weight, then tie an 18-inch leader on behind with a small hook and a strip of squid or shrimp for bait. The wooden bobber will keep the bait right up at the surface. The slim shape will provide the least amount of resistance when the needlefish takes the bait.

Cast the bobber and reel it slowly, just fast enough for the bait to travel along just under the surface. As soon as you feel the tug of the strike, relax the line to keep the fish from feeling any extra tension. The best way to do this quickly is to hold your rod parallel to the shore when you are reeling, then point the rod at the fish as soon as he strikes. This will give him four or five feet of loose line.

Give the fish three or four seconds to gulp the bait, then pull the rod back. If you've hooked him, he'll go straight up into the air. Be sure you keep your bait moving. Needlefish don't seem to like a drifting dead bait. They like action.

Wahanui

Fork-Tailed Snapper

Our next fish seems to have only one thing in common with the 'aha — its long jaws and big mouth. As a matter of fact, this fish is known as the "wahanui," which means "big mouth." It's also called the "fork-tailed snapperfish," and, by scientists, *Aphareus furcatus*. It is one of the very few snappers found in shallow water here in Hawai'i.

It belongs to the same family as the 'opakapaka, onaga and uku, and it looks quite a bit like the 'opakapaka. The most important difference is the color and the flatness of the body. The wahanui is usually bluegrey, dirty violet or a purplish-brown.

These hungry feeders are usually found in small schools just outside the reef. Most of the ones I've caught have been hooked when I have been trolling for papio in water 10 to 20 feet deep on the outer edges of coral reefs. These fish were caught on very small swimming plugs and spoons, each less than 1½ inches long.

For best action with wahanui, you must use extremely light tackle. The biggest wahanui are rarely more than a foot long. Their small size keeps them from putting up much of a struggle when they are outgunned by heavy tackle.

Because of their big mouths, they are very easy to hook. They feed greedily. They are one of the best examples of that old rule that fish and people would stay out of trouble if they would just keep their mouths shut.

Hahalalu

Young, Big-Eyed Scad

"It's not the size of the dog in the fight, it's the size of the fight in the dog." That old saying could be the motto of the hahalalu. This little silvery fish is a tough fighter. He forgets about how small he is when he is hungry and pounces on a bait the way big game fish do. A hooked hahalalu never stops fighting until you knock him on the head and toss him into the ice chest.

Most hahalalu fishermen don't get their sport from the fight, however. They pick tackle heavy enough to jerk the fish out of the water as soon as he bites. For them, the sport is the large number of fish that can be caught quickly when the hahalalu are biting.

Hahalalu fishing is most fun when the fisherman uses the lightest tackle made. Even so, hahalalu are so small (a big one is 6 or 7 inches) that the fight is almost always won by the fisherman. Sometimes the hahalalu gets hooked in the lip and tears the hook loose. But most swallow the bait down deep.

The hahalalu is the same fish as the akule (*Trachurops crumenophthalmus*). Hahalalu is the name used for these fish during their first year of life. After they are a year old, they are about 9 inches long. When they are young, they live in shallow bays, coves and harbors.

The adult akule lay their eggs from February through August. The early hatchers from the February spawning show up in harbors beginning in July. From July through December new hahalalu continue to show up in shallow water. These are fish that hatched later and have just grown to the right size to bite a hook.

Fishermen catch them by whipping and by bobber fishing. To be a successful hahalalu fisherman, you need to know how to use both methods. Sometimes one method works best. At other times, the other method is best. The hahalalu change their feeding habits throughout the day, and you must be able to change with them.

SCHOOLING HAHALALU

Bobber fishermen use a long flexible pole. A pole of 10 to 15 feet is good if it has a very light tip. Some of these poles, called "telescoping" poles, are very easy to use. They come in sections that slide back into each other for easy carrying.

To use a long pole for bobber fishing, tie a length of line to the tip. The line should be about the same length as the pole, which makes it easy for you to cast. Use a light line of 2- to 4-pound test and you won't need a special leader.

Tie a hook to the other end of the line. Pick a #10 limerick hook. Pinch on a light split shot about five inches above the hook. Now attach a small, round cork bobber about three feet above the split shot.

Always be careful in tying knots in light nylon line. The knots break easily if you pull just the slightest bit too hard. You need the light line, by the way, because hahalalu have big, sharp eyes. They won't bite on a hook or bait if they see the line that is tied to it.

For bait, use an inch-long strip of squid. You can buy frozen squid in most food stores. It is often sold under the Japanese name "ika" or the Italian name "calamari."

Picking a spot to fish is easy. If the hahalalu are around and biting, someone else will always be there no matter what time of day you set out. Hahalalu always attract crowds.

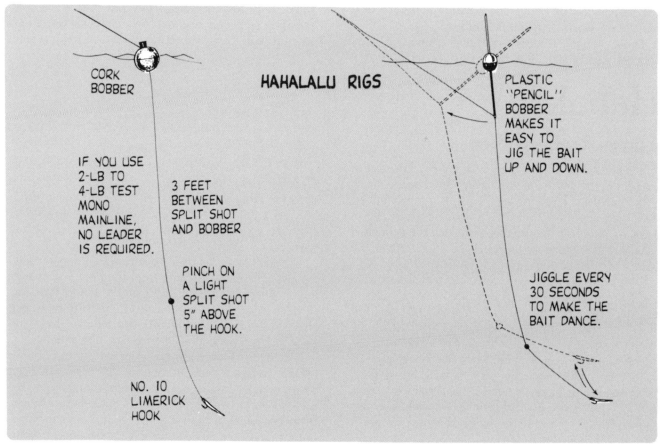

CORK BOBBER

HAHALALU RIGS

PLASTIC "PENCIL" BOBBER MAKES IT EASY TO JIG THE BAIT UP AND DOWN.

IF YOU USE 2-LB TO 4-LB TEST MONO MAINLINE, NO LEADER IS REQUIRED.

3 FEET BETWEEN SPLIT SHOT AND BOBBER

PINCH ON A LIGHT SPLIT SHOT 5" ABOVE THE HOOK.

JIGGLE EVERY 30 SECONDS TO MAKE THE BAIT DANCE.

NO. 10 LIMERICK HOOK

Fish your bobber rig by swinging the bait out as far from shore as you can. Then let the split shot pull the bait down until the bobber stops it. Watch the bobber carefully. If a hahalalu strikes, he'll pull the bobber under. If a hahalalu does not strike within about a half a minute, jiggle the bobber to make the bait dance. The dancing bait will often make a hahalalu strike immediately.

When the bobber goes down, set the hook right away. Most pole fishermen pull the hahalalu right out of the water before it gets a chance to fight. Their main idea is to catch a lot of fish to eat. And it does take a lot of hahalalu to feed a family a good dinner.

You can bobber fish with an ultra-light spinning rod and have the fun of reeling in the hahalalu as it pulls from side to side. I like to do this when I have young friends and relatives fishing with me.

If you can't get a cork bobber, try using a plastic "pencil" bobber. These are long and slim. They dive under the water quickly when a fish bites. They are also very easy to see. I like them because they make it easy to jig the bait up and down when the fish aren't biting right away.

I like to bait fish for hahalalu with one of my very light fly rods which I use to fish for small trout when I'm traveling. Fly rods are great for hahalalu. I use a floating fly line in place of a bobber. And I use a light leader with no split shot. I flip the bait out with the heavy line, let the bait settle and then twitch it gently through the water. When a fish hits, the line twitches backwards on its own. Then I can play the fish without weight or bobber to slow him.

Bobber fishing works best when the fish are feeding in schools right near shore. When they stop biting along a harbor edge, you may still be able to catch them by whipping.

To do this, you'll need a light spinning rod with 4- to 6-pound test line. (You can probably get away with 2-pound test, but sometimes you'll hook a papio that will break your line.)

To the end of your line, attach a small ¼- or ½-ounce torpedo-shaped casting weight. On the other end of the weight, tie on a 5-foot leader of 2-pound test nylon. At the end of the leader, tie on a No. 10 limerick hook.

For bait, you can use squid, but I prefer a tiny minnow strip. Cut a thin strip about an inch long. The best kind is the clear plastic that is filled with tiny silver sparkles. In the late afternoon, glow green strips also work very well.

Put the strip on the hook carefully so that it doesn't spin when you pull it through the water.

The advantage to whipping is that your bait can cover a lot of water. By whipping, you can find hahalalu that are roaming over a wide area.

Toss your lead as far as it will go and reel your line in steadily. Keep the rod tip low. It should only be a foot or two above the surface. As you reel, twitch your rod tip in short jerks of six to eight inches. This makes your bait jump forward like a frightened shrimp or small nehu.

When a hahalalu bites, don't jerk the rod tip to set the hook. If you do, you'll tear the fish's mouth. Fight the fish lightly. Hahalalu usually take a moving bait in the front of their mouths where the hook can pull out easily.

Cast to many different places until you find the spot where the hahalalu are feeding. But watch the bobber fishermen. When the bobbers start diving again, switch back. The fish have again changed their feeding habits.

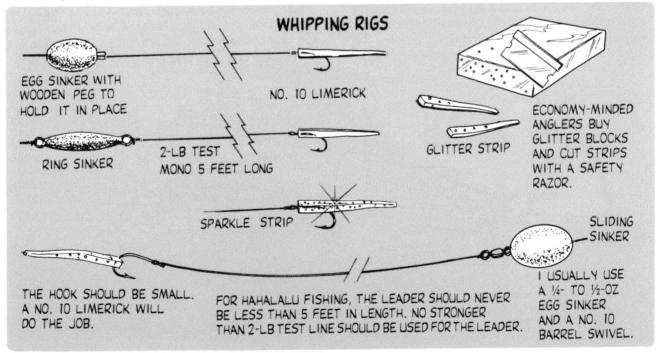

WHIPPING RIGS

EGG SINKER WITH WOODEN PEG TO HOLD IT IN PLACE

NO. 10 LIMERICK

RING SINKER

2-LB TEST MONO 5 FEET LONG

GLITTER STRIP

ECONOMY-MINDED ANGLERS BUY GLITTER BLOCKS AND CUT STRIPS WITH A SAFETY RAZOR.

SPARKLE STRIP

THE HOOK SHOULD BE SMALL. A NO. 10 LIMERICK WILL DO THE JOB.

FOR HAHALALU FISHING, THE LEADER SHOULD NEVER BE LESS THAN 5 FEET IN LENGTH. NO STRONGER THAN 2-LB TEST LINE SHOULD BE USED FOR THE LEADER.

SLIDING SINKER

I USUALLY USE A ¼- TO ½-OZ EGG SINKER AND A NO. 10 BARREL SWIVEL.

Akule

Big-Eyed Scad

Akule are a fish of many names and pleasures. We've already talked about the hahalalu, the akule of 4 to 6 inches. Smaller ones are known as pa'a'a. On the Big Island, 5- to 7-inchers are also called ma'au. Bigger ones (they grow to 15 inches) are simply known as akule. Scientists refer to them with the jaw-breaking name of *Trachurops crumenophthalmus*. Fishermen know them as a good-tasting sport fish and an excellent live bait.

Because they travel in large schools, akule were the most important commercial species of fish in the early 1900s, a time when simple methods were effective with easily caught fish.

During the year, akule and 'opelu (their close kin) alternate in abundance — each species being most common during the half year when the other is scarce. March through August seems to be akule season. Akule bite most readily during their spawning cycle with June and July being especially good months. Spawning seems to incite schooling behavior and draws akule into shallower waters, 15 to 30 fathoms deep. By contrast, akule hang out in 25 to 50 fathoms during January, February and March.

Fishing for akule is most successful during the dark phases of the moon (the first and last quarters) when they can be caught at night by attracting them to a drifting or anchored boat with a submerged light (a dim light being better than a bright one).

Actually, the light does not attract akule directly, but draws small fish, shrimp, crabs and other tiny creatures. Akule are voracious predators and will eat anything meaty and tasty. Once these "bugs," as akule fishermen call them, have congregated in the pool of light, akule gather to feed. Several hours may elapse from the time a light is first submerged until akule arrive and start biting.

At other times of the month, when the moon is brighter, natural light is well spread throughout the water and artificial light loses its power to attract.

Look for akule over rocky bottoms. A depth recorder helps not only to find the jagged bottom features but to show the gathered schools. When akule are at the surface, however, no electronics are needed to spot them. You can hear the snap of their mouths as they feed at the surface and see the V-shaped wakes of their fins.

Pick a tide when the current is slow or still, which may happen at the change of tide in some places or on the incoming or outgoing tide in others. Slack water with little current is essential to allow the lines to stay down under the boat.

Drift over your selected bottom with the light over the side until akule gather. Then anchor to hold position.

Many types of lures work very well. The traditional akule lure is a bit of nylon floss tied with red thread to a #10 or #12 limerick-style hook. Other floss colors are good, especially red, blue and green. Some fishermen

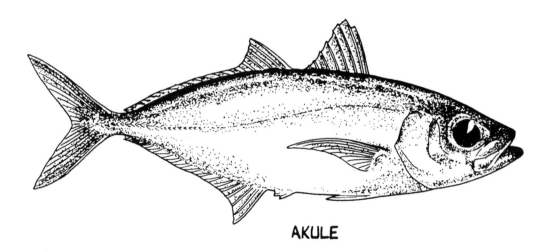

AKULE

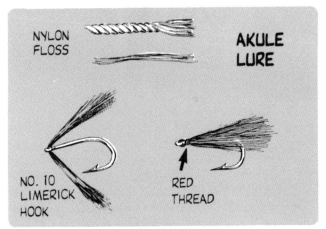

NYLON FLOSS

AKULE LURE

NO. 10 LIMERICK HOOK

RED THREAD

mix flies of different colors to suit all preferences, using, for example, a six fly trace with two whites, two reds and two blues or greens.

Akule will readily strike several kinds of bait including small bait fish and strips cut from the dried skin of other akule. To prepare the latter, skin an akule, stretch the skin on wax paper and cure it in a cool, dry, covered spot.

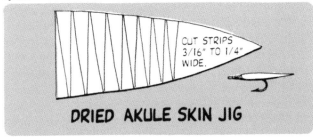

CUT STRIPS 3/16" TO 1/4" WIDE.

DRIED AKULE SKIN JIG

When akule are feeding at the surface, they will greedily strike a bait made from the top lip of another akule. Grasp the lip of an akule with your fingers and pull it free. Attach it to a hook of suitable size and draw the lip back and forth across the circle of light from the edge to the center and back. Make the bait swim like an escaping bait fish or shrimp. When a chasing akule approaches, stop the lip so he can catch it.

When akule are feeding deeper, you'll need to drop your spread of flies down to them. Tie the flies to short leaders of 4-pound test clear monofilament nylon. Then attach these to dropper loops on your mainline, spacing the flies at least a foot apart. Spreading them two to three feet apart sometimes works better because you fish a wider range of depths, and it is easier to free a hooked akule while other hooked akule remain in the water.

To sink the flies, use as much lead as your rig can handle. On a spinning rod, for example, you may only be able to use a few ounces. On heavier gear or on a handline, you might go as high as 8 to 10 ounces.

Jig the lures to give them action. With akule, action stimulates action and the husky akule of a pound or more can wear you out with their fight and the frequency of their strikes.

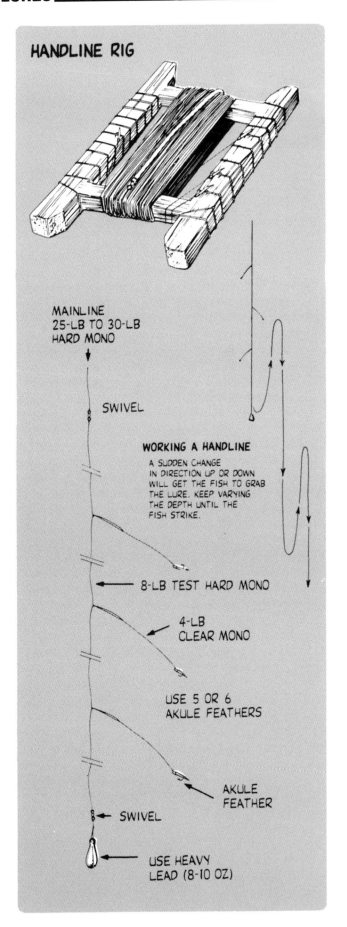

HANDLINE RIG

MAINLINE 25-LB TO 30-LB HARD MONO

SWIVEL

WORKING A HANDLINE

A SUDDEN CHANGE IN DIRECTION UP OR DOWN WILL GET THE FISH TO GRAB THE LURE. KEEP VARYING THE DEPTH UNTIL THE FISH STRIKE.

8-LB TEST HARD MONO

4-LB CLEAR MONO

USE 5 OR 6 AKULE FEATHERS

AKULE FEATHER

SWIVEL

USE HEAVY LEAD (8-10 OZ)

'Opelu

Mackerel Scad

The closest cousin to the hahalalu is the 'opelu, or mackerel scad *(Decapterus pinnulatus)*.

The 'opelu is small but mighty — among the mightiest fish in the sea if it be judged by its true worth on the offshore grounds. If you are what you eat, then the marlin, ahi, ono, mahimahi, ulua, kaku, kahala, kawakawa, aku and all other kinds of fish we love to catch are 'opelu. Because all count the 'opelu among their favorite foods.

As a matter of fact, so does the 'opelu, itself. Small pieces of 'opelu make great baits for catching other 'opelu.

'Opelu is good eating to everything that swims. There may be no fish that won't take a bite if offered. Bottom fishermen use small strips to catch everything from reef fish to onaga. Full filets are readily gobbled by mahimahi gathered around floating debris and kahala roaming the depths. Whole 'opelu tempt ahi to grab the hooks of handliners who "drop stones" and long-liners who stretch their rigs across miles of ocean.

It is not quite the perfect bait because its softness makes it fall apart with most attempts to rig it for trolling and makes it too easily stolen when used for bottom fishing. But saying 'opelu is not the perfect bait merely means there is no perfect bait.

The 'opelu is a member of the same family as the ulua, amberjack and rainbow runner, though it never gets big enough to be more than a full belly for its large cousins. Occasionally an 'opelu will grow to 2 pounds and 14 or 15 inches, but most of the fish found in the large schools off Hawai'i's coasts are a foot or less.

It takes two years for an 'opelu to reach 12 inches in length, that is, if it can evade all the fish that feed on it and all the fishermen who trick it into their nets.

February marks the end of the season of abundant 'opelu, though some can be caught all year round. According to the commercial catch statistics kept by the Division of Aquatic Resources, times are lean for 'opelu fishermen until September when the average monthly catch jumps from around 14,000 pounds to over 30,000.

The civilization of the early Hawaiians so heavily depended on the 'opelu that tabus were established to manage this resource. According to David Malo, writing in the 1830s, 'opelu were kapu half the year with open season for the other six months. The lifting of the kapu each year was significant enough to be marked by a human sacrifice, according to Malo.

The kapus were designed to protect 'opelu during the spawning season, according to Margaret Titcomb, writing in the book *Native Use of Fish in Hawaii*. If so, the kapu must have included the period from March through the end of August. Most spawning occurs during May, June and July. Information on Hawaiian calendars as to the actual months of the kapu is misleading since each island had a different calendar, using the same names for the months but locating them at different times of the year.

An 'opelu is ready to spawn by the time it is a year old and 9 inches long. This 9-inch fish lays about 82,000 eggs. Spawning occurs in waters near shore with depths ranging from 50 to 300 feet, the same depths netters often find most productive.

The eggs become part of the plankton until they hatch. Newly hatched 'opelu swim far offshore where they remain until they are about 5 inches long, after which they swim inshore to the depths of their birth.

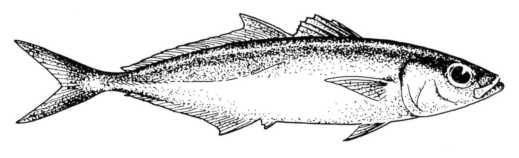

'OPELU

The plankton of its birth then becomes the food on which it lives. Gosline and Brock, in their *Handbook of Hawaiian Fishes*, write that the food of the 'opelu consists mostly of arrowworms, fish larvae and the crustcean elements of the plankton, such as amphipods and larval crabs.

Netters exploit the 'opelu's gentle trusting nature. Each day during the fishing season they go to the 'opelu's favorite places, the 'opelu ko'a, and feed them with a palu bag full of chum. The 'opelu become very tame and willing to follow the palu bag anywhere, even when it is over the open mouth of a large net.

'Opelu can be so trusting that they become downright disappointed when a boat stops along the 'opelu ko'a for fishing or diving and doesn't feed them. They approach the boat in swarms, reluctantly moving away when they realize no one is going to give them a handout.

During the dark of the moon, 'opelu are attracted by lights and can be caught on handlines. Some people prefer 'opelu caught on a hook because the netting operation bruises the fish.

By sheer force of numbers, the 'opelu live out their lives in the most hostile and least protected environment of the sea while still managing to survive from generation to generation — to the great relief of all the other creatures of the sea, as well as you and me.

Many experienced fishermen don't know that you can catch 'opelu on a hook. As a result, they miss out on a lot of fun. Catching 'opelu on spinning tackle is great sport.

To catch 'opelu, you need to know what tackle to use and where to fish. Let's begin by choosing our equipment.

First of all, pick a spinning rod that is stiff enough to handle a 2-ounce sinker. You need that much weight to sink your line down to the bottom.

You'll need a spinning reel big enough to hold 150 yards of line. Your line should be between 10- and 15-pound test. I like to use 10-pound test line because the sinker can pull it down more quickly.

Strong line isn't really needed. 'Opelu are good fighters, but they don't really get very big. Most of the 'opelu we catch are under a pound. But the rig we are going to show you has several hooks on it. That means that sometimes you'll catch three or four 'opelu at once. When you do, you'll be glad that you aren't using line that is weaker than 10-pound test.

To make the 'opelu rig, you'll need a length of 50-pound test nylon monofilament to start. I like to fish about five hooks at once, so I cut a 10-foot piece of 50-pound test. Choose clear, colorless monofilament.

Now make a simple loop at one end. Then tie a barrel swivel on the other end. Measuring from the swivel end, make a dropper loop about every two feet. The drawings will show you how to make a dropper loop.

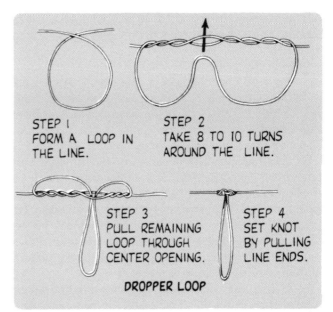

STEP 1
FORM A LOOP IN THE LINE.

STEP 2
TAKE 8 TO 10 TURNS AROUND THE LINE.

STEP 3
PULL REMAINING LOOP THROUGH CENTER OPENING.

STEP 4
SET KNOT BY PULLING LINE ENDS.

DROPPER LOOP

Next, you'll need some 6- to 8-pound test nylon monofilament to make leaders for your hooks. Again, choose clear, colorless monofilament. Nylon leader material is made in several different ways. Some leaders are very soft and flexible. Others are hard and stiff. For our rig, we want hard, stiff nylon.

These leaders will be about 6 to 8 inches long. Cut sections about a foot long. Once all the knots are tied, the finished leader will be the right length.

Next, you'll need some " 'opelu flies." You can buy these or make them yourself. If you cannot buy or make flies, don't worry. We'll introduce you to another type of lure that is just as good.

'Opelu flies are tied on a No. 10 limerick hook. To make them, you need a short length of white nylon floss. Nylon floss is made from very thin fibers. You can buy nylon floss at fishing tackle stores or at sewing stores. Some fishermen use fibers from nylon ropes.

To make your own fly, gather just enough floss to fit through the eye of the hook. Push one end of the floss through the eye of the hook and pull both ends back along the hook shank. Then tie the floss: wrap the thread around the floss just behind the eye of the hook and tie the ends of the thread.

For a bit of color, use red or yellow tying thread. White will do nicely. Some fishermen like to use the light green color that is popular for tennis balls.

If you don't want to bother with flies, you can substitute the soft plastic used to make "minnow strips." Your best choice is the clear plastic with tiny silver sparkles. It is sold in blocks or already cut into strips. The strips are usually too big and must be cut in half. I take a standard size minnow strip and cut it across the middle. The thin half is just the right size. The fat half can be cut down the middle to make two thin halves that are also just right. One minnow strip makes three good 'opelu lures.

The minnow strips use No. 10 limerick hooks just as flies do. For my secret weapon, I put a minnow strip on with a fly.

Attach the hooks to the leader with a palomar knot. Tie a loop in the other end of the leader. Attach the leaders to the dropper loops with a double link. Using a double loop link helps make the leader stand away from the main line to keep it from tangling. The stiff leader also helps keep the hooks from tangling.

Attach a length of light leader to your sinker. Four-pound test would be good. If your sinker gets stuck on the bottom, you can break the sinker off the rig without losing the flies. Using a 3- or 4-foot section of leader on your sinker is best. That way, your hooks will still be three or four feet above the bottom when your sinker touches. If the plastic strips get too near the bottom the hinalea (wrasse) will chew them off.

Now that your rig is ready, you'll need to find a spot where 'opelu hang out. The 'opelu grounds are called " 'opelu ko'a."

'Opelu like to live in water between 50 and 150 feet deep. Knowing the depth of the water you are in will help you find 'opelu. But the best sign of an 'opelu ko'a is the sight of other 'opelu fishermen.

Commercial 'opelu fishermen drift for 'opelu in long narrow boats and canoes. They drop chum overboard to attract the 'opelu. Then they lower nets from the side of the boat.

If you see boats doing this, you know you have found an 'opelu ground. You don't need to go near the boats to catch 'opelu. You should stay at least 200 feet away from other 'opelu boats to keep from disturbing the schools of fish they are gathering. You'll still be able to catch all you need, especially if you stay on the down-current side.

The 'opelu schools may be near the bottom, at the surface or anywhere in between. When I have found an 'opelu ko'a, I shut off my engine and lower the rig all the way to the bottom. As soon as I feel the sinker touch, I jig the line a few times. Then I reel the sinker up about 10 feet. I jig a few more times. if there have been no bites, I reel up another 10 feet. I keep this up until I can see the flies below me. If I still have no bites near the surface, I drop the rig back to the bottom and start all over.

When you find the 'opelu school, you often catch a fish on every hook. Pulling in several 'opelu at once is very thrilling. But you must fight the 'opelu gently. Their mouths tear easily and you will lose as many as you catch.

Often, when you are on the 'opelu grounds, you can see fish rolling in the water below you. Frequently, these will be 'opelu kala, another type of fish that travels with the 'opelu. 'Opelu kala see the boat and are reminded of the free food they get from the commercial netters. But they rarely try to eat the flies or minnow strips. I've

never caught an 'opelu kala when trying for 'opelu, but I have caught several other kinds of fish. Down near the bottom, I've hooked weke-'ula, papio and small uku.

Sometimes ulua, kahala, kaku and mahimahi have pulled 'opelu off my lines when I've been too slow in getting them up to the boat.

The 'opelu grounds are an exciting place to fish. The 'opelu are a sporting, handsome and delicious fish to catch.

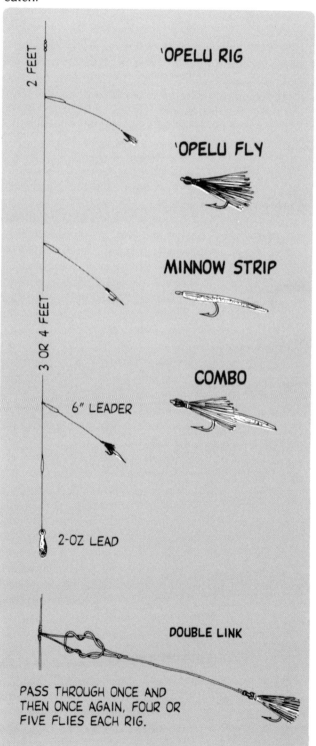

'OPELU RIG

'OPELU FLY

MINNOW STRIP

COMBO

2 FEET

3 OR 4 FEET

6" LEADER

2-OZ LEAD

DOUBLE LINK

PASS THROUGH ONCE AND THEN ONCE AGAIN, FOUR OR FIVE FLIES EACH RIG.

Aku

Skipjack Tuna

Catching aku is a good way to begin to learn about the sport of trolling. Aku put up a good fight. They can be caught on very light tackle. And fishing action is often fast enough to keep beginning fishermen from getting bored. What's more, when aku are plentiful, there's room to make mistakes without anyone getting too upset if a fish is lost.

The aku is the skipjack tuna with the scientific name *Katsuwonus pelamis*. It is found in Hawaiian waters all year around, but you are most likely to catch it when the big schools arrive during the late spring and summer months. Some places, like the area off Ke-ahole Point along the Kona Coast, are home to large schools that are almost always around when the current is right. The fish aggregating buoys are also good places to find aku.

Most aku are between 3 and 6 pounds in weight. The biggest ones reach about 40 pounds.

Aku are handsome and sporty looking fish. Their bright silver sides flash in the sun when they strike a lure. Dark blue stripes on their bellies give them a racy look. The deep and brilliant blue of their backs blends well with the color of the sea, making them hard to spot in the water. When aku are excited, their sides shine with light pink highlights.

Your first clue that aku are around is usually a swarm of black birds. These are called terns or, in Hawaiian, *noio*. If you see noio flying steadily along without stopping it may mean that the aku are somewhere around but the noio haven't found them yet either. When noio find aku, they swarm above them in a pack. When you see them off in the distance, the birds look like they are shuttling back and forth from left to right. They are actually circling above the school.

When the aku chase small bait fish up to the surface, the noio pounce on the bait fish as they try to escape along the surface. The birds beat their wings rapidly to control their flight and swoop down to the surface. Under them, you'll see the splashes of feeding aku.

If your boat is the first on the scene, you should have little trouble catching aku. If, on the other hand, other boats have run back and forth through the aku school, the fish become frightened and dive down when they hear a boat coming. At such times, they are very hard to catch. Sometimes they frighten easily even when other boats are not around.

The secret to catching aku is to borrow a rule that trout fishermen follow: fish fine and far off. This means to use a small lure with a very light leader and to put the lure very far behind the boat. It also helps to circle the school, keeping the boat away from the fish while you are pulling your lures through the school.

What tackle should you use? We'll go through your gear one item at a time, beginning with the outer end, the hook.

Fishermen are divided over whether to use a single hook, with one point, or a double hook, with two points. I like the single hook even though the double hook holds the fish better. The single hook usually works just as well. It is easier to get out of the aku's mouth (a good point if you are going to use the aku for live bait).

Sometimes the double hook prevents the aku from closing its mouth when it is hooked. Since it can't close

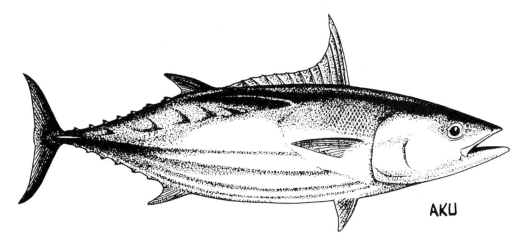

AKU

its mouth, it drowns as you pull it through the water and does not give its best fight. And, of course, should you catch a world record size aku on a double hook, it wouldn't count.

DOUBLE HOOK

TWO POINTS HOLD THE FISH BETTER.

SINGLE HOOK IS BEST IF YOU ARE BAIT FISHING.

Your lure should be a ⅛- or ¼-ounce feather jig. This is the type with a hole through the center and no hook. The best jigs seem to be those with pearl heads, but the lead heads with the red glass eyes or red shell eyes are also very good.

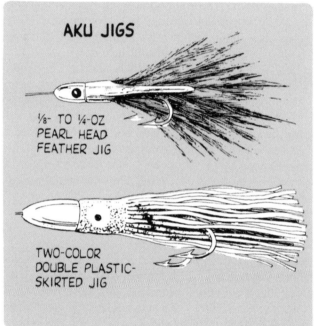

AKU JIGS

⅛- TO ¼-OZ PEARL HEAD FEATHER JIG

TWO-COLOR DOUBLE PLASTIC-SKIRTED JIG

The feather skirts are attractive to fish, but many fishermen prefer to use plastic skirts. A double skirt of two different colors works well. I've had good luck with pink over white, red over pink, red over yellow, pink over red and lime green over pink. Lately, my best aku lure has been one with a pink underskirt and a clear overskirt with an orange stripe down each side. This lure may copy the colors of an excited squid.

Your leader should be clear nylon. Wire will catch aku sometimes, but it will scare away many more fish than it will hook. I rig my lures with 50-pound test leaders that are at least 15 feet long. The long leader puts plenty of distance between the swivel and the lure. Sometimes the swivel will scare fish away as it bounces along ahead of the lure.

When aku are very hard to catch, I switch over to rods that have 20-pound test line or lighter. Then I tie the lure directly to the line with no swivel. When I put the lure out, I trail it 50 to 100 yards behind the boat.

Then I jig the line to make the lure dart forward and drop back as the boat pulls it along. Lifting the rod tip a foot or two and dropping it back quickly gives the lure an action that aku like.

Spinning tackle or a very light trolling rod gives the aku a chance to put up a good fight. You do have to match your tackle to the fishing plan, however. If the rest of the people on the boat want to catch a lot of fish in a hurry, light tackle may take too long to bring the fish in.

I enjoy using a light 7-foot spinning rod with 15-pound test line and a medium-sized spinning reel. But when I'm catching aku to be used for bait, I use a 20-pound class trolling rod and reel.

When an aku is hooked, it is wise to slow the boat to half-speed right away. Otherwise, the hook will tear out.

If you are trolling with several aku lines, you will probably get several strikes at once. Even if only one line is struck, slow the boat and jig the other lines. The others should fill up with aku right away.

Because the mouth tears easily, you should boat an aku with a landing net. If you don't you'll lose an occasional fish because the hook tears out as you try to lift him aboard.

Boating an aku is more difficult if you are using a long leader. Once the swivel reaches the tip of the rod, you have to pull the leader in by hand. If you fish without a swivel and tie the lure directly to the line, you can reel the fish right up to the net.

Trolling without a swivel will sometimes twist the line. After your lure has been in the water for 10 or 15 minutes, reel it back in. Then grab the line at the first guide and pull it back toward the reel to make a loop of slack. If the line is twisted, the loop will wrap around itself. If it isn't twisted, the line will just hang loose. To keep your line from twisting, check the hook to make sure it hangs straight on the knot and isn't being pulled to one side.

Sometimes you will catch aku "blind." That means you'll get a strike without seeing any birds, splashes or others signs of action. You were just lucky and trolled across the path of a traveling school.

At other times, you will see aku jumping in the air. When they leap out of the water, they aren't feeding. There is an old legend that says that the aku who waves his tail in the air at you is really just waving goodbye.

When you see signs of aku but are not getting any strikes, they just aren't feeding. But that can change quickly. Often, aku will start feeding during and after a change in the tide.

Another good fishing time is very early in the morning. Like many other kinds of tuna, aku like to feed in the hours just after dawn. The Kona charter fishing boats, for example, like to race up to the fishing grounds as early as they can to catch their bait fish while the aku are still eating breakfast.

Aku should be chilled immediately after being caught. The meat will spoil rapidly otherwise.

During some seasons of the year, aku have small parasites or "worms" in the meat around their bellies. These look like small white seeds. You can usually get rid of them by cutting off the belly section. The meat in the body usually does not have worms.

Where do you go to find big aku? It probably doesn't matter because no matter where you CAN go, the chances are they won't be there.

That may sound like double-talk, but it's based on some surprising conclusions about the aku's temperature and oxygen requirements, especially the physiological needs of the biggest aku.

Aku grow to 40 pounds (the IGFA all-tackle world record is just shy of 40 pounds and 1 inch short of 40 inches). Hawai'i sees fish of other species near or greater than their existing records almost every year — marlin and yellowfin tuna, for example. When was the last time you heard of an aku much over 30 pounds, let alone over 40?

An article by Richard Barkley, William H. Neill and Reginald M. Gooding in the U.S. Fisheries Bulletin 76 (3), 1978, suggests the reason.

Barkley, Neill and Gooding challenge conventional wisdom that aku live in the warm surface waters of the tropical and subtropical oceans. That's because when you see them, that's where they are. If you don't see them, chances are you believe they are in the warm surface waters of some other tropical or subtropical place.

Captured aku have been observed and experimented with in tanks with subsequent measurements made on the kind of water they prefer, particularly its temperature and the amount of dissolved oxygen it contains.

Their conclusion? Small aku seem comfortable in waters from 64° to 86°F; that is a very broad range encompassing a wide spectrum of surface conditions. Large aku, however, have a much smaller range of temperature preference, only up to about 68°F. That water temperature is lower than is customary at the surface in Hawai'i nearly year round.

The colder the water is, the more oxygen there is dissolved in it. You've had the experience with warm soda — it loses its dissolved gasses a lot more quickly than cold soda does. Aku seem to require unusually high concentrations of dissolved oxygen for long term survival. That, in itself, means a need for colder water.

According to the scientists, "If our laboratory findings with captive skipjack tuna accurately reflect their natural habitat, only the smallest of these aku can inhabit the warm surface waters of the tropics and those larger than 4.5 kilograms (about 10 pounds) must inhabit the thermocline."

The thermocline in Hawai'i varies in depth depending on the season but is between 100 and 200 feet deep throughout the year.

Does that surprise you? It didn't necessarily surprise the scientists. Their comment, "Our hypothesis, and it can be tested, explains many features of the distribution of skipjack tuna in the eastern and central Pacific Ocean."

So the next time you hook up with a big aku (over 20 pounds) be thankful for the unusual opportunity — and ask yourself why the fish was someplace he wasn't supposed to be.

Many of the lessons you learn by catching aku will make you a better fisherman no matter what type of fishing you do next. The aku is a good teacher.

FEEDING AKU

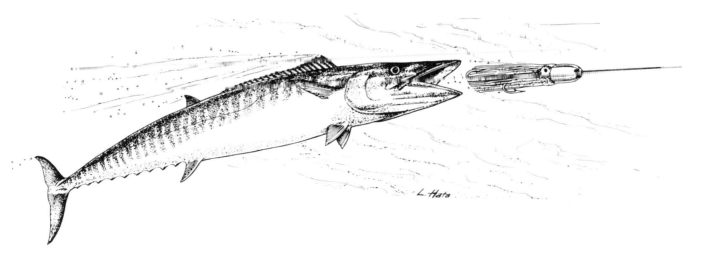

Ono

Pacific Ono or Wahoo

The slashing strike of an ono is an exciting event. Ono pull hard and run fast. They strip line from the reel so rapidly that the reel screams as though frightened.

Ono are usually caught by trolling with jets, heavy lead-headed feather jigs or plastic trolling plugs. The strike of an ono on a plug is the most exciting to watch. The plug splashes across the surface behind the boat. To catch it, the ono must race across the surface with it. Sometimes you can see an ono shove the upper half of its body out of the water as it tries to snatch the plug. Water streams across the ono's brightly barred sides and shoots back across its streamlined head.

Often, the striking fish misses the bait and you are treated to a second spectacular strike. The angry fish, enraged because the bait got away, charges it again with even more force.

All of this action usually happens very close to the boat. Ono seem to prefer the lures trolled right in the wake, not too far behind the transom. Some fishermen feel that ono are attracted by the whirling propellers and the churning white water. On the other hand, some days ono seem to want to stay away from the boat and all strikes are on the outrigger lures pulled 75 to 100 yards behind the boat.

More ono are caught on jets and leadheads than on plugs. Being heavy metal lures, they travel in a straight line, which makes them easy for ono to catch. They also run deeper under the surface. Ono seem to like lures that travel between 1 and 5 feet down.

I have several fishing outfits (rods, reels, lines, lures and hooks) that I use only for ono fishing. My favorite lure is a six-hole jet. This lure is solid brass with chrome plating. Four of its six holes go straight through the lure from front to back. The other two holes start at the front and angle out the sides. The head is rounded like a bullet.

I trim the lure with two skirts. First, I tie on a white skirt. Over this, I tie on a pink skirt with blue sparkles. Other colors that are good for ono are red and yellow, pink and white, pink and green, and black and pink.

To protect the wrappings from the ono's sharp teeth, I wrap the skirt with Monel wire. Monel wire is rustproof and wraps easily. The ono's teeth cannot cut these wrappings.

I rig the lure with two stainless steel hooks. And because the ono's teeth are so sharp, I use braided stainless steel wire for my leader. Many fishermen would rather use nylon monofilament. They think they get more strikes on nylon because it is harder for the fish to see. But an ono can chew through nylon. When he does, you lose the fish and the hooks and lure as well.

When I'm fishing only for ono, I use short leaders, between 7 and 10 feet long. That's long enough to catch the biggest ono. But it is also short enough to allow you to reel the fish right up to the side of the boat for easy gaffing.

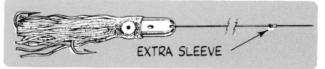

EXTRA SLEEVE

I always crimp on an extra sleeve right in the middle of the leader. This keeps the lure from sliding all the way back on the leader when a fish is hooked. Before I started doing this, I lost many ono. The problem was that the lure would slide all the way back to the swivel when a hooked fish ran away from the boat. If a second ono was watching, it would take off after the lure as it was pulled along behind the hooked ono. Then the second ono would chomp down on the lure and cut the line right next to it.

The rod I choose is a 30-pound class rod. It has a flexible tip with lots of bend to it. Because the rod bends easily, I enjoy the fight more.

I like to use a 6/0 reel with this rod. The 6/0 will hold 500 to 600 yards of 50-pound test line. That's plenty of line for ono fishing. As a matter of fact, 50-pound test line is strong enough to catch any ono that swims. The IGFA world record for 50-pound line is 124 pounds. It has been a long time since anyone has caught one that big in Hawai'i.

Most of the really big ono are caught in the tropical Atlantic Ocean near Bermuda, the Virgin Islands or the Bahamas. These Atlantic fish are called wahoo, though they are the same species as our Pacific ono. Scientists call both the ono and the wahoo *Acanthycybium solandri*.

Wherever ono are found, they seem to prefer shallow water around islands. My favorite spots are in water between 120 and 300 feet deep. This depth is usually too shallow for marlin and ahi, so I only fish it when I know that I want ono. It is just as well that my thoughts are only on ono. A marlin would break the short leader with his tail. An ahi would probably turn up his nose at the lure when he spotted the wire leader.

I like to troll a pattern of zigzags back and forth between the 120- and 300-foot lines, cutting back and forth across the current.

If I don't have time to zigzag, I try to troll along the coastline staying between 160 and 240 feet. Staying in this depth makes good sense because the ono's favorite food is 'opelu. 'Opelu hang out in 20 to 30 fathoms.

To give the ono a choice, I troll four different lures. I always put the six-hole jet with the pink and blue skirt about 30 yards behind the boat. My boat is an outboard and the propeller makes a cone of bubbles that leads back to a point just about 30 yards behind the engine. The jet swims along just to the side of this point.

Sometimes an ono will strike a lure and pull out some line without getting hooked. I always immediately start reeling the line in until the lure is back in position. Often, I'll get a second strike as soon as the lure is back in the right spot.

When an ono is hooked, it makes a very strong first run. It usually will not fight much after that. On heavy marlin tackle, the battle is over very fast. That's one reason I like the rods with the flexible tips; you get more fight from the fish.

When you bring an ono up to the boat, always remember how dangerous this fish is. It has a row of sharp-edged teeth on both sides of its top and bottom jaws. These come together like the edges of a pair of scissors. Always gaff the ono behind the head so you can control those jaws with their razor teeth. Then stun the fish with a billy club before you bring it aboard. The ono should be safely placed in a fishbox. No attempt should be made to take the hook out of its mouth until you are sure the fish is dead.

Ono are more common than most kinds of fish in Hawai'i. They are a good match for a beginning angler with a lot of enthusiasm and a little bit of know-how.

ONO PREFER LURES
TROLLED RIGHT IN THE WAKE

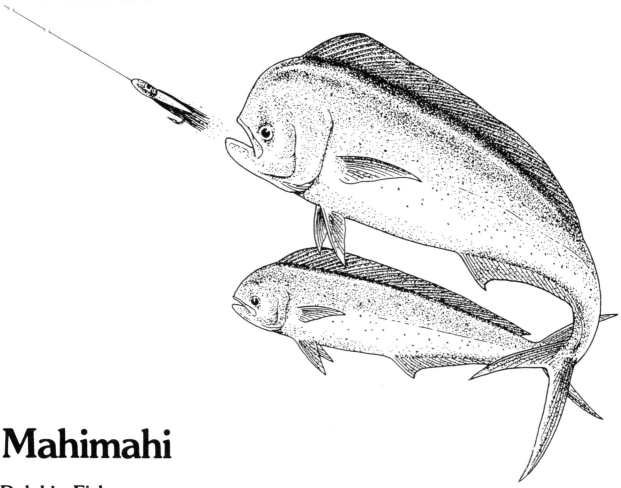

Mahimahi

Dolphin Fish

"The mahimahi is a stupid fish. He'll eat anything. That's why he is so easy to catch." These words were said to me by the editor of a well-known fishing magazine. I don't agree with him.

It's true that sometimes mahimahi *are* very easy to catch. Then, all you have to do is drag a lure in front of them and they'll strike it immediately. Almost any lure will work.

At other times, mahimahi seem to turn their noses up at everything you try to get them to eat. Even when they are hungry, they do seem to prefer one type of lure instead of another. The last mahimahi I caught burst out of the water in the middle of my wake and swam right past two very good-looking lures. Fortunately for me, he liked the third one and gulped it down with no hesitation.

I said "he" in describing this mahimahi because it is easy to tell the girls from the boys. You can spot the difference even from far off. Male mahimahi have a square forehead that seems almost to jut forward. That's why they are called "bulls." The head of a female

mahimahi slopes backward. It is more graceful and streamlined.

"Bulls" have a reputation for fighting harder. The shape of the head may be the reason. Pulling against a bull mahimahi is like pulling against a broad, flat oar blade. The square, flat surface has a lot of resistance to the water.

Whether male or female, any mahimahi fights very hard. That's why fishermen like to catch them. They don't just pull hard. They don't just run through the water very fast. They jump — in high spectacular leaps.

Their leaps are so thrilling they shock some anglers speechless. Other fishermen yell with excitement when a mahimahi first breaks water.

Most mahimahi are caught trolling. Over the years, I've caught mahimahi on every kind of trolling lure. They strike marlin plugs, jets, leadhead jigs, swimming plugs and even the small feather jigs used for aku.

The first mahimahi I ever caught was on a small wooden plug I made when I was about 12 years old. This lure was shaped from a dowel. It had a front end cut at an angle to pull it down underwater and make it wobble from side to side. Its rear end was tapered like the back of a fish. I finished it off by painting it yellow. Yellow has proved to be one of my best colors for mahimahi ever since.

My biggest mahimahi was caught on one of my smallest lures. This fish weighed over 50 pounds, but it struck a ½-ounce pearl-headed jig with a feather skirt.

I like to catch mahimahi on small lures because I run the small lures on my light rods. Mahimahi are the most fun when they are caught on rods and reels that give them a chance to fight their best. Unfortunately, many mahimahi are caught on marlin fishing tackle. Though they do their best, a mahimahi can't give very much sport on tackle built for fish 10 or 20 times as big.

For the beginning anglers who fish on my boat, I always choose a special rig when mahimahi are around. This is a 20-pound class rod with a flexible tip. The reel is a 4/0 size high-speed reel with 30-pound test line. The lure I choose is a 1- to 3-ounce pearl head with any of several different colors. I like yellow, red, pink, blue, green, or a combination of any two of these.

The rod is flexible enough to take an exciting bend when a fish is hooked. The bend also makes up for some of the mistakes the fisherman might make while trying to fight the fish.

But the rod is stiff enough to pull the mahimahi toward you when he sulks. Sometimes mahimahi stop running and jumping and just "dog it." They turn their sides toward you to keep you from pulling them in. They just use water resistance to try to tire you out.

The 30-pound test line is strong enough to catch just about any mahimahi that swims. I always use fresh line that is in good condition. Old line that has seen hard use will break easily. And the reel I use is big enough to hold enough line to outlast any mahimahi run.

The small lures are insurance that you won't catch too big a fish. Big marlin and ahi will generally leave a small- to medium-sized feather jig alone. But you can't always be sure. We occasionally do have the big ones hit the tiny lure — and then just strip the reel with a mighty run. The small lures also give you a much better hookup. The mahimahi has narrow jaws, which sometimes make it difficult for him to swallow the hooks of a big lure. Many mahimahi that are caught on big lures are hooked outside the mouth.

Fishermen quickly learn that mahimahi like to gather around floating objects. A drifting log that has been in the water a long time is almost certain to be surrounded by mahimahi.

Most mahimahi, however, are caught by "blind" trolling. The fish strikes with no warning. The angler has seen no signs of fish or possible action before the strike.

Mahimahi travel together in schools. Sometimes only one fish from a school will strike. Usually, several will hit at once. Sometimes, every one of your trolling lines will go off as you go through a school.

When a mahimahi is pulled in towards the boat, other mahimahi often follow it. These "followers" can be caught by a fisherman who is alert and well prepared. I keep a spare rod ready with a small feather jig that has a strip of bait on the hook. The bait is whatever I have handy. It might be squid, a piece from an 'opelu, akule or kawakawa or even a section cut from the belly of another mahimahi. After a mahimahi strikes and all the empty lines are pulled in, I toss out the baited jig. I let out 40 or 50 feet of line and put the rod in the holder while we fight the first mahimahi. Often, we'll hook a follower on the baited line while we're pulling in the first mahimahi. I've even had times when a mahimahi has followed a hooked ono. It pays to be prepared.

Some of the excitement of chasing schools of mahimahi as they feed on flyingfish is to watch the antics of the always present 'iwa birds. These giant birds act in harmony with the mahimahi and with the angler, for whom they are often the first sign that fish are present.

From their high vantage points, drifting with the air currents far above the sea surface, the 'iwa is the first observer to spot the neon blue mahimahi fins cruising the sea below. As the mahimahi come up to feed, the 'iwa descend to the surface to await the unsuspecting malolo (flyingfish) that the mahimahi unwittingly deliver to them.

The 'iwa birds know the malolo and its habits well. Last week as I scurried to work my baits into a position ahead of the school, I watched the 'iwa as they out-thought the startled malolo. Like linebackers back-stepping to judge where a quarterback would deliver the ball, these 'iwa birds scrabbled backwards a few feet above the waves. Maintaining their downwind position, they waited for the malolo to spring bewildered from their inhospitable watery home — sometimes with the mahimahi right behind.

Wonder of wonders, we even saw a mahimahi firmly clamped to the tail of a big malolo as an 'iwa snatched its head. And it was the mahimahi that let go.

Perhaps it was just as well that the mahimahi lost the battle. Or, perhaps we should say, escaped, because sea birds do eat mahimahi.

And, not just sea birds as big as the 'iwa.

Fishery biologist Thomas S. Hida, of the National Marine Fisheries Service, has been studying the food habits of sea birds, based on the examination of regurgitated material; not a pretty study, I'm sure, but an interesting one.

Hida has found the remains of small mahimahi in the stomachs of such small sea birds as the black noddy tern and the gray-backed tern.

Mahimahi can be caught drift fishing with live or dead bait. Drift fishing is especially good on a windy day, if the water is not too rough. When the wind pushes the boat along at a good rate, it gives a drifted bait a little action.

Also, the wind pushes the boat to new places so you are always trying different waters.

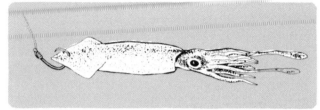

By drift fishing, I've caught mahimahi on whole squid, on dead akule and 'opelu, and, best of all, on live 'opelu or live akule. When drift fishing with live bait, the hook should be pushed through the eye socket in front of the eye. This will not kill the bait, and the movement of the boat will keep the bait swimming forward. When drift fishing on a still day, it is wise to hook a live bait through the middle of the back. When hooked just under the back skin, the bait keeps moving as it tries to swim downward to get away.

Mahimahi are well-known as the best dish on the menu at the most expensive restaurants. A dinner of grilled or sauteed mahimahi can be the end of a perfect fishing day or the beginning of an angler's lifelong devotion to catching this thrilling sport fish.

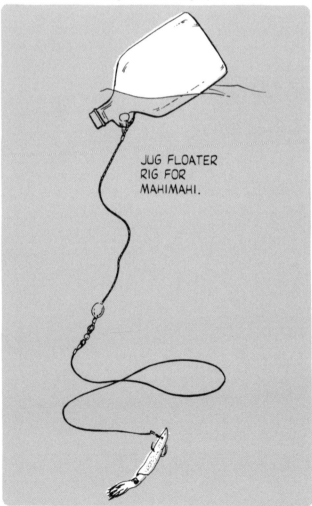

JUG FLOATER RIG FOR MAHIMAHI.

Keep a plastic jug floater rig aboard when you are trolling in mahimahi water and you'll increase your catch. To make one, start with a plastic one-gallon juice or bleach jug (empty, of course) with an airtight cap. Securely tie a 10-foot length of heavy braided line to the handle. I prefer 130-pound test. To the other end, attach a swivel and a light (an ounce or two) weight.

Then tie on about six feet of 80- to 100-pound test nylon monofilament leader. To the end of the leader, attach a large Tankichi hook. Wrap the line and leader around the jug, and keep it handy.

When a mahimahi strikes a trolling line, immediately slip a bait on the hook, unroll the line and toss a float overboard. The bait can be a thawed squid or an 'opelu or akule filet. If your mahimahi has traveling companions, one of them will take the bait.

When you've boated your hooked mahimahi, go back and troll past your floater. The float will keep track of the location of the school for you as the hooked companion stays with the school (or they with it).

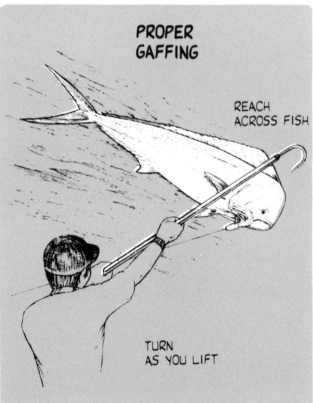

PROPER GAFFING

REACH ACROSS FISH

TURN AS YOU LIFT

When gaffing a fish, go for the head. Reach across the fish with the hook point down. Set the gaff hook with a pull that keeps on coming with a follow-through that lifts the fish out of the water and into the boat (marlin and tuna, of course, are exceptions). Turn the gaff as you lift so that the point is up — this helps prevent the fish from getting off the gaff. The sooner the fish is in the fishbox, the better. A live fish still flinging hooks around is least dangerous when you've got the lid and walls of the fishbox between you and it.

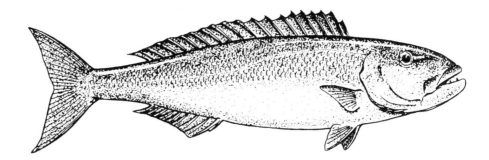

Uku

Grey Snapper

Hawai'i's grey snapper is the black sheep of the snapper family. All of its Hawaiian cousins are brightly colored fish with hues ranging from rosy to bright red, occasionally offset with silvers, oranges and yellows. The grey snapper, on the other hand, is about as drably dressed as a fish can be — light grey with bluish or greenish tints and, occasionally, slightly darker bars. All of its Hawaiian cousins are shy creatures, hiding away in the great depths where they are among the deepest-living of Hawai'i's food fish. The brash grey snapper, however, boldly invades the shallower waters, where it occasionally comes within reach of shore-casters.

And it carries a Hawaiian name that immediately alarms those of us who know that it shares its name (uku) with a not-too-nice little bug that is fond of crawling around on human heads.

Even its English name is misleading. Hawai'i's grey snapper is nothing at all like the grey snappers that are better known from catches made by Atlantic Ocean fishermen.

The grey snapper is a scrapper. It is a tough-fighting fish that does not give up from the moment it is hooked until you finally gaff or net it to pull it into the boat. Unlike the rest of the family, which are gracefully proportioned fish with handsome head profiles, the uku has a head with a snout almost like a dog's. The snout even has grooves along each side.

Uku are caught year-round, but the best months are May through July, according to records kept by the Department of Aquatic Resources.

Most uku are caught in water between 180 and 300 feet deep. But uku are rule-breakers. I once caught an uku on Moloka'i in a sandy channel 5 feet deep. And I have caught many uku trolling small plugs in 15 to 20 feet of water over the reefs on the Big Island. And still more uku have bitten my downrigger baits in 60 to 100 feet depths.

The biggest uku I ever caught snatched a live 'opelu bait fished 600 feet down.

But the places that are most fun to fish are between 180 and 240 feet deep. The depth is great enough to give you more uku to catch. And it's deep enough to discourage many of the smaller fish that peck away your baits. But it's not too deep to make you put away your light tackle and switch to handlines or winches. On calm fishing days, as a matter of fact, I use spinning tackle and still reach the bottom to hook uku.

A good all-purpose fishing rig for uku that is heavy enough to pull up the big ones but still light enough to have some fun with them, that's my "meat" rig. It is a 30-pound-class rod with a high-speed 6/0 trolling reel full of 30-pound test monofilament line.

A 10- or 15-pound uku will put a very good bend in the rod. The line is strong enough to take the pull of the biggest uku in the ocean (if you set the drag right). The reel is fast enough to haul up the line quickly between catches when you want to get the hooks back fast to change baits.

Heavier line would be safer to use, of course. That's because the uku spots are also places where huge kahala and ulua lurk. But the thin line will drop to the bottom quickly with 6 or 8 ounces of lead. Heavy lines require more weight to keep them down.

Whenever I'm bottom fishing I like to use more than one hook, for two reasons. First, there is a lot of work in getting a line down and back up. It's nice to have several baits down to make the elevator ride more worthwhile in case the baits get stolen. Second, fish don't feed on the bottom. Some spread out above the bottom. Uku are like that, and it helps to have hooks in several places.

I use four to six hooks spread out a few feet apart. The hooks are tied to short leaders no more than 15 inches long and made from 80-pound test nylon. The leaders are tied to three-way swivels. The swivels are separated by two to three feet of 80-pound test mono.

The bottom swivel is tied to the sinker by a 2- or 3-foot length of 10- to 20-pound test nylon. This dropper loop to the sinker is light enough to break if the sinker gets stuck. The top swivel is tied to the line.

I use Tankichi hooks in size 18 or larger. The size depends on the size of the uku. The biggest uku weigh nearly 40 pounds and have mouths big enough to swallow marlin hooks.

The best baits are strips of squid, octopus, 'opelu, aku, kawakawa, akule or ahi. Frozen squid is the easiest to get because you can buy it at most food stores. Look for ika (the Japanese name) or calamari (the Italian name). Squid is commonly sold using either or both names.

If you can, use several different types of bait on the same line. Sometimes uku are fussy and change their tastes. And, of course, there are many other types of fish that feed in the same spot. Different baits will catch different fish.

The bigger uku like live baits, with live akule and live 'opelu being best. A struggling bait fish will excite even the most uninterested bottom-hunter.

The best times for uku fishing are just before dawn and just after dark. That's when the live baits are especially good. Uku can be caught at just about any time of the day, however.

If you have a sturdy boat and a strong stomach, you'll be able to fish the very best of the uku grounds. Uku are most common on the broken bottoms of inter-island channels where strong currents and winds make rough and miserable fishing conditions.

Some fishermen find their best sporting success in drift fishing for uku with whole squid as bait on heavy spinning gear. These fishermen attach a 1- or 2-ounce torpedo sinker to their line, then tie on a 3-foot leader of 100-pound test nylon. Their hook is a No. 28 Tankichi, since they are after the really big ones. Remember the bait is a whole squid, hooked once through the end.

The small torpedo weights aren't heavy enough to pull the bait all the way to the bottom. If the fisherman lets out 150 to 200 feet of line, the bait will settle and drift through the mid-depths. Big uku come up from the bottom to hunt. And these are the same waters that big mahimahi will dive to in their search for food. This is a good way to fish for several different kinds of fish at the same time, especially on those days when the wind shoves the boat along too fast to hold bottom with sport-fishing tackle.

Uku are very tasty fish to eat; their meat is white, firm and delicious. Served as sashimi, uku seems to taste best if you catch it one day, refrigerate it overnight and serve it the next day on a plate with sliced, purple (for color) cabbage. Eat it with a spicy mustard and shoyu dipping sauce.

The uku may be the black sheep of the snapper family in some ways, but its flavor makes it the equal of all of its cousins.

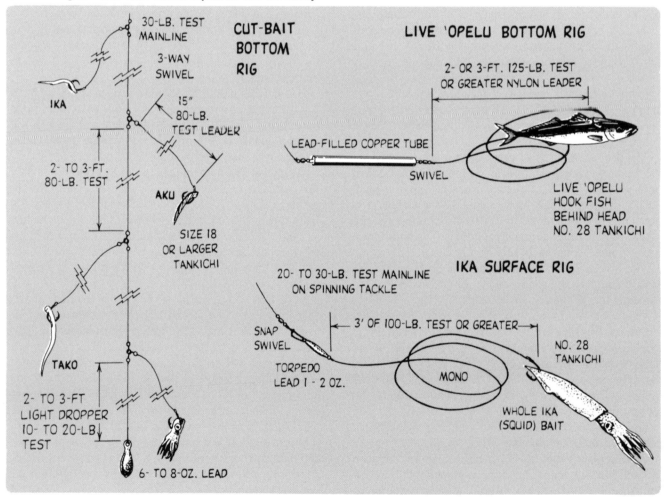

Tuna and Billfish
Hydrodynamic Refinement

In the mind of the reader, it's the writer of the "three-dot column" who has the glamour job on any newspaper. The reader imagines a bon vivant whose "research" takes him to the best places, where he hobnobs with the talented, the famous, the prestigious and the powerful; he's privy to their secrets, their successes and their idiosyncracies.

What a life! Let me imagine for a moment that it is mine. But what would I write a three-dot column about? The secrets, accomplishments and idiosyncracies of the talented, famous, prestigious and powerful that I know are all about fish and fishing.

Aha! Hang on for a three-dot column of a different kind — with nary a mention of Jackie O., Carol B., the "Duke," Frank F. or any other luminary of non-piscatorial (and, therefore, superficial) fame.

The following items are guaranteed to be non-scandalous, not based on rumor and thoroughly informative to anyone whose idea of excitement is a sea full of shimmering fish rather than a discotheque full of writhing dancers. We will spurn the "superficial" for the "super-fish-all" (sorry, but a three-dot column has to have at least one pun).

Tuna and billfish are the ultimate in hydrodynamic refinement. Even their eyes are set flush with their heads to form a perfectly smooth surface. Their fins retract into grooves in their bodies so that no break mars the perfectly streamlined shape. . .Even at their slowest, the tuna must move a distance that is at least the length of its body each second. For a human that would mean six feet a second, or about four miles an hour, which is faster than a human can swim.

If a tuna stopped swimming, it would suffocate. Tuna need to swim to continue to pass water over their gills to extract oxygen. . .Tuna are heavier than sea water. if they stop swimming, they sink.

Because tuna swim constantly, they consume enormous amounts of energy and must eat about one-fourth of their body weight each day. That means a 200-pound tuna must eat 50 pounds of smaller fish and squid. To do this, a tuna must always be hungry, a great boon to the fisherman.

Most fish are coldblooded, matching their body temperature to that of the surrounding sea. Tuna are "warmblooded," meaning they can raise their body temperature until it's as much as 15 degrees warmer than the sea. . .High body temperatures help the tuna use their energy more efficiently, but some tuna get so hot during periods of distress and great energy use that they begin to "cook" their own flesh. This sometimes happens when a fish is caught on rod and reel. . .

Tuna in schools talk to each other. Their snapping and grunting noises are signals to other members of the school. . .The eyes of a tuna, like those of hawks and wolves, are specially designed for high-speed pursuit and capture of prey. They have what is called "binocular or stereoscopic vision."

Tuna and billfish migrate continuously, transversing the length of an ocean within a few months. . .They often return to the same spots during their migrations. Tagged fish that are recovered (after a long period of time) near the spot of their tagging are believed to be ones that have returned to that spot, rather than fish that have lived there continuously. . .

However, a 107-pound ahi tagged off Kona in 1978 was recovered six and a half months later only 42 miles south of the tagging point, suggesting that ahi spend a great deal more of their migrating time in Hawai'i than many people have considered to be the case.

Half of the world's tuna catch is made by two countries, Japan and the United States, despite the fact that tuna are commercially important to the fishing fleets of 70 coastal and inland nations. . .

Tuna is a high protein food that is also high in cost. The typical price per pound throughout the world is nearly as much as the cost of beef. . .The highest price for bluefin tuna is paid in Japan, where it is used for sashimi. Bluefin tuna has sold for as much as $26,000 per ton on the Japanese market. . .

The female tuna lays millions of eggs annually, yet the odds against their survival in the open sea are so great that only two of the eggs laid by a female ever become adult tuna.

Canned tuna is usually albacore, ahi, aku or bigeye tuna. . .Among the members of the tuna family are species with such exotic names as the "leaping bonito," the "frigate" tuna and the "butterfly kingfish". . .Forty-eight different species of fish are included with the tuna in the family *Scombridae*, under the order scientists call *Perciformes* or "perch-like fish."

The bill of the billfish is an extension of its upper jaw and is used as a weapon and to kill food. It also serves to help the billfish swim faster, the way a rocket's aerodynamic shape is improved by its coned nose.

Tuna and billfish live in what is called the "mixed layer" of the ocean. This surface layer is churned by wave and current action and has a fairly uniform temperature throughout. It extends from the surface down to the "thermocline," which can be anywhere from 100 feet to 500 feet down, depending on the geographic area.

And being the three-dot columnist is not really the best job on a newspaper. When I breathe in, I like to smell clean air, lightly salted, not the smoky suffocating stuffiness of a crowded barroom. And for background music to my research, I prefer the clear ringing tone of a singing reel.

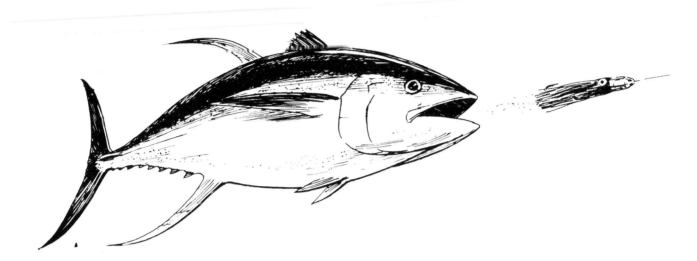

Ahi

Yellowfin Tuna

Fishing is finding, fooling and fighting fish. One of the hardest fish to find, fool or fight is the yellowfin tuna, or ahi.

Ahi are found in Hawaiian waters most of the year. But the greatest numbers arrive with the spring run in May and June and stay through August. Even in the months when large schools are here, ahi can be hard to find. Most are caught by trolling "blind" around places where fish have been found in past years.

Ahi are hard to fool because they have excellent eyesight. In clear water, ahi can spot a big lure or bait from as far away as the length of a football field. They can spot a fast-moving lure even when they are traveling just as fast themselves. What's more, they see a heavy wire leader and are smart enough to know something is wrong. Many fishermen use nylon leaders instead of wire because they fool more ahi.

Ahi are hard to fight because they are strong, streamlined and smart battlers. Their bodies are packed with tough muscles. The muscles are linked to a rigid backbone and tail. This muscle, bone and tail system drives the fish forward with great power.

The ahi's body shape splits the water cleanly like a rocket splits the air. He uses his strength and shape to fight smart. The ahi does not waste energy by throwing himself into the air like a marlin or a mahimahi. He puts all of his power against the rod, reel and line in strong pulls. Ahi are tackle smashers. They break away by breaking lines, rods, reels and fishermen.

Hawai'i's great summer ahi average 200 pounds and grow as big as 300 pounds. They are more than many young anglers can handle. The big ahi can fight a full grown man or woman angler for many hours.

Most of Hawai'i's school ahi are under 100 pounds, and many are between 5 and 20 pounds. These small ahi are great sport for anglers of all sizes, skills and strengths. They are usually caught on light tackle, which adds to the thrill.

Giant ahi are caught on heavy trolling tackle. Serious ahi fishermen troll with 80- and 130-pound class tackle. Some even use 180-pound line. Reels are lever action 80s, 80 Wides, and 130s or star drag 12/0, 14/0 and 16/0 Penn Senators. Rods are heavy-duty with roller guides and aluminum butts.

Jets are the most successful giant tuna lures. Ahi jets are skirted with two or three plastic squids. Good color combinations are blue and silver over yellow; pink and silver over blue; red and blue over white; pink over white; and brown over yellow and black.

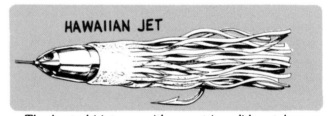

HAWAIIAN JET

The best ahi jets are either cast in solid metal or are hollow and weighted with lead. Ahi jets should be heavy enough to stay below the surface even when trolled at high speeds. Ahi fishermen sometimes troll at 10 to 15 miles per hour. Fast trolling speeds keep the fisherman moving quickly from place to place as he tests new spots for ahi.

Jets are rigged on strong nylon leaders. Good ahi leaders can lift 250 pounds or more without breaking. The lures are rigged with two 10/0-sized hooks. Some fishermen use only one hook because an ahi swallows a lure completely and is easily hooked even with only one point.

Each year, many ahi are caught on plastic trolling plugs, but tournament catch records show that plugs don't catch as many ahi as jets. Ahi are also caught on large leadhead jigs. This is the type of lure that is also known as the "Japanese feather." These jigs have a chrome-plated head with a single red glass eye on each side. The big ahi jigs weigh a pound or more. Before jets, the Japanese feather jigs were the most popular ahi lures. In those days, their skirts were made from long colored chicken feathers. Now, fishermen use plastic skirts on these lures too.

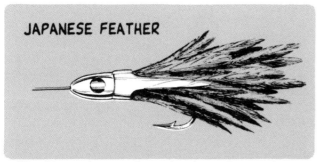

JAPANESE FEATHER

Big ahi are also caught on live bait when anglers are fishing for marlin. Ahi will often take a live aku (skipjack tuna) rigged with a bridle. Some fishermen use live 'opelu.

Even smaller ahi of 30 to 100 pounds will strike big jet lures. But fish under 30 pounds are more often caught on small jets and leadheads. Sometimes these fish attack tiny aku jigs of as little as one-quarter or one-half of an ounce. The best lures, however, for ahi under 30 pounds are the leadheaded jigs from 1 to 3 ounces. Pearl heads in small sizes are also good. Rapalas, Rebels, Redfins and other swimming plugs also work well.

The fun of catching smaller ahi is in using light tackle. With 20-pound class tackle and some patience, you can easily enjoy the thrill of catching a tough fish that won't give up until it's too tired to wiggle a fin.

Since the smaller ahi travel in schools, you will often get several strikes at once. Fighting several fish at once is exciting as each angler uses his skill to keep his fish from tangling with other lines.

Sometimes the skipper can keep track of where the school goes. Then he can troll back through the school and hook up again.

When an ahi strikes, be prepared for a long run. Giant ahi will nearly empty the reel spool with a sizzling charge of 600 or 700 yards. Once the fisherman stops the fish from running, the ahi tries a new trick. His new trick is to dive down as far as your line will let him. This is the time to keep the boat moving away from the fish, which keeps the angle of the line pulling the fish back toward the surface.

To haul the fish to the boat, you must pump. To do this, raise your rod tip; this pulls the fish toward you. Then lower the rod tip quickly and smoothly, turning the reel handle rapidly to crank line back onto the reel.

As the ahi is pulled in, it will dive down below the boat and circle around in the depths. When the fish circles, it means he is almost too tired to run anymore, but be prepared for a last gasp and a last run.

When the fish is close enough for a deckhand to grab the leader, all of the gaffing equipment should be ready. The deckhand should be wearing his gloves. One or more gaffs should be ready to grab, and the billy club should also be at hand.

Once the crew grabs the leader, it is important to keep the ahi coming right to the boat. If it is not gaffed immediately when it breaks the surface, the ahi will usually try to dive again. The gaff should be pulled into the cheek as soon as the head comes up. A second gaff should be set by a second crew member. The fish should be rapped on the head with the billy club to stun it. Its throat should be cut to bleed off the heat built up inside the fish's body during the fight. And then the ahi should be hauled aboard and packed in ice. The ahi should be chilled as fast as possible to keep the meat from spoiling.

After all of the work of finding, fooling and fighting an ahi, any fisherman, regardless of his or her age, can be very proud.

Dropping Stone for Ahi

"Dropping stone" is a highly productive fishing method unique to, but widespread throughout, the Pacific islands. It is a favorite method of local fishermen where yellowfin tuna tend to school up well below the surface in particular places called "ko'a." Stone-droppers fish the ko'a, the fish-aggregation buoys and porpoise schools (ahi are frequently found feeding under porpoise). Stone-droppers catch ahi, bigeye, aku, albacore, kahala and marlin, among others.

As with any technique that has evolved in widespread and isolated places with different fishing conditions, stone dropping has many variations. No two fishermen do it the same way, including partners who fish from the same boat.

Little has ever been written or published about the method, and the veteran fishermen who have earned their skill through line-scarred hands and years of experimentation like it that way.

We'll describe a basic method — one that works very well and is in common practice. All methods employ the same basic device: a stone attached to the handline with a slip knot. The stone pulls a baited hook rapidly to a predetermined depth, and the slip knot releases it so that the line is unencumbered for the presentation of the bait. The hook and leader are wrapped around the stone to prevent tangling during the descent. The leader is, in addition, wrapped around palu (cut-up chum), which disperses after the slip knot frees and, thereby, attracts fish to the bait

The stone-droppers' gear includes a hook, leader, swivel, handline, lead weight (to hold the bait down once the stone is released), line markers, a stone and a line-gathering basket. Bait is almost always 'opelu, either a filet, tail section or small whole fish. Chopped 'opelu is also first choice for chum.

The Hook: One of the variations in stone-dropping is the size and style of hook used.

Tankichi hooks are the best choice as a compromise in hooking ease and strength. Japanese Maruto hooks are easier hookers but sometimes break. Norwegian hooks are stronger but harder to hook with.

When fishing smaller ahi (fish of up to 80 pounds) in the ko'a and around the buoys, anglers pick sizes 30, 32 or 34. For the bigger ahi, especially in porpoise schools, the preference is for sizes 36, 38 and 40 and sometimes larger.

The Leader: Considerations are length, strength, and type of material.

Flexible and supple types of nylon monofilament are preferred. Wire is out — ahi see it easily. Hard and stiff mono formulations seem to break more easily.

Small ko'a ahi require lighter leaders of 80- to 125-pound test. Larger fish require 250- to 400-pound test. The lighter leaders (250-pound test) will get more bites, but you'll break off a lot of fish. Surprisingly, fishermen report they break 250-pound leaders on the strike if the line is held by a heavy rubber band.

Leader length varies from 12 to 30 feet. Since the leader is the slipperiest part of the gear to pull, some fishermen prefer the shorter length.

The Swivel: Strong barrel swivels are essential. These need not be the expensive ball-bearing type, but they must be strong enough to take the strain of hand-to-hand combat with big fish.

The Line: Some prefer hard braids of non-stretching materials. Others like the give of braided nylon. Since the latter is less expensive, it makes a good starting point. Line of 300- to 400-pound test will do the job.

The Lead: An 8-ounce bank sinker is enough. Remember, the stone will pull the bait down to the right depth. You just need enough weight to hold it there.

Line Markings: Here's a use for those plastic legs the ono leave you after they've chopped off most of the skirt of a trolling lure. Use different colors to mark different depths. A single, short strand of 3 inches will do.

The Stone: Some prefer dense, smooth beach pebbles. Unless wrapped carefully, however, the line will slip off. Blocky chunks of aa lava, oblong with rectangular faces, are easy to wrap, especially if they have a flat surface for the bait and chum. Dimensions of the stone should be, roughly, 8" x 4" x 2", or the size of a brick.

DROPPING STONE FOR AHI

1. BAIT HOOK WITH AN 'OPELU FILET.

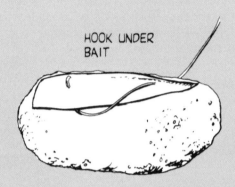

HOOK UNDER BAIT

2. PLACE BAIT ON STONE **HOOK SIDE DOWN**.

3. PILE SOME PALU ON BAIT ABOVE THE HOOK POINT TO HELP HOLD THE BAITED HOOK IN PLACE.

4. PULL LEADER ACROSS CORNER AND AROUND STONE TO THE UNDERSIDE WHERE THE HOOK IS.

5. FIRST WRAP IS OVER BAIT AND PALU ABOVE HOOK. CONTINUE WRAPS FROM LEFT TO RIGHT ACROSS BAIT, ADDING SOME PALU EVERY FEW WRAPS.

6. WRAP TO SINKER AND THEN TAKE TWO MORE WRAPS, STAYING TO RIGHT OF SINKER.

FIRST LOOP

BACK WRAP

7. CATCH LINE AROUND FINGER OF LEFT HAND TO MAKE A LOOP AND THEN BACKWRAP TWICE.

FIRST LOOP   MAINLINE

SECOND LOOP

TWO WRAPS BETWEEN LOOPS (OPPOSITE DIRECTION FROM FIRST WRAPS)

8. FORM A SECOND LOOP OPPOSITE TO THE FIRST.

9. TWIST LOOPS AROUND EACH OTHER THREE TIMES.

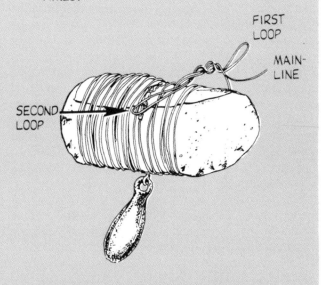

FIRST LOOP

MAIN-LINE

SECOND LOOP

10. KNOT WILL HOLD FOR DROP BUT WILL SLIP EASILY WHEN LINE IS PULLED.

The Gathering Box: Large plastic milk crates are common. They are the right size and have open sides to allow the line to dry.

Fishing depth varies from place to place and species to species. At some koʻa, the ahi are relatively shallow, striking at 25 fathoms. At the buoys, they are usually deeper: 40 to 50 fathoms. When running with porpoise schools, 40 fathoms is a good depth to try. Drop way down for albacore; you'll find them at 60 or 70 fathoms.

Follow the directions for assembling your gear, baiting hooks, and tying the slip knot. Once you've lowered your stone over the side, don't touch the line until the stone has reached the right depth (otherwise, the knot may release prematurely). Tie off your handline with a ¼-inch rubber band and get ready. Don't try to grab the handline when it goes over the side on the strike. If you do, you'll get a vivid lesson in why the early Hawaiians named this fish "ahi" for "fire."

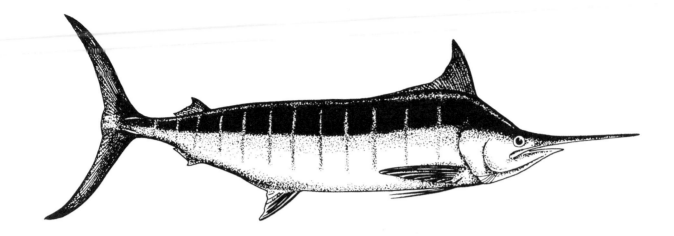

A'u

Pacific Blue Marlin

Marlin make Hawai'i's fishing spectacular. Without this king-of-all game fish, Hawai'i's angling would be just interesting, not explosive. It's the marlin that brings the big game fishing elite from all over the world. It's the marlin that brings Hawai'i's own fishermen to their feet in exhilaration and to their knees in exhaustion.

For proof of Hawai'i's supremacy as the world's blue marlin capital look to the record books. Currently, of the 11 existing IGFA line class records, seven are Hawai'i catches. And the record books don't even show the really big catches, like the 1,450-pound blue boated on 80-pound test line on Tom Rogers' *KONA SEAFARI* and the 1,805-pound monster caught on Cornelius Choy's *COREENE-C*.

What's more, Hawai'i is the proving ground for modern marlin fishing methods. Big game trolling lures were invented here, and local lure makers lead the continuing process of refinement and evolution of trolling attractors.

In addition, Hawai'i's offshore specialists discovered and developed the most effective methods of rigging and fishing live baits. So productive are these home-grown techniques, the traditional methods of other fishing grounds have never received more than casual interest from Hawai'i's anglers.

But blue marlin aren't the whole billfish story. Hawai'i is also a tourist stop for migrating striped marlin, black marlin, shortbill spearfish and, occasionally, Pacific sailfish.

Three factors contribute to Hawai'i's success with blue marlin: our location on a well-traveled migration route, extremely deep water near shore and a regular abundance of marlin food — particularly the toothsome skipjack tuna.

Furthermore, calm, clear waters surrounding the islands aid fishing. The waters are so clean, a sharp-eyed marlin can spot a rapidly trolled lure as much as a hundred yards off. And, on most days, the seas are so flat the fisherman is as comfortable as he would be at home in a rocking chair.

Much of this book is relevant to marlin fishing. The techniques of making and rigging lures, bridling live baits, fishing with outriggers, and many other methods used in catching marlin have been described on the pages pertinent to Hawai'i-style fishing in general. In addition to information found elsewhere in the book, here are some tips especially pertinent to marlin fishing:

1. Look for marlin where they live. Rarely are they caught in waters much less than a hundred fathoms deep. They prefer to feed where the hunting is easy and will trail schools of skipjack and yellowfin tuna. Sometimes, they'll take up positions above underwater ledges where bait schools often come, knowing lunch will show up eventually. Most marlin seem to be caught by trolling "blind." But, when a marlin is hooked, even though it may seem to be almost at random, there is usually a reason for the marlin to have been there, and the student of marlin fishing marks the spot.

2. Record hunting is good in Hawai'i. Know the rules and follow them. Following the IGFA rules presents no real handicap and may inscribe your name in the record books.

3. Never forget that marlin are an aggressive fish. This will help you understand how to catch them. Most fishermen feel that the marlin's attack on a lure is an act of destruction — but sometimes it's no more than an instinctive response similar to that of a cat fascinated with a piece of dragged yarn.

4. Learn every method you can for catching marlin and know how to use them. Be an expert with lures, live bait, skip baits, swimming dead baits and anything else you can discover. Don't just fish live baits on the surface. Know how to fish them deep. Consider other types of live baits besides aku. Marlin have been taken on 'opelu, akule, ahi, ke'o ke'o and even on ono and mahimahi.

5. Stay alert to what's happening in your wake. Seeing a fish before the strike can mean the difference between hooking it and losing it. Some marlin, for example, will follow a lure for a long time without striking. These can be teased into taking by releasing the drag and dropping the lure back into the marlin's face.

6. Stick with it. Marlin aren't caught every day. Statistics from the Hawaiian International Billfish Tournament show that in the best years tournament fishermen average one marlin every two to three boat days. In the worst year, it was one marlin for 36 boat days.

7. Keep your tackle in good repair. Once hooked, a marlin's major goal is to take your gear apart. Preventing that painful separation means inspection and maintenance long before the strike. Replace frayed or abraded line. Retie knots. Lubricate rollers. Examine drags and replace worn parts. That's just a start. You are never really finished.

8. Set your drag with a scale until you can tell the proper setting on your own. Run the line through the guides and tie the end of the line to a hand-held spring scale. Striking drag should be one-fourth to one-third of the breaking strength of the line.

9. Fish your lures in a pattern. One effective four-lure pattern features one plug that stays on top, splashing all the time, two more that pop and dive, pulling a continuous stream of bubbles, and a final lure that is very erratic with lots of underwater action. The active lure is fished closest to the transom. The splasher is run on the short outrigger. The two straight-running poppers are fished on the second and last rods back.

10. Experiment with lure colors, but know that blue has proven to be a consistent winner.

11. Experiment with outriggers. Some skippers feel that all lures should be run from outriggers for the best action. Others run all lures from flat lines because outriggers don't give enough jolt on the strike. Try several different strategies to see what works best for you.

12. On your outriggers, use tag lines rather than snaps. You may save your teeth on a strike. A tag line whipped back into your face will just sting. A snap will clear out your upper plate.

13. The size of bait fish you select to bridle for marlin is limited only to the size you can catch and are willing to handle. Many small marlin have been suckered by baits as big as 20 to 25 pounds. On the other hand, Tom

Rogers' 1,450 blue ate a bait that weighed less than two pounds.

14. Respect the power of the billfish, a creature one scientist described as having "evolved to the limit of hydrodynamic refinement." Marlin can swim as fast as 50 to 60 miles per hour. They generate so much force, they can drive their bills into two feet of wood and four inches of steel (both feats have been proven by aggressive fish).

15. Most marlin are solitary fish, lone strikers, but be ready for the multiple strike. At times marlin pair up, even school up, and packs of billfish have been known to hit everything in sight.

16. Sharp hooks are essential. The striking end of a marlin is all bone.

17. When setting your lines for trolling, wind the last few turns on a diagonal with the final wraps lying across the others. The cross turns help keep the line from digging into the spool on a strike.

18. Hook the fish. Nothing is more frustrating than fighting a fish for 15 minutes and then watching it spit out the bait because he's just been toying with you. Make sure you put enough pressure on the fish to drive the point into something solid. If you are going to pull the hook out, do it early before you've wasted your energy, and then get back to fishing. When lure fishing, make sure your fish has the opportunity to turn and run from the boat. His turned head will help you slide the hook back into the corner of his mouth where it has the best chance of getting a firm bite.

19. On the strike, run the boat ahead until the hooked fish is behind all lines and lures. Then clear the remaining lines to give yourself maneuvering room.

20. As the fish runs out line, don't increase the drag setting. The pressure on the fish is increasing automatically from the diminishing diameter of the spool and the increasing friction of line in the water. The only change you should make is to reduce the drag.

21. Don't fight the fish directly behind the boat. Keep the boat to one side. He'll tire more quickly if he's forced to continuously exhaust the muscles along one side rather than being able to rest one set by switching to the other side.

22. Don't winch — pump! Pry the fish toward you by lifting the rod smoothly. Pick up line by reeling quickly as you lower the rod. Keep your pumping action smooth. Keep the line tight on the fish — don't ever release the tension on the line by dropping the rod tip too quickly.

23. Short lines invite breakoffs. The closer the fish is to the boat, the shorter the line and the more likely it is that an error will cost you the fish. Be extra alert when the fish is ready for gaffing.

24. Many hands (deckhands, of course) make light work. For best results, a fishing team should have a boat handler, leader puller and gaff man in addition to

the angler. Such luxury may be impossible, but it does pay off. Safety is of paramount importance. If possible, the leader man should drop the recovered leader back over the transom and into the water to prevent the danger of a loose loop wrapping an unwary ankle. The gaff man should stand behind the wire puller so he can reach the fish at the right moment. The gaff man should strike the fish on the same side of the wire man that the

gaff rope is anchored. Otherwise, he'll lasso the wire man, roping him to a powerful and angry fish.

25. Gaff the marlin by reaching across the fish's shoulder and gaffing him in the hump. the hump is a firm anchoring point. The angle of the pull will exert pressure on the fish to angle it away from the boat while continuously pulling the fish off balance and onto its side.

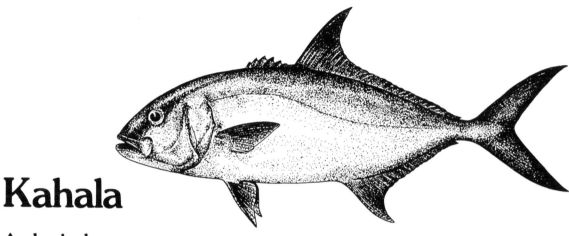

Kahala

Amberjack

More of these big tough jacks are caught during January, February and March than any other time of year. You'll like the kahala if you enjoy sport fishing for a hard fighting game fish on light tackle. You may not like it at all if you are a commercial fisherman and your favorite ahi ko'a has been taken over by schools of wormy fish with poor market value and a reputation for carrying ciguatera toxin.

A chat with one disgruntled handline fisherman disclosed that he had taken almost two dozen kahala between 20 and 50 pounds on a January outing for ahi. Each strike, a hoped for tuna, soon telegraphed disappointment with the characteristic short, hard runs ending in head-shaking jerks. (Ahi, on the other hand, tend to pull smoothly, strongly and steadily right up to the surface.)

Their poor market value aside, kahala are a great sport fish. The big ones, running up to 150 pounds or more, fight hard even on fairly heavy tackle. Furthermore, they are an attractive fish, well-shaped and handsomely colored with tinges of green, brown, purple and yellow.

Your best chance of catching one on sporting gear is probably off Ke-ahole airport. To do so, catch a live aku (small ones are better), bridle it and let it swim straight down from a drifting boat. The aku tend to school up in about 90 fathoms, and that's where you are likely to find the kahala. Kahala are a deep-water fish ranging up from the bottom to about 50 fathoms. Be prepared to have your aku intercepted by a tough fish while the bait

is racing down. It could happen anywhere from 50 fathoms on down to the bottom.

You'll know you've got a strike if your bait speeds up a great deal. The first spurt of speed will be the extra escape velocity of the aku when a fish makes a pass at it. Once the kahala grabs the bait, your line will sizzle from the run.

Be prepared for huge fish. Sometimes this kahala - aku cat-and-mouse game gets interrupted by a marlin or ahi.

There isn't really much you can do with big kahala. They do tend to be riddled with worms, making them most distasteful in appearance when you are cleaning them. With the fish cooked, the worms are no problem, but they are there — a nagging dissuasion to the appetite. Worse yet, some kahala have been implicated in cases of ciguatera poisoning.

There is no quick test for ciguatera. If you are going to chance eating a suspect fish, try feeding a piece to the cat. If the cat gets sick, chances are you'll get sicker. The symptoms include nausea, vomiting, abdominal pain and diarrhea. A numbness and tingling around the mouth, later extending to the limbs, is also common. You will also feel weak with muscular aches and pains. A headache, dizziness and nightmares also may hit you. And, generally, you'll get a reverse temperature sensation: cold water makes the palms of your hands and the soles of your feet tingle.

Altogether, it just means that the best way to enjoy a kahala is on the end of the line, not on the end of a fork.

Ulua

Giant Trevally
the Ultimate Shore-Casting Challenge

The ulua is everyman's fish, yet no man's fish.

Everyman's? Ulua are caught using every fishing device from spears to spinning gear, every method from trolling to slide-baiting, and at every depth from shallow water dunking to deep-sea bottom-fishing.

No man's? The ulua is master of most encounters. Strong and stubborn, this pugnacious battler beats the angler physically even when the man's tackle outlasts the fish and the man's skill and muscle bring him to victory. Not only that, but the capture of a big ulua grips the angler and never really releases him. The encounter remains vivid and is relived continually anytime someone can be forced to listen.

Few fishermen catch a lot of ulua. Some try with fanatic determination, yet must be satisfied with a few fish for a year's effort. The best anglers are those who break the twin hundred marks for 12 months of trying: 100 fish and a 100-pound fish. In the carefully kept records of the Hilo Casting Club, each annual champion has surpassed the hundred fish mark, with the best record being 120 fish.

Furthermore, because ulua grow to heroic proportions, the dedicated angler's dream is to beat the 100-pounder. Rarely is this mark broken by much. Just as the four-minute mile seemed unbeatable to runners

decade after decade, ulua catches hit the barrier at 135 pounds, give or take a few, and then only once every few years. Old stories of bigger fish were routinely discounted as living only in fertile imaginations of old men. Then a 179-pounder was caught by bottom fishing, followed soon after by the spearing of a 191-pounder. Unbelievable catches, yet backed up by well-publicized photos and full documentation. Ulua fishermen now hear the tales of giant fish caught by early Hawaiians and dream of the 200-pound monster, maybe even believing that they could stop one if they hooked it.

How do you stand your best chance of catching an ulua? The answer varies from island to island, from fisherman to fisherman, and from circumstance to circumstance. No matter what one fisherman may say is the best way, some listeners will shake their heads in disagreement while others will get angry over the disclosure of closely held secrets. The fishing writer treads this territory with great trepidation, knowing that whatever he writes, he cannot really win.

Though the biggest ulua have been caught bottom fishing from boats, the most productive method is slide-baiting, a specialized technique developed in Hawai'i just for ulua.

Slide-baiting

This is a method for fishing large baits on heavy tackle where rocky cliffs overhang very deep water. The tackle features oversized reels, long and stout casting rods, heavy test lines, intricate terminal tackle, giant casting weights and a novel way of baiting the line *after* the cast has been made and the sinker anchored.

In selecting tackle, the fisherman must not only match the size of the fish but also the angler's own physical needs. Among the ranks of successful slide-baiters are women and youngsters with gear chosen to suit their size.

Logically, gear selection begins with the size of your casting weight and the strength (therefore the diameter) of your line. An ulua fisherman wants to be able to toss a 12-ounce sinker a hundred yards on 80-pound test line, and some can actually do it.

The rod. For many years the most common rod was the marriage of a trolling rod blank to a heavy section of bamboo, with the total length approximately 11 to 12 feet. These "half-and-half" rods were frequently home-made, but stores specializing in ulua fishing gear sell ready-made versions. Many ulua fishermen now use full-length fiberglass rods. If properly selected for strength and stiffness, these are real workhorses.

The reel. The most common "right out of the box" reels are Penn Senator trolling reels in the 4/0 or 6/0 sizes with the latter getting the nod when line capacity is important. Experienced ulua fishermen modify the 4/0 reels by "stretching" them. This is accomplished with a Newell broadbill conversion kit consisting of a wider spool and reel seat and longer extension bars. The result is a 4/0 with almost the width of a 6/0.

Some fishermen use the newer model Senators and the Daiwa sealine trolling reels. Among other advantages, these reels have aluminum spools, making them easier to cast. For the wealthier fishermen, the Penn International reels are the choice. The tradition-alists pick Pfleuger Templars and Atlapac reels. Both are collector's items since they are no longer made.

The line. Eighty-pound monofilament is nearly standard for the 6/0 sized reel. Fifty-pound test is a better choice on the 4/0 because of the smaller line capacity.

Terminal tackle. Here's where the arguments start. Each fisherman has his own special minor preferences, but some of the general features differ markedly from island to island. We've illustrated the basic rig with all the extras and a guide to variations.

Most of the variations affect what the ulua fisherman calls his "leader," a different use of this term than is common in fishing. The typical slide-bait leader has two or three separate sections. One section, the part most fishermen identify with the word "leader," is the piece between the slide buckle and the hook. The second and, if used, third parts, are the connections between the mainline and the swivel stop. Together, these help prevent the ulua from cutting the line by chafing it with his body or rubbing it against the rocks. The total length of leader an angler may feel necessary can depend on bottom conditions and how high the angler is above the fish. Shorter leaders tend to be much easier to cast. Long leaders require special splices that allow the end of the leader to be reeled right up onto the spool and to be cast easily through the guides.

Bait. Bait will depend a great deal on what is available. On the Big Island, the first choice is eel. The brown-spotted moray eel (puhi) is most often used, but many fishermen will pick the "white eel" (tohei) if they can get it. Ulua love octopus (tako) baits, but so do eels. Whole live fish of just about any kind work well. Ulua will sometimes eat a dead bait fish; however, using such is a desperation measure for anyone who can't get a better bait. Occasionally, big ulua are even caught on lobster and 'a'ama crab.

Those are the slide-baiting basics. Look to the tips at the end of this seciton for some important additions.

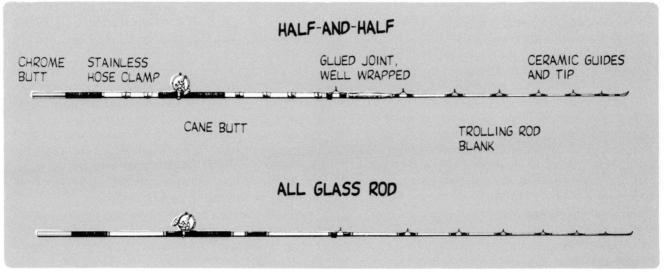

HALF-AND-HALF

CHROME BUTT · STAINLESS HOSE CLAMP · GLUED JOINT, WELL WRAPPED · CERAMIC GUIDES AND TIP

CANE BUTT · TROLLING ROD BLANK

ALL GLASS ROD

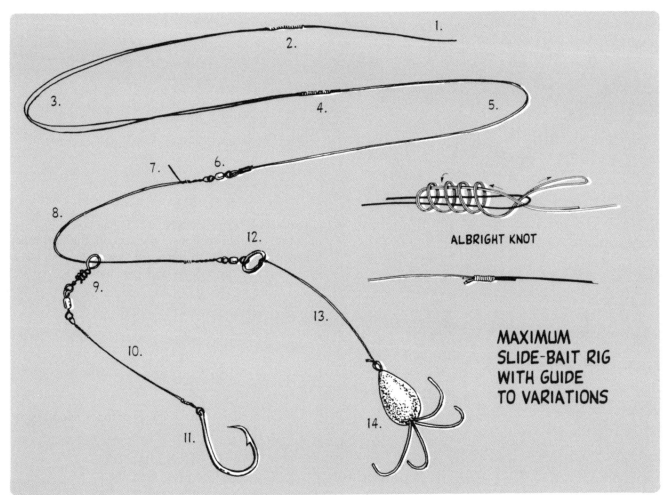

ALBRIGHT KNOT

MAXIMUM
SLIDE-BAIT RIG
WITH GUIDE
TO VARIATIONS

Slide-bait Rig with Guide to Variations

Illustrated above is the slide-bait rig with some of its many variations. Following the numbers you'll first see (1) the mainline. This is usually 80-pound test monofilament for a 6/0 reel and 50-pound test for a 4/0 reel. Next is the double line knot (2) formed by using either a bimini, spider or braid knot. Whichever you choose, be sure to make it tight and smooth so it will easily pass through the rod guides.

The double line itself (3) may be only a few inches long — just enough to provide two lengths of mainline to be attached to the next leader section — or it can, by IGFA rules, be as long as 30 feet, providing that the double line and leader combined do not exceed 40 feet.

The albright knot (4) is used only if the first leader section (5) is used. This leader section is optional; some fishermen prefer to use it while others don't. It consists of plastic-coated cable wire (Sevalon) of 90- to 100-pound test or of nylon monofilament of 200- to 300-pound test. This section can be long enough to run onto the reel. But don't overlook the IGFA rules about total double line/leader length allowed.

Use a 3/0 swivel (6) and a wire retainer (7) when attaching the second leader section (8). The retainer, formed from wire from the second leader section, keeps the bait off the bottom by stopping the slide buckle (pig tail) (9) from passing onto the second leader section until a fish strikes. The second leader section is made of stainless piano wire (#10). It can be a few inches to as much as six feet long, depending on the length the caster can handle.

The third leader section (10) consists of either piano wire (#15), nylon-coated cable or heavy monofilament. Its length can be from a few inches to a few feet. A Tankichi hook (11) of #48 to #50 size is tied to the end of this leader.

A swivel with brazed stop ring (12) joins the second leader section to the anchor line (13). The swivel with brazed stop ring can be store bought or it can be assembled from a barrel swivel (3/0 for strength) and large split rings (two for strength).

The anchor line consists of a 20- or 30-pound test cord. The length of the cord depends on the length of the second leader section. The combined length of the two should not be so long that casting ease will be hampered.

Complete the rig by using an anchoring sinker with wire claws (14). The sinker can be from 6 to 12 ounces, depending on the size of the angler and the tackle he (or she) is using.

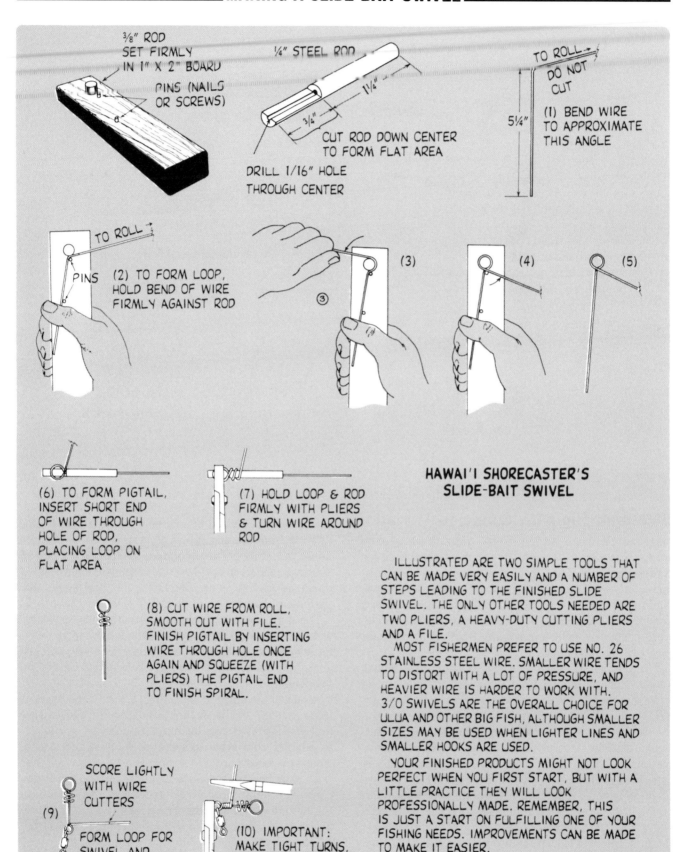

3/8" ROD SET FIRMLY IN 1" X 2" BOARD

PINS (NAILS OR SCREWS)

1/4" STEEL ROD

1/4"

3/4"

CUT ROD DOWN CENTER TO FORM FLAT AREA

DRILL 1/16" HOLE THROUGH CENTER

TO ROLL

DO NOT CUT

5 1/4"

(1) BEND WIRE TO APPROXIMATE THIS ANGLE

TO ROLL

PINS

(2) TO FORM LOOP, HOLD BEND OF WIRE FIRMLY AGAINST ROD

(3)

(4)

(5)

(6) TO FORM PIGTAIL, INSERT SHORT END OF WIRE THROUGH HOLE OF ROD, PLACING LOOP ON FLAT AREA

(7) HOLD LOOP & ROD FIRMLY WITH PLIERS & TURN WIRE AROUND ROD

HAWAI'I SHORECASTER'S SLIDE-BAIT SWIVEL

(8) CUT WIRE FROM ROLL, SMOOTH OUT WITH FILE. FINISH PIGTAIL BY INSERTING WIRE THROUGH HOLE ONCE AGAIN AND SQUEEZE (WITH PLIERS) THE PIGTAIL END TO FINISH SPIRAL.

SCORE LIGHTLY WITH WIRE CUTTERS

(9)

FORM LOOP FOR SWIVEL AND INSERT SWIVEL

(10) IMPORTANT: MAKE TIGHT TURNS, WIRE SHOULD SNAP AT SCORE.

ILLUSTRATED ARE TWO SIMPLE TOOLS THAT CAN BE MADE VERY EASILY AND A NUMBER OF STEPS LEADING TO THE FINISHED SLIDE SWIVEL. THE ONLY OTHER TOOLS NEEDED ARE TWO PLIERS, A HEAVY-DUTY CUTTING PLIERS AND A FILE.

MOST FISHERMEN PREFER TO USE NO. 26 STAINLESS STEEL WIRE. SMALLER WIRE TENDS TO DISTORT WITH A LOT OF PRESSURE, AND HEAVIER WIRE IS HARDER TO WORK WITH. 3/0 SWIVELS ARE THE OVERALL CHOICE FOR ULUA AND OTHER BIG FISH, ALTHOUGH SMALLER SIZES MAY BE USED WHEN LIGHTER LINES AND SMALLER HOOKS ARE USED.

YOUR FINISHED PRODUCTS MIGHT NOT LOOK PERFECT WHEN YOU FIRST START, BUT WITH A LITTLE PRACTICE THEY WILL LOOK PROFESSIONALLY MADE. REMEMBER, THIS IS JUST A START ON FULFILLING ONE OF YOUR FISHING NEEDS. IMPROVEMENTS CAN BE MADE TO MAKE IT EASIER.

Dunking

Heavy-duty spinning gear provides a sporting alternative to slide-baiting in areas where the ulua grounds are shallow, sandy bottomed and sloping. Rods may still be 10 to 12 feet long, but are much more flexible, requiring a lot less casting effort. That's important because the dunker will do far more casting than the bait slider. Smaller baits are essential; the bait rides the cast with the sinker. Lines may be as tough as 50-pound test, yet many dunkers prefer lines testing 20 to 30. Large capacity reels are essential with good gearing systems for fast and dependable line pickup and strong, smooth drags to maintain steady pressure. Large capacity may mean a spool that can hold 400 yards of 20-pound test line, but any ulua that drags that much away from a fisherman with his heels dug into the sand will rarely be landed.

The diagrams show the basic dunking rig with a description of variations appealing to different tastes.

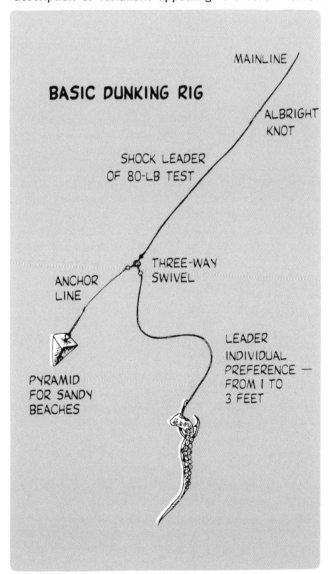

BASIC DUNKING RIG

MAINLINE

ALBRIGHT KNOT

SHOCK LEADER OF 80-LB TEST

ANCHOR LINE

THREE-WAY SWIVEL

LEADER INDIVIDUAL PREFERENCE — FROM 1 TO 3 FEET

PYRAMID FOR SANDY BEACHES

Dunking is the least productive and, therefore, least interesting method for ulua. Most fishermen who dunk are after 'o'io, large papio or smaller ulua. The problem is that dunkers generally work shallow sandy places during the daytime. These aren't the prime ulua conditions. Furthermore, dunking limits the size of the bait offered. You can only cast a relatively small bait. Occasionally a big fish will grab a slice of squid or an octopus tentacle (good dunking baits), but generally they like a real mouthful.

To dunk for ulua, pick deep sandy channels that open out on deep water. Or drop your bait in the depression between the surf and the low rise of sand that forms outside the surf line.

If you want to put your rod in a sand spike, make sure the spike is several feet long and your drag is set loose enough to let line go before the spike is pulled from the sand. Lots of wonderful dunking rods have been lost when the sand spike gave way.

Fish early in the morning at the crack of dawn or late in the afternoon.

Whipping

For many, whipping is the ultimate challenge, the best test of skill, strategy and technique. Anglers who struggle with 60- and 70-pound ulua on slide-baiting gear know what it is like to wrestle giants, yet some slay these Goliaths with a pea-shooter. After all, the IGFA awarded a world record to Big Island fisherman Hugh Fleming for a 54-pound ulua caught on 16-pound test line, proof (for those who need it) that it can be done.

Sixteen-pound test line, however, is living dangerously. If the fish won't break it, the reef usually will. Most whippers use at least 20-pound test with 25 to 30 being closer to the standard. Whipping from a boat toward shore gives the angler enough advantage to allow a greater chance with lighter line.

Follow the rules, if you want to whip the big ones.

Use a well-built rod with hard smooth guides. You have to be able to trust your tackle to stay together in a long fight and your guides to protect your line from chafing.

Pick a reel with good line capacity, strong gearing and a fast retrieve. The latter is especially important because ulua like fast-moving lures.

Beef up your line with as long a leader as you can cast. For most people, this is about three to four feet. For a longer leader, don't use a swivel (it won't go through the guides) and knot the line directly to the leader with an albright knot. This joint can be reeled through the guides and down onto the spool. Fifty- to 80-pound test nylon leaders are the minimum.

Vary the size of your lures. Sometimes, the ulua will only charge after a 6- or 7-inch chugger. Other times, a ½-ounce jig works best. Have different, in-between sized lures.

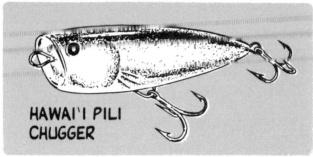

HAWAI'I PILI CHUGGER

Vary your retrieve. On some days, the ulua want a lure to race across the surface. At other times, they'll only show interest in a sinking lure jigged along the bottom.

Work deeper water along the edges of broken bottom with coral heads showing a few feet under the surface. Shallow water is rarely the home for ulua. They like to lurk in deeper water, coursing along the edges of steep cliffs.

Keep your hooks sharp. Ulua don't always swallow a lure when they strike. Occasionally, they try to shove it around with their shoulders. Sharp hooks will get you extra fish through accidental snagging.

Trolling

The secret to trolling success is in fishing the right areas. Most spots easily accessible to trollers have been plowed through so many times that the big fish dive for the bottom any time they hear the sound of an engine. The only way to fish easily accessible spots is with live bait rigged to swim as deep as possible. Such live baits can be 'opelu, akule, small aku or any other small member of the tuna family.

In the remote regions where ulua are still unaccustomed to being raked over by passing boats, they will hit just about anything offered. We've taken them on every kind of trolling lure including jets, plastic-headed big-game plugs, swimming minnow lures, spoons, trolling feathers and fixed-hook jigs. Our greatest successes have been with swimming minnow plugs and trolling feathers rigged with strips of bait.

Best results have come in waters 40 feet deep or less and at trolling speeds of 4 or 5 knots. To fish the most likely spots, around rocks and coral heads rising up from the bottom, we maneuver the boat in the deeper water and swing the trolling lines as close to the rocks as we can get them.

Bottom Fishing

Ulua are caught from lines dropped from boats in many different depths from a few fathoms down to a hundred fathoms or more. The most productive depth seems to be between 20 and 30 fathoms. The giant 179-pound ulua caught off Makena, Maui, for example, was hooked in 125 feet of water. It took a live 'opelu, by the way, and struck at one o'clock in the afternoon.

Though many large ulua are caught bottom fishing during the day, the most successful times seem to be during the night with the half-hour before dawn being especially good in many places.

Live baits, especially 'opelu and akule, are best, but any bait freshly cut from 'opelu, akule, squid, octopus or tuna will do the job.

Any bottom fishing rig will work, from simple spreaders on up through the stone-dropping gear used by ahi fishermen.

Get the ulua away from the bottom as quickly as possible once he is hooked. Ulua are known to dive for caves once they've realized they've just grabbed an indigestible mouthful of hook and leader.

Thirty-five Tips on Fishing for Ulua

1. For heavy-duty whipping, pick a fast taper rod to match your size. I'm 6 feet tall, 200 pounds and prefer a 9- to 10-foot graphite rod with plenty of backbone. I can toss a 2-ounce lure a respectable distance on 30-pound test line. But what is right for me may not be as good for you as something else will.

2. Get the feel of how much pressure your tackle can stand before a fish tells you that you don't know. You'll need a partner to help. Tie your line to a spring scale. Give the scale to your partner to hold. Back off to fighting distance — say, 30 yards or more — and try pumping against your partner. Your partner should read the scale, giving you the readings for each pump. With this information, you should be able to adjust your drag for maximum power. Add the results of a second experiment to your equation. With your drag set where you think you want it, have your partner walk away. First, you'll be surprised at how fast your spool spins at normal walking speed and how hard it is to keep your rod tip up with only 10 or 15 pounds of drag showing on the scale. You should come away with a better appreciation of how hard you can fight your fish.

3. Don't overlook sandy beaches as whipping spots. Big ulua will come into the surf to chase bait fish tumbled around by the churning waves. This is especially true in the early morning or evening. As the light shines through breaking waves, you'll enjoy the thrill of seeing the menacing shadow coursing through the wall of water to crash your lure.

4. Ulua are "opportunistic feeders," meaning they'll eat anything that looks good. Remember that when you pick lures. Ulua can be caught whipping with underwater plugs (Mirr-O-Lures and Rapalas, for example), surface disturbers (any kind of chugger, even homemade jobs like the Moloka'i ulua plug), and darters (the Pfleuger Ballerina has a long record of success). They'll eat spoons and jigs. They'll eat any kind of standard trolling lure. They'll charge anything that moves. And this is the key. It's got to move if it's going to move fish.

MOLOKA'I ULUA PLUG

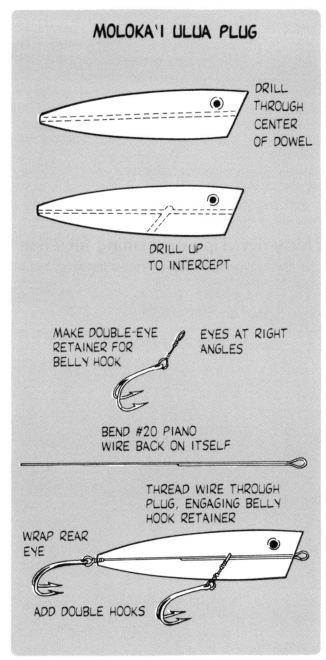

DRILL THROUGH CENTER OF DOWEL

DRILL UP TO INTERCEPT

MAKE DOUBLE-EYE RETAINER FOR BELLY HOOK

EYES AT RIGHT ANGLES

BEND #20 PIANO WIRE BACK ON ITSELF

THREAD WIRE THROUGH PLUG, ENGAGING BELLY HOOK RETAINER

WRAP REAR EYE

ADD DOUBLE HOOKS

8. Be ready with the proper gaff for the job. When casting from sea-level perches, carry a small hand gaff. If you fish more than a few feet above the water, you'll need a longer pole gaff. For high perches, equip yourself with a sliding gaff. This type of gaff was developed on the mainland for fishing from bridges, but the Hawaiian version is even better. The bridge gaff is simply a grapnel with four prongs. You attach it to your line with a snap or a slide buckle. The gaff should be attached to a heavy cord strong enough to haul in a big fish. It should also be attached to a floater buoyant enough to keep it at the surface. Slide the gaff down the line and hope the floater holds it in position to snatch your fish. The Hawaiian version is a double hooker with slide rings positioned to orient the hooks toward the fish.

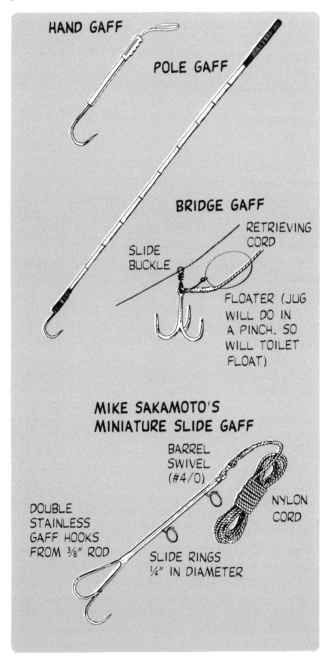

HAND GAFF

POLE GAFF

BRIDGE GAFF

SLIDE BUCKLE

RETRIEVING CORD

FLOATER (JUG WILL DO IN A PINCH. SO WILL TOILET FLOAT)

MIKE SAKAMOTO'S MINIATURE SLIDE GAFF

BARREL SWIVEL (#4/0)

NYLON CORD

DOUBLE STAINLESS GAFF HOOKS FROM 3/8" ROD

SLIDE RINGS 1/4" IN DIAMETER

5. Whenever possible, select lures with wire-through construction. Lures with screw eyes are notorious for losing fish as the screws pull out. Standard hooks can also be too weak for big fish. Remove any lightweight treble hooks and replace them with sturdy double hooks.

6. When using spoons, be sure to have both gold and silver lures. Because of the way fish see light and the way the characteristics of light change throughout the day, sometimes the gold will work much better than the silver.

7. When slide-baiting, use a safety line to secure your pole. Heavy ulua strikes break rods. Anchor the safety line to the rocks with a railroad spike or other heavy metal bar.

9. When setting your drag, make it lighter than the maximum you feel you can get away with. You can always add more pressure as needed by cupping the spool of a spinning reel or pressing your thumbs against the spool sides of a conventional reel. This allows you to increase your drag, but still keeps it light enough to respond to a sudden strong surge by the fish.

10. When sliding bait or whipping the shore, be prepared to catch anything. Ulua fishermen are occasionally surprised by mahimahi, ahi, aku, kawakawa, barracuda, sea bass, kahala and uku — not to mention a lot of sharks and eels.

11. At night, ulua shy away from light. Shining lights on the water will chase them away, but you can use this to your advantage in herding a hooked ulua away from underwater obstacles. If your fish runs toward a known coral head, shine a light on it and the fish will veer away.

12. When sliding bait from the beach, you may need to use a longer rod (13 feet or more). The long rod may give you more casting distance and will get the line angle up higher for easier sliding. You'll need the distance to reach deeper waters, of course. For example, Moloka'i surf-caster Lolly Agliam caught his biggest ulua, 135 pounds, with a 15-foot rod and a 9/0 surf reel fished from a sandy beach.

13. Many anglers believe ulua bite best during the tide change. They adjust their fishing schedule to make sure their lines are in position ahead of time with a fresh bait.

14. Catching tohei for bait is easiest at night. You can often find them while torching on reefs. As a matter of fact, night torching will provide lots of different kinds of creatures for bait including puhi, tako and small fishes.

15. Conditions that are perfect for fishing may not be very good for catching. Many anglers report that nights of glassy smooth seas bring poor catches. Rough choppy seas bring the ulua.

16. Another thing that brings the ulua is palu. Chum with pounded bait, but do the pounding at the water's edge. The smell and taste of the bits of pounded eel and other bait fish form an enticing slick, but the sound of the pounding seems to attract ulua, too. That's not just conjecture. SCUBA divers in search of ulua will sometimes employ a similar trick. They sit on the bottom and bang rocks together. Ulua swim in to find out what is going on. Some fishing spots in use for ages have depressions ground into the rocks from centuries of palu pounding.

17. Don't assume you can't fish slide-bait if you are young, small or female. You may need help with the casting, but not with the other chores, including fighting the fish. Pauline Sugimoto, for example, caught a potential women's world record for 80-pound class tackle. Her 58½-pound fish was caught on a 10-foot rod and a 6/0 reel using an 8-ounce casting weight. Study those dimensions and you'll see that the gear was scaled

down to fit her 5'2" size. That's the secret, just as it was the secret to success for 9 year old Reyn Hata. At that early age, Reyn could already boast a 36-pounder. His scaled down gear included a 9-foot rod, 3/0 reel, 50-pound test line and a 6-ounce sinker.

18. The three types of ulua you are most likely to catch are the white ulua, 'omilu and kagami. some places produce a lot of kagami, a diamond-shaped fish with a bright silvery skin, flat body and long fin filaments. Shallow waters are the home of the 'omilu, or blue trevally. 'Omilu are the smallest of the big ulua, rarely going much over 20 pounds. The whites are the largest, found in the deepest water and well-deserving of their name "giant trevally."

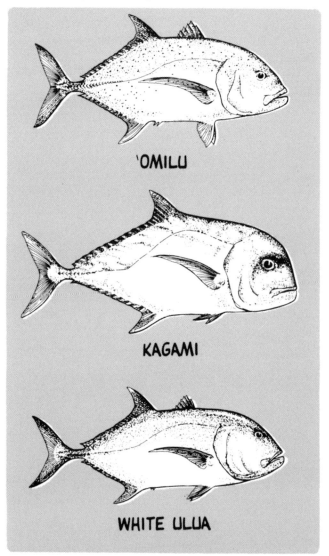

'OMILU

KAGAMI

WHITE ULUA

19. Inevitably in ulua fishing, a hooked fish will reach safety in the rocks, snagging your line in the process. That's not necessarily the end of the battle. Release the tension on the line, loosen the drag and wait. Frequently, the ulua will free himself and the fight resumes. Be prepared to wait for hours, if necessary. It can take that long.

20. When trolling for ulua, keep the drag set as strongly as the line and leader can take. A striking ulua will try to head for the rocks below. A firm drag can prevent him from turning his head. This will give you a chance to pull him out into deeper water, increasing your chances of boating him.

21. When akule are swarming in shallow water, trolling a live akule on a downrigger can be a sure-fire method of picking up ulua and large papio. In some spots, you only need to get the akule down 20 or 30 feet.

AKULE FISHED FROM DOWNRIGGER

22. If eel is such a great bait for sliding, why not use it for trolling or whipping? Either way, the eel can be rigged quickly with an open-eye bait needle and a short leader that matches the length of the eel from snout to vent. A flexible leader such as heavy mono or light cable wire is best, with the latter being almost too stiff. Crimp a loop in one end of the leader and hang a hook on the other. With the loop end of the leader on the needle, insert the point in the vent, and thread the leader through the bait. When the loop is inside the mouth, thread the main wire leader through the top of the head, engage the loop, and then push the main leader out the bottom jaw. Twist the main leader back on itself to form a tight loop, clamping the mouth firmly shut.

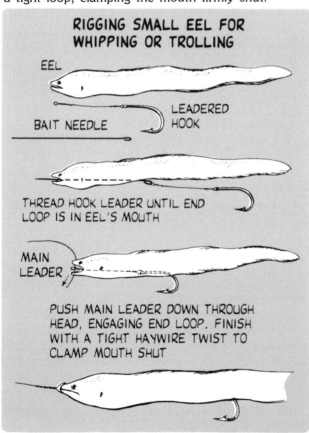

RIGGING SMALL EEL FOR WHIPPING OR TROLLING

EEL

BAIT NEEDLE

LEADERED HOOK

THREAD HOOK LEADER UNTIL END LOOP IS IN EEL'S MOUTH

MAIN LEADER

PUSH MAIN LEADER DOWN THROUGH HEAD, ENGAGING END LOOP. FINISH WITH A TIGHT HAYWIRE TWIST TO CLAMP MOUTH SHUT

Troll it slowly so it swims, or skip it. If you want to whip with an eel, pick the smallest kind, no more than a foot or so long. It's hard to cast, but worth the extra effort.

FISHERMAN HAULING ULUA ON BACKPACK FRAME

23. Be prepared. Ulua are big and you'll generally catch them a long walk from the nearest jeep trail. Experienced fishermen bring backpack frames to haul out the big ones.

24. The best ulua fishermen have bags under their eyes. Ulua bite best at night, meaning that the guys who are into fish don't get much sleep. But many big ulua are caught in daylight hours. Don't give up just because the sun is shining.

25. Slide-baiting allows you to put out a fresh bait without reeling in the line and recasting. As a result, you may have two or more baits on the same line, both waiting for ulua. Since ulua generally travel with partners, you'll occasionally hook them in pairs. The wire retainer on the leader can help keep the top ulua from running the slide buckle back up the line when the bottom ulua heads in the opposite direction.

26. Ulua like to strike from ambush. They wouldn't get much to eat if they advertised their presence to the reef fish they feed on. In selecting waters to whip, bear that in mind. Look for deep-water places surrounding coral heads that might provide cover. At night, ulua are more likely to come out into the open. That's why good whipping spots aren't always good slide-baiting grounds and vice versa.

27. Whipping from a boat gives the fisherman a special advantage over the fish, but only if the boaters remember to stay in deep water and cast toward the shallows. Watch for the strike as the lure leaves the protection of the reef and races out into the exposed depths. When an ulua charges up from the bottom to intercept the lure, the whipper can plane the fish away from the bottom by making the ulua pull in an arc with the boat in the center. Try that from shore and the fish dives right into the bottom, cutting the line in the process.

DIVE TAKES ULUA AWAY FROM SHALLOW OBSTRUCTIONS, **ADVANTAGE:** ANGLER

28. When baiting a Tankichi hook, always keep as much of the hook exposed as possible. The hook depends on its shape to trap the fish's jawbone. If the hook opening is clogged up with bait, you'll get a skimpy purchase on the jaw, at best. Hook the bait lightly; then tie it on, if necessary, to hold it securely.

29. Don't try to make an all-out cast with a dry line. Your first cast with a revolving spool reel should be to get the line wet. Make it gentle. Casting a dry line is hard on the thumb and the equipment. Once the line is wet, it is softer, lays better on the reel and flows through the guides more easily.

30. Some whippers believe that ulua will not feed in the surfline unless the water is warm to the touch — from the mid 70s to the mid 80s. This can vary from place to place. Keep track of the water temperature to see if it is a factor on your favorite grounds.

31. Like many species of fish, ulua will taste better if it is bled immediately after capture. East Coast fishermen bleed jacks by cutting the tail stump, but there is a much better way. Cut into the border of the gill opening behind the gills. Cut deep enough to release a heavy flow of blood. The blood will carry away some of the heat of the fish. It is also the blood that spoils quickest in the body tissue.

32. Whippers sometimes need additional weight for casting distance. Several types of lures can be altered effectively by adding weight. Hollow-bodied lures like the Mirr-O-Lure, for example, can be filled with a mixture of lead pieces and epoxy resin. Some types of lures can be fished effectively when trailed behind a torpedo casting lead if the leader between lead and lure is long enough (three feet or more). Swimming plugs and spoons are good examples. So are curly-tailed plastic worms and grubs.

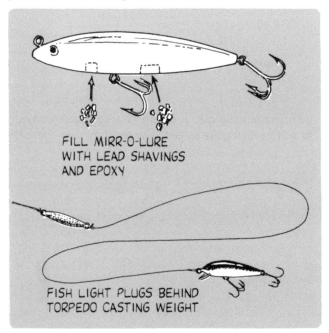

FILL MIRR-O-LURE WITH LEAD SHAVINGS AND EPOXY

FISH LIGHT PLUGS BEHIND TORPEDO CASTING WEIGHT

33. Don't attach your leader to the lure with a snap. Use a split ring or an ice-tong connector. Ulua mangle simple safety pin connectors.

USE SPLIT RING OR ICE TONG BUT NEVER SAFETY PIN

34. To keep your slide bait up off the bottom, you can increase the length of your anchor line without increasing your casting problems. First, make up a tight roll of quick-dissolving toilet paper (the kind sold for use in marine and RV heads). Make your wad at least as big around as your thumb. Wrap your long (as much as 10 feet or more) anchor line around the wad, securing the last wraps with half hitches. Cast the sinker, and when the toilet paper dissolves, the anchor line will stretch out to full length. Wait till this happens before you slide your bait.

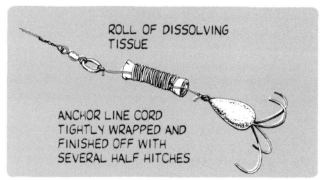

ROLL OF DISSOLVING TISSUE

ANCHOR LINE CORD TIGHTLY WRAPPED AND FINISHED OFF WITH SEVERAL HALF HITCHES

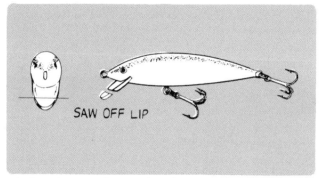

SAW OFF LIP

35. When trolling or whipping with Rapalas or other lipped swimming plugs, try shortening the lip. The modified version can be pulled through the water faster without spinning out. It doesn't roll so much from side to side or kick quite as fast. The shortened lip offers less wind resistance for casting, increasing your distance. To shorten the lip, clamp it firmly in a vise, making sure the lure is perfectly upright in its swimming position. Saw carefully with a fine-toothed blade and finish off with a file.

Seasickness

The Offshore Blues

For many years I fished from shore and avoided boats for an embarrassing and painful reason: I got seasick just about as fast as the boat could get out the harbor mouth, remained in agony throughout the entire trip and never really returned to normal for two or three days.

I agree thoroughly with that classic description of *mal de mer*, "first you are afraid you're going to die, then you're afraid you won't."

But the lure of the big catches offshore made me determined to beat the problem. Fortunately, through a program I designed for myself, I've conquered my seasickness so well that I've been comfortable fishing for salmon off the tempestuous Columbia River bar, marlin in raging seas off New Zealand and bluefish in the stormy North Atlantic.

Knowing (and it is true) that seasickness "is all in your head" is small comfort for the man whose guts are twisting violently in continuous spasms timed to the roll and pitch of every wave.

Getting it out of your head is the first step in beating seasickness, but how can you get it out of your head if you are so worried about it that it is the only thing you can think about?

There is an unfortunate rule of the sea: if you are afraid of getting seasick, you will. Worrying about it is the major contributing factor.

The fishing population may be separated into those who hang over the rail and those who don't, but it is not divided up into those who always get seasick and those who never feel a twinge. Any person who has a healthy balance system (controlled by the semicircular canals in the inner ear) will get seasick under certain combinations of conditions.

You are in good company if you get seasick. Lord Nelson was supposedly so seasick at the Battle of Trafalgar that he was confined to his cabin during one of his greatest sea victories.

As a matter of fact, oceanic researchers have proved to their own satisfaction that seasickness can even be induced in fish!

Obviously, your goal is to reach that point where you take boat rides in comfort without ever even thinking about seasickness, because thinking about it is your first step toward the rail.

The only way this can be done is through positive experiences with the sea — a succession of trips that build up your confidence. Once you've earned your "sea legs" through comfortable trips during which you've held onto your stomach, you'll find that seasickness never enters your mind.

But how can you ensure that your first few trips will be good experiences? The answer for me was a combination of medication and common-sense do's and don'ts.

First the medication. I was able to do it without prescription drugs, but there is a powerful combination of vertigo fighters you can get through your doctor. If he does not know of any you might suggest a preparation of phenergan and epiedrine.

These drugs should only be taken after a physical examination and may have some side effects you won't like. Phenergan, for example, may cause drowsiness. It may also make you retain bodily fluids, a problem if you have difficulties in your urinary tract, notably, prostatitis.

Two over-the-counter drugs may be of help under the normal sea conditions common along our lee coasts.

These are sold under the trade names Dramamine and Marezine. I've had especially good luck with the latter, and it was a major part of my own cure. Surprisingly, these drugs are antihistamines, though that may not be startling to anyone who knows chemotherapy a lot better than I do.

Now for the common sense:

(1) Don't assume that you are automatically going to get seasick because you experienced motion sickness (car sickness, for example) as a child. Kids are much more susceptible to motion sickness, and you have already outgrown that susceptibility.

(2) Watch what you eat, but do eat! Eat plain foods in moderation. Avoid greasy or highly seasoned foods. I'm big on peanut butter and jelly sandwiches for my seagoing lunches, after a cereal and toast breakfast. As a matter of fact, I'll often go all day munching on a back-packer's blend of granola, a trick I picked up when the camping editor of *Field and Stream* was a guest on my boat.

If you don't eat, your blood sugar level goes down and you may feel sick just from that. When mine goes down, I get headaches and an acid stomach. Those are similar enough to some of the first symptoms of seasickness that it is easy for me to convince myself that I'm on the way to seasickness when I'm only hungry.

(3) Don't drink alcohol, but do drink! Alcohol may affect your balance system, and that is the control center for motion sickness. Dehydration, on the other hand, from lack of fluid intake and exposure to the sun can start a blinding headache which starts a cycle of misery that ends up in your guts.

(4) Pick your day. Those first few trips should be on a gentle sea. Don't be afraid to bow out of a trip if the sea turns rough. You've got long years of fishing ahead of you once you've got your stomach under control.

(5) Make your first trips short ones. Plan a few half-day trips to start with, and you will have a lot less anxiety.

(6) Pick your spot. Choose a place on the boat where you can get plenty of fresh air, free of the smelly fumes of fuel and dead fish or bait, and where you can keep a clear view of the horizon. The latter is important in helping you keep your head and neck stable, thus minimizing the sloshing around of the fluid in your semi-circular canals.

(7) Keep your visibility clear. Wear sunglasses to protect your eyes from surrounding glare that might give you a headache, and keep those glasses wiped clean of the fog of salt spray. If you normally wear prescription glasses or contact lenses, be sure to wear them fishing. When you can see the horizon clearly and are able to keep your surroundings in focus, you'll have a much better chance of avoiding the loss of internal control that leads to nausea.

(8) Stay out of the sun. Anything that may tend to make you feel uncomfortable will increase your chances of getting sick. Just in case the boat does not have a cover, bring a baseball cap, sunglasses and a light-colored, long sleeved shirt to block out those hot, penetrating rays.

You know you've beaten it when you can board ship with someone else who is sick and your only gut feeling is sympathy for the poor devil.

Cleaning Your Catch

Fish Preparation Begins with the Hookup

The second best reason to go fishing is to bring home something good to eat. If you have to ask what the very best reason is, you have no future as a "sport" fisherman.

Fish is good food. But it is only good if it is prepared right. Proper preparation doesn't mean just cooking. After all, one of the best ways of enjoying the flavor of fish is to eat it raw as sashimi.

Preparation means all of the things you do from the time your fish is safely landed until the time it is served.

Kill your fish quickly. Letting it die slowly from lack of oxygen can affect the flavor of the meat. Tuna fishermen will tell you that even the effect of a long fight can spoil the meat of ahi.

Knock the fish on the head with a billy to stun it. Then cool it as quickly as possible. If you can, put it on ice in a cooler or in an insulated bag that has ice.

If you cannot put it on ice, put it in a damp cloth bag. Splash water on the bag occasionally. As the water evaporates, it will steal heat from the fish and keep the fish cooler than the air. As much as possible, keep your fish in the shade. The cooler you can keep your catch, the longer it will keep its flavor and the better it will taste.

After your fishing trip is over, clean your fish before storing it in the refrigerator or freezer.

Let's go through the steps of cleaning a fish. Every fisherman has his own special methods. I'm going to describe the steps I think are easiest. You'll learn other methods as you become more experienced. And you'll learn special methods for cleaning special types of fish.

Your tools are a knife, a cleaning board and a fish scaler. The best knives are special fileting knives. They have a long, slender, curved blade that comes to a

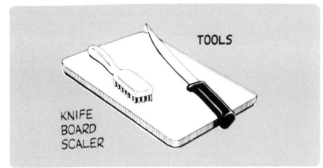

sharp point. My favorite knife has a spoon that sticks out of the handle. The spoon helps me scrape the blood out of the stomach cavity. A cleaning board can be wood or plastic. Plastic boards are easier to clean. The fish scaler has triangular teeth, which pulls the scales loose from the skin as you scrape them gently across the outside of the fish.

Scaling is the first thing to do if you wish to cook the fish with the skin. In some dishes, the skin adds flavor to the food. In others, the skin helps keep the fish from falling apart during cooking. But in dishes such as sashimi or fish kabobs, the skin should be removed so it need not be scaled. To scale the fish, scrape all parts with the scaler and rinse the loose scales off with fresh water.

The next step is to remove the head, gills and entrails. This is done by making three cuts. The first cut (cut A) is made through the belly skin behind the belly fins. Cut B is along the side, starting above the vent and slicing forward to meet cut A. Cut C is made by slicing in at an angle behind the side fins. Cuts A and C should be made on both sides.

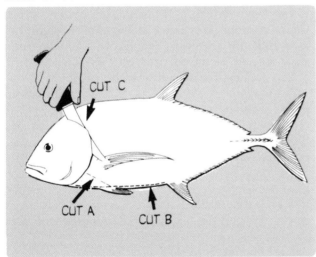

The knife should be angled forward, and the slice should be made deep enough to reach the backbone. The entrails should be broken (or cut) free at the back end of the stomach by reaching into cut B. Break the backbone by forcing the severed head sideways. Now the head can be pulled free. With it will come the gills and entrails altogether.

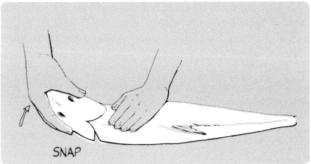

If the fish is small, you will not want to filet it. You'll want to cook it whole. Clean the inside of the stomach cavity. Scrape and rinse out the blood along the top of the stomach cavity. Remove the tail fins by cutting through the backbone where the tail joins the body. Remove the back and belly fins by slicing into the body on both sides of the fins and pulling the fins out.

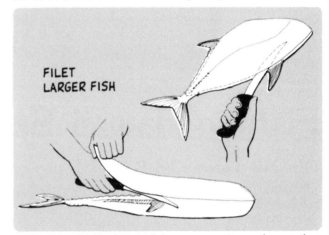

You should filet larger fish to get sections of meat that are boneless. To filet a large fish, slide the knife along the backbone with the tip reaching in to touch the spine. Slice in from the back and then up from the belly. The filets should be loose except where they attach to the spine itself. To free the filet, lift the loose part near the tail and slide the knife along the spine as you lift the filet.

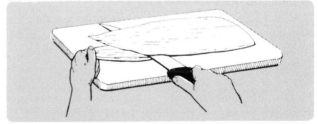

The skin should still be on the filet. If you want to skin the filet but still leave each side in one piece, put the filet on the cutting board with the skin side down. Loosen the skin near the tail by slicing with your knife. Then grab the skin with your left hand. Press the knife against the board on a slight angle and pull the skin, wiggling it as you pull. The knife should slice the skin free as the filet is pulled toward you.

Now cut off the rib cage and you have a clean skinless filet. It won't be completely boneless. There is a thin ridge of bones that runs down along the center of each filet.

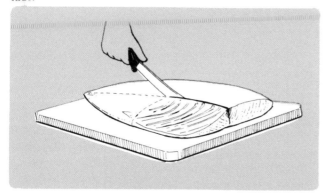

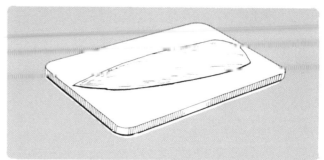

For a boneless, skinless section of fish, like the kind you need for sashimi, let's go back to the step where we have a filet with the skin still on it. Place the filet skin side down. Slice down through the filet next to the center ridge of bones. Don't cut through the skin. When your knife blade reaches the skin, turn the blade sideways and slice out along the skin.

Now you've got a clean skinless and boneless piece of fish. This section can be sliced thinly and served as a pupu on shredded cabbage with a shoyu and mustard sauce. Or you can slice it into thicker chunks, marinate it in teriyaki sauce, thread it on wooden skewers and grill it over charcoal as fish kabobs. Or you can bread it in tempura batter and deep fry it for tempura fish. Or you can sprinkle it with corn meal, parmesan cheese and salt and then pan fry it. Or you can. . . The ideas for cooking fish can go on forever.

Every way of cooking fish is tasty and flavorful as long as the fish is well cared for by the fisherman before the cook takes over.

Fishing Hawaii Style

Oh, The Good Old Days!

Hawai'i's potential as a sport fishing center first achieved national prominence in the late 1930s and early 1940s with the publication of books by S. Kip Farrington Jr. and Harlan Major.

To be sure, Hawai'i's great fishing had been heard of around the world before then; in fact three Hawaiian catches were already on the record books as world beaters. The first of these was a 125-pound ono caught by George Stickney off O'ahu. The record has been repeatedly broken and now stands at 149-pounds, but all of these bigger fish have been caught at other spots around the world — not Hawai'i.

When was the last time you heard of a Hawaiian ono weighing more than 100 pounds? Farrington, in his book, *Pacific Gamefishing,* published in 1942, by Coward-McCann, Inc., reported that 100-pounders were not unusual in Hawai'i. By that time a lot of mainlanders had already gotten the chance to experience Hawai'i's fishing — and other kinds of excitement — firsthand when Uncle Sam sent them out here as fighting men. Fish fighting wasn't exactly what Uncle Sam had in mind, but intrepid anglers everywhere know how to cash in on opportunities, and some of them brought back fascinating stories about big Hawaiian fish.

Another world record from Hawai'i in this era was for a 67½-pound mahimahi caught by Freddy McNamarra.

Fortunately for modern Hawai'i fishermen, it is still possible to catch mahimahi of this size; however, the diminishing numbers of mahimahi taken from Hawai'i waters in recent years are a cause of alarm.

The third record, a 184-pound ahi caught by Mrs. Charles Cooke, was listed as the largest Allison tuna ever taken by a woman. This record is broken almost monthly, and the top ahi catch by a woman now stands at 254 pounds. Fittingly, it was also caught in Hawai'i.

Farrington has been hailed as one of the all-time greats of fishing and outdoor writing at a time when his competitors included guys like Zane Grey and Van Campen Heilner. His *Pacific Game Fishing* is a collector's item.

The book's chapter on fishing in the Hawaiian Islands gave mainlanders a different view of these islands than that appearing daily on the front pages of newspapers across the world — Hawai'i, the staging area for war in the Pacific.

The chapter is replete with pictures: record fish, Farrington fighting an ahi from the deck of Dudley Lewis's *Piko*, early wooden and feather trolling lures, fishing for mullet from fishing chairs along the Ala Wai, a converted U.S. Navy launch trolling off Pearl Harbor, etc.

Farrington touted the Islands as a place where 10 varieties of game fish grew to sizes unheard of in the rest of the world. For Farrington, Hawai'i had everything: big fish, deep clear water and no sharks to mutilate your catch. Superb accommodations? One took that for granted in Hawai'i, despite the beastly hostilities.

Farrington considered the yellowfin tuna the star performer of the Hawaiian Islands "and well worth the 2,200 miles from the Pacific Coast to catch."

Unfortunately, his advice was not always worth taking despite his recognized expertise. He claimed that visitors would find the best fishing in Kona during the winter months and that not many ahi had been taken off the Kona coast. Maybe he was giving an accurate report for that time in history, but both statements viewed in present terms are the reverse of the true picture.

He also claimed that ahi of up to 500 pounds had been taken by commercial fishermen while flagline fishing in depths of 30 fathoms. This was a period of time in marine biology where fish were routinely misidentified, and it is easy to confuse the ahi (Allison yellowfin tuna) with the po'onui (bigeye tuna). Both species have yellow fins and robust bodies, but the bigeye tuna is definitely the larger species and can conceivably grow to 500 pounds. Record bigeyes of over 400 pounds have been boated off Peru.

Farrington cautioned that ahi trollers should hold the rod in their hands to be ready for the strike with the butt in the gimbals and the harness already attached. Given the blazing speed and locomotive power of the ahi, this would seem to be a good practice only for the fisherman willing to fight his fish by swimming after it; he would certainly end up in the drink if he relaxed at the moment the fish hit.

These were days when blue marlin were caught daily, yet anglers refused to believe the blue was found in the Pacific. Hawai'i's big billfish were called "silver marlin."

Farrington wrote, "There is practically no noticeable difference between the blue and the silver marlin so far as shape is concerned." He added, "If you saw one alongside the boat or even on the dock, you would, I'm sure, believe it was a blue marlin."

Marine biologists have, of course, proved him right. Yet, despite the evidence in their eyes, fishermen called these billfish "silver marlin" because of the bright metallic sheen displayed when they jump out of the water during the fight.

Perhaps the fish that captured Farrington's imagination most was the bonefish, our 'o'io. The world record for bonefish at that time was a 13¾-pound fish caught at Bimini. "This fish is the world's record only because bonefishermen of the Hawaiian Islands have never sent in affidavits of the fish they have taken," Farrington wrote. Then he stunned the bonefishermen of the Atlantic by reporting his own personal observation of bonefish exceeding 25 pounds!

Hawai'i's fishing lures also impressed Farrington. He wrote of the "many kinds of beautiful native feather baits" of so many varieties "that most of their cabins look like chicken coops." The pearl shell Polynesian trolling lures intrigued him so much he tried to buy one, but its owner refused the princely sum of $25 for it, a figure that would be close to $200 today, assuming the constant rate of inflation over the intervening years.

Harlan Major's book, *Salt Water Fishing Tackle*, seems an unlikely place to find information about fishing in Hawai'i. However, in 1939, when the book was written, Major was a field correspondent for the Bishop Museum and was very interested in the methods used throughout Polynesia.

Like Farrington, Major was especially fascinated by the pearl lures. In regards to the catching of aku, Major claimed, "Time and again I have tried every modern lure in my tackle box against one of these 'pearls' as they are called, but the modern bait could do no better than one fish to about five for the pearl."

So concerned were the fishermen of the day about the possibility of losing these "super lures," that when the more modern practitioners began to substitute metal hooks for the bone points of the pearl lure, they made the hooks of soft wire. Major was told that the reason for this was that no fisherman would chance losing his pearl to a big fish. Better that the **fish** be lost!

"In the making (the pearl) is guarded from the eyes of anyone not in the family, and no outsider is allowed to see it until it has taken a fish. No one must yawn while it is being made, because the aku will also yawn when he is about to take it and will not be hooked," Major reported.

Pre-World War II Hawai'i was certainly an exciting and interesting time for fishing, but were they the "good old days?"

I don't think so. By any standard you choose, the "good old days" of big game fishing in Hawai'i are **now**. Never in the history of Hawai'i's fishing has the angler had a better chance of catching a marlin or tuna on sport fishing tackle than he does today. At times in recent years, the spring run of marlin and tuna off Kona has never been excelled in that port's history.

But that's only half the reason big game fishing now is greater sport than ever. The rest is in the equipment. The equipment today's angler has at his command has increased the odds that the chase and the challenge will produce success.

Improvements in boats and tackle have enhanced the fisherman's chances of finding fish, hooking them and bringing them to gaff, while contributing to creature comforts that make today's fishing outing akin to a day spent at the country club.

Three dozen years ago, when the potential of Hawai'i's waters as a serious sport fishing center was only beginning to be recognized, anglers took to sea in ponderous wooden boats adapted from Japanese sampans and designed to batter their way through the heavy seas of inter-island channels. Top speed might have been a groaning 10 knots, providing an acceptable range for trolling but not for getting to and from far-flung fishing grounds in time for a tournament weigh-in.

Fishing amenities were crude. Utilitarian bamboo outriggers were the rule, and it helped to have access to a bamboo forest to replace the dry sticks broken regularly on heavy strikes.

A rod holder was something you talked a machine shop into customizing for you from a heavy metal pipe on special order.

A wooden fishbox served both as a fighting chair and a (usually unsanitary) place to store a fish out of the direct rays of the sun. Gimbals bolted to the lid of the box acted as a rudimentary aid to help support the weight of the unwieldy (and often unreliable) winch that passed as a fishing reel.

Today's big water fisherman launches his attack on King Neptune's legions from a chariot that would awe any Hawaiian god. The boat's grace and regal elegance, its responsiveness to command, its speed and service-ability, its luxurious appointments — all combine to make it truly a floating palace.

Adorned with fiberglass outriggers, tips dipping and dancing as they activate bait trailing in the foaming wake, trimmed with glistening chrome fittings and sporting an umblemished skin of space-age chemicals, they advance at the beck and call of captains who become a bit more than mere mortals as they ascend to the heights of tuna towers to survey their domain.

With 20 knots (or more) of speed at the touch of his hand, today's fisherman doubles his fishing range, but such a capability is magnified tenfold by the array of communications equipment monitoring the sea and relaying reports back to the master spy at "communications central," the helm.

A completely outfitted boat has equipment that not only tells sea temperature and the ocean's depth and underwater structure, but also will take charge of steering the boat if the captain chooses to devote his attention to other duties.

Scanning sonar on many boats is the ultimate fish-finder, capable of spotting any fish for a thousand feet around and below the boat.

The comforts of home may also be found aboard most of these so-called "fishing machines," even if your home is a mansion. Carpeting, a bar, a complete galley, bathroom facilities (yes, even for taking a bath!), a television set — all are found on some of the "better-appointed" fishing boats of the Hawaiian fleet.

Once a fish is hooked, he is fought from a specially designed fighting chair. Padded for comfort and bolted to the deck for stability, this swiveling seat can be pointed right toward the fish, no matter which direction it runs or what maneuver the captain employs to stay

with him. Attached to the seat is an adjustable footrest to brace against for additional lifting efficiency.

A gaffed fish is safely secured, out of the reach of sharks, on a "swim step," a platform mounted on the transom above the waterline. Some boats have a door in the transom through which big fish can be pulled in-board to avoid any chance of loss.

Other boats are equipped with live wells on the transom to contain smaller catches such as mahimahi and ono. Many have refrigerated units accessible through the deck for cold storage, guaranteeing perfect condition of your catch after a full day at sea.

Tackle has kept pace with progress. The bamboo rods of yore have been replaced by strong, resilient, reliable shafts of plastic fibers impregnated with epoxy resin, the so-called "fiberglass" fishing rods.

As technology advances, even these superior fighting tools will eventually give way to the now extravagantly expensive graphite rods. Rod butts are no longer just modified shovel handles. Some are curved to maximize fighting leverage. Many are made of lightweight, virtually unbreakable materials such as fiberglass or aluminum to avoid the loss of rod, reel, lure and fish on an exceptionally heavy strike.

Anglers need no longer contend with ring guides that cut like butter under the knife edge of a thin line sliced across them at high speed or corrode into rough-toothed surfaces that can rasp a line into a strand of fluff. Modern guides have rotating bearings of super hardened metals. The rollers turn at high speed to decrease the friction on the line shooting across them.

Twisted linen lines, with their propensity to rot and break at a touch, have been replaced by uniformly fabricated strands of synthetic polymers: nylon and dacron. These form a bond between fish and fisherman that is exactly as strong as it has to be while being just weak enough to qualify in designated line test categories.

So much progess has been made in other aspects of fishing that the improvement developed in ways of getting big fish to grab hooks in the first place may be no more than icing on the already delectable cake.

Yet this is precisely the aspect of fishing that has gotten the most attention. The original "pearl" lures notwithstanding, the pioneers of artificial lure fishing would be ecstatic over today's imitation baits. Once artificial lures for marlin and ahi were carved of wood or cut from a piece of plumbing pipe in hopes of duplicating the effective action of some already proven prototype; today's plugs are turned out with uniform attractiveness from molded plastic, each with the exact appearance and action of the tested original.

Though it was not a modern angler who discovered that a live bonito dragged slowly behind a boat would interest a marlin or tuna, this technique of live baiting has now been refined into a *modus operandi* that would be outlawed by any court with a billfish jury.

Yet the good fishing of today threatens to become merely the "good old days" of tomorrow. Scientists have already begun to proclaim that the blue marlin are overfished, and the ahi, being a pelagic species of world-wide economic interest, are receiving no protection from conventions established by the 200-mile limit laws.

In the 1930s and 1940s, S. Kip Farrington Jr. was able to boast about the bonefishery in Hawai'i. Today, if any fisherman dared to compare what was available to the shore fisherman then and what is available to him now, he would find the results very disturbing. The claims of today's big game fishing may be headed toward a similarly bleak future.

Let's Go Fishing

After All, Fishing Is Amusement

Once you've mastered the methods, there is still more to learn before you can qualify as an expert fisherman. Regardless of your fishing record, you must be able to adopt the manner of the master angler — you must know how to talk and act.

First, you must have the right attitude, namely that fishing is serious enough to consume your every waking thought but never so serious that you cannot disguise your interest with casual disdain.

Take humorist Max Shulman, for example. He had the right outlook, and I offer in evidence his five simple truths garnered from his vast experience in big game fishing:

1. **Fishing boats leak.**
2. **Fishermen drink.**
3. **Any fish you lose is a marlin.**
4. **Fishing was always better the day before you got there.**
5. **Though deep-sea fishing is a very difficult sport, it can be mastered by any man or woman with average strength and inherited money.**

Clearly the man is a true disciple. He has, as they say, "been there."

Second, you must be keenly interested in learning as much as you can, but never **appear** to be eager. Not, that is, unless you want to be the unwitting foil and straight man for all kinds of tall tales told by an assortment of tour guides and local wits who relish the thought of educating you.

Consider the young fisherman out on a trolling trip who spotted a disabled 'opakapaka swimming near a handline fisherman's skiff and asked his captain for an explanation.

Now, as every bottom fisherman knows, it sometimes happens that a fish will get off the hook before it can be reeled completely to the surface. When this happens, the fish will keep coming right to the top because its air bladder inflates as the fish is drawn out of the heavy pressure of the depths. Such fish surface and remain alive but helpless.

But that's not the story the skipper told the beginner. The skipper swore him to secrecy, telling him he

would give him the true explanation about a strange new fishing method.

According to this skipper, the bottom fisherman had commissioned an artist to paint an exact replica of a school of bait fish on the bottom of his boat. Fish swimming under the boat saw this attractive gathering of succulent and available food and rushed upward in a feeding frenzy. So eager were they to snatch up the tasty morsels that they slammed against the bottom of the boat and knocked themselves out.

The fisherman had only to doze in the sun until awakened by a bump, then scoop the fish in with a hand net.

Another novice angler made the mistake of asking whether the high mercury level in fish still was the problem it once was. He was told that local fishermen had at last developed a way to rid the fish of mercury and turn a profit in the process.

The secret is to hang the fish in the ice house, tail down. When the temperature in the ice house falls to zero, the mercury in the fish will drop like the mercury in a thermometer. All you have to do then is cut off the tails. The ice house operator can then gather all of the tails and boil them until the mercury rises again. The mercury can then be skimmed off the top and sold to a thermometer company.

Still another neophyte, while gasping in incredulity over the size of the first marlin he had ever seen, was told that it really wasn't much compared to the largest billfish ever caught in Kona. This giant marlin was reportedly boated back in the days when there wasn't a scale big enough to weigh it, not even a truck scale. The commercial fisherman who caught it, fileted the meat from the bones and hung the skeleton for display. They say that the shadow of the skeleton alone weighed 50 pounds.

Occasionally, if someone thinks you look gullible enough, you are likely to hear the story of the twin Hawaiian boys who were identical in every way except their fishing luck. The lucky one fished from the starboard side of the boat and filled his fishbox every trip. The unlucky one never felt a nibble.

Finally, they decided to switch sides. After an hour of continued frustration, the unlucky twin was startled by a huge fish that swam straight to the surface. Instead of grabbing his bait, the fish popped its head out of the water and asked, "Where did your brother go?"

And finally there was a fellow sitting down at the dock with a shotgun, a bag of Mexican jumping beans and his pet golden retriever. Every now and then he'd toss a handful of beans into the water whenever a school of fish would swim by. The fish would gobble the jumping beans. Within minutes the beans would do their stuff and there would be fish leaping up and down all over the bay in front of him.

Then he'd pop them with his shotgun and send the dog out to bring in the catch.

One last bit of advice, no matter how good you are at some pursuit, it is, of course, impossible to be called an "expert" unless you can speak the jargon — the technical language known only to the cognoscente. For example, knowing the right words and how to use them correctly can earn you all the accolades of an expert fisherman even if your only association with a fish is a passion for tuna salad sandwiches.

To separate the true believers from the counterfeiters, fishermen have evolved an especially complicated pattern of passwords. These are words designed to trip up the faker. Their catch is 1) they have more than one meaning, 2) they have meanings that depend only on how they are used, or 3) they have meanings that are just the opposite of what you might expect.

Some examples will suffice.

Consider the word "sportfisherman." Easy, you say. That's a guy who fishes for sport. Oh yeah? Then what the devil is a 45-foot sportfisherman with tuna tower and twin diesels? A "sportfisherman," you see, is a boat outfitted for big game fishing. In other words, a sport fisherman can own a sportfisherman to take out friends who are sport fishermen but who may not own sportfishermen of their own. Makes sense if you are a sport fisherman even if you don't own a sportfisherman.

Strike. That's another of those words. Strike is what a fish does when it snatches a lure or bait. "Strike" may be what the skipper yells to signify that a fish has grabbed the hook, but don't you dare strike the fish without further orders. Confusing? Not if you know that "strike" also describes what you do when you haul back on the rod to drive the point of the hook into the fish's jaw. But that's ok. Most fish caught by fast-trolling strike themselves when they strike the lure. You only have to strike the fish when the fish strikes a live bait and, even then, your skipper may want to strike the fish with the boat. Of course, if he shakes the hook, you've struck out.

Bait? Lure? Well, you see, you can lure a fish to a hook by using a strip of fish or squid, or a whole fish, which are called baits. But you could also lure a fish to a hook with a fake device made to look and act like a fish or squid. That artificial bait is called a lure. You see how easy it is to keep the words lure and bait straightened out. A lure that is natural is a bait, and a bait that's artificial is a lure. But, if you get confused, you can call one an artificial bait and the other a natural bait. Or you can call one a natural lure and the other an artificial lure. But you have to understand that when you say artificial you don't mean it isn't real. After all, you can't catch a fish with your imagination (though, I guess I know some people who have) and everything you lure a fish with is real.

Let's take something easy like "land" and "boat." Now to "boat" a fish means to land it from a boat and to "land" a fish means to boat it from land. But no one really holds with these distinctions and you hear fishermen talking about landing marlin (bringing up a picture of an angler tied to a tree with his heels dug in the sand while a leaping billfish blasts through the surf). So, I guess you are safe. So let's leave boat and land and think about something more clear-cut like "billfish."

Now the common billfish we catch in Hawai'i is the marlin. But not all billfish are marlin, even though that's the only kind we catch here — although, as a matter of fact, a billfish doesn't have to have a bill to be a billfish. For that matter it doesn't even have to be a marlin to be a marlin. Oh dear. I haven't straightened you out much, have I?

Let me try again. When we say "billfish," we mean marlin (which have long noses called "bills"), swordfish (which have long noses called "swords"), sailfish (which have long noses called — gee, I don't know what fishermen call them) and spearfish (which don't have long noses, but we call their noses "spears," anyways).

Now the marlin (we've got two kinds, the Pacific blue and the black) are true billfishes and belong to the family bearing the Latin name *Makaira*. We also have something we call the striped marlin, but it's not really a marlin. It's got a bill, all right. And it looks so much like a blue marlin that a lot of fishermen have a hard time telling the difference. But it's really a member of the genus *Tetrapterus* (you don't have to learn that — it's Latin and nobody ever learns fishing Latin because fishing English is complicated enough). The *Tetrapterus* are the spearfishes, which will probably fool you because the striped marlin doesn't look like a spearfish. The spearfishes have this big sail along their back and really look a lot more like a sailfish, which is what every fisherman thinks when he catches his first one (first spearfish, that is) even as he wonders what happened to the bill (or whatever you call the long skinny nose a sailfish has — it isn't really thick enough to be called a bill).

See how easy fishing becomes when it's put into words by an expert?

. . . **Jim Rizzuto**

No Fisherman's Library is Complete without Fishing Hawai'i Style Volume 1, 2 & 3!

Volume 2 of "FISHING Hawaii Style®" is an authoritative guide to advanced fishing methods practiced by successful fishermen of the Central Pacific. Beautifully illustrated by Les Hata, it contains more than 500 detailed drawings that are accurate representations of fish, rigs, tackle and techniques. Les's drawings show not only his consumate skill as an artist but also his intimate knowledge of fish and fishing.

The volume is packed with lore not available elsewhere in book form. It describes how to catch game fish of the shoreline and deep seas, and even includes sections on shrimping, crabbing, lobstering and squidding.

You'll find comprehensive and detailed descriptions of surfcasting for ulua (slide-baiting and dunking), drifting sand bars for 'o'io, locating and catching deep-water snapper, fighting big game fish on light and heavy tackle, catching tuna at night under lights (the ika-shibi fishery), trolling green sticks, making and using popping plugs for whipping, fishing from boards powered by sails and small motors, jigging with flies for akule and live-baiting amberjack and other giant deep-sea denizens, and a wide range of practical and useful information that will increase your fishing skills.

Charts and fishing forecasts track the cycles of abundance for Hawai'i's fish telling you the months of best fishing for each species. A fact-packed fish description section tells the characteristics and habits of all of the major species of the Central Pacific. Les Hata's carefully detailed illustrations make accurate identification of each species easy.

In this volume, you'll find advice and information from dozens of Hawai'i's most successful fishermen. Their lore is passed along in an entertaining and interesting style, relying heavily on their own words in presenting anecdotes and instructions.

Read it for your enjoyment. Most of all, read it to become a better fisherman.

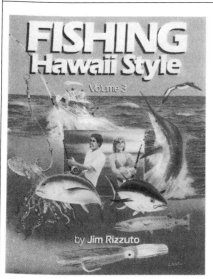

Fishermen continuously adapt, invent, innovate, improvise, modify, modernize, create, construct, contrive, devise, fabricate– the list is as endless as the results of their ingenuity. We've collected thousands of these ideas, selecting hundreds of the best to include in Volume III of this best-selling "FISHING Hawaii Style" series.

Here you will find tips, tricks, techniques and projects to make your fishing more enjoyable and successful. Regardless of whether you fish from a boat or shore, the surface or the depths, big game or small, you'll find useful suggestions and helpful advice.

These ideas spring from the experiences of many of Hawai'i's most successful fishermen, and the staff of HAWAII FISHING NEWS is grateful for their help. As you look through this book, you'll see the names of great fishermen–and of others whose ingenuity shows they are well on the way to being great.

Use the lore and wisdom in these pages as starting points for your own special fishing ideas and unforgettable fishing adventures.

For ordering information, contact: **HAWAII FISHING NEWS**
P.O. Box 25488 • Honolulu, Hawai'i 96825 • Phone: (808) 395-4499 • Fax: (808) 396-FISH
Visit us at our website at <hawaiifishingnews.com> or E-mail <fishnews@hawaii.rr.com>

Over 300 Ways To Prepare The Fresh Catches Of The Day

FRESH CATCH OF THE DAY ...*from the* FISHWIFE *by Shirley Rizzuto*

Novice cooks and gourmet seafood chefs will love the tempting simplicity of the more than three hundred recipes that are offered in **"FRESH CATCH OF THE DAY ...from the FISHWIFE."**

An extensive array of **Fishwife's Tips** will guide readers to success–from choosing fresh seafood, to safe handling and preparation, to innovative cooking in the kitchen and barbecuing and smoking seafood outdoors.

This, the second work of author and "Fishwife" Shirley Rizzuto, spanned the last decade of the 20th century. As we enter the next millennium and increasing attention is given to healthy living for longer life, scientists and dietitians predict we will turn more and more to the oceans of the world for healthy eating.

With this in mind, "FRESH CATCH OF THE DAY" will most certainly become a popular and necessary part of every culinary library.

The author's first work, "Fish Dishes of the Pacific. . . from the FISHWIFE" was widely acclaimed as "the best of its breed," "a fish preparation book without equal."

We at *HAWAII FISHING NEWS* are sure that this second cookbook with its all-new recipes featuring the diversity of Hawai'i and the island nations of the Central Pacific and a sampling of the best of the Northwest and Alaska will elevate seafood preparation to new heights and increase appreciation for seafood cookery.

Within these pages are a fabulous and varied collection of recipes for the many types of seafood available to the angler and at local seafood counters. The intent is that cooks will never again have to ponder what to do with their "FRESH CATCH OF THE DAY."

17 CHAPTERS AND OVER 300 RECIPES

- TUNA (Bigeye, Yellowfin, Albacore, Skipjack)
- BILLFISH (Swordfish, Marlin, Sailfish, Spearfish)
- MAHIMAHI (Dolphin Fish)
- ONO (Wahoo)
- OPAH (Moonfish)
- SNAPPER (Onaga, Ehu, Opakapaka, Uku)
- SALMON (King, Silver, Red, Chum, Pink)
- SHRIMP (and Freshwater Prawns)
- SQUID AND OCTOPUS (Ika, Tako)
- SEAFOOD PASTA DINNERS
- SOUPS, STEWS & COMBOS
- SAUCES, MARINADES & RELISHES
- HERBS
- GUIDE TO MICROWAVE COOKERY
- SMOKING YOUR CATCH
- TIPS ON FISH & COOKING

For ordering information, contact: **HAWAII FISHING NEWS**

P.O. Box 25488 • Honolulu, Hawai'i 96825 • Phone: (808) 395-4499 • Fax: (808) 396-FISH
Visit us at our website at <hawaiifishingnews.com> or E-mail <fishnews@hawaii.rr.com>